*Routledge Revivals*

# Spenser's Faerie Queene and the Cult of Elizabeth

First published in 1983, *Spenser's Faerie Queene and the Cult of Elizabeth* presents *The Faerie Queene* as a central document in the cult of Elizabeth. It shows how Spenser combines the resources of medieval iconography and Renaissance rhetoric in celebrating the Queen as the predestined ruler of an elect nation. In its introductory discussion of Renaissance poetics, the book emphasises the contemporary belief in the moral function of praise. Particular attention is given to the popular identification of Elizabeth with the Virgin Mary. If Elizabeth's gender created problems for a poet writing in the heroic mode, at the same time it made available to him a form of praise that no secular poet had been able to use before. While the book contains material of interest to the Renaissance specialist, its lucid style and the valuable background material it provides will appeal to undergraduates reading Spenser for the first time.

# Spenser's *Faerie Queene* and the Cult of Elizabeth

Robin Headlam Wells

Routledge
Taylor & Francis Group

First published in 1983
By Croom Helm Ltd.

This edition first published in 2023 by Routledge
4 Park Square, Milton Park, Abingdon, Oxon, OX14 4RN
and by Routledge
605 Third Avenue, New York, NY 10017

*Routledge is an imprint of the Taylor & Francis Group, an informa business*



**Publisher's Note**

The publisher has gone to great lengths to ensure the quality of this reprint but points out that some imperfections in the original copies may be apparent.

**Disclaimer**

The publisher has made every effort to trace copyright holders and welcomes correspondence from those they have been unable to contact.

A Library of Congress record exists under ISBN: 0709927614

ISBN: 978-1-032-63529-3 (hbk)
ISBN: 978-1-032-63532-3 (ebk)
ISBN: 978-1-032-63531-6 (pbk)

Book DOI 10.4324/9781032635323

# Spenser's *Faerie Queene* and the Cult of Elizabeth

Robin Headlam Wells

CROOM HELM
London & Canberra

BARNES & NOBLE BOOKS
Totowa, New Jersey

Croom Helm Ltd, Provident House, Burrell Row, Beckenham, Kent BR3 1AT

British Library Cataloguing in Publication Data

Wells, Robin Headlam
Spenser's Faerie queene and the cult of Elizabeth.
1. Spenser, Edmund. Faerie queene
2. Elizabeth I, *Queen of England* – Poetry
I. Title
821'.3 PR2358

ISBN 0-7099-2761-4

First published in the USA 1983 by
Barnes and Noble Books,
81 Adams Drive,
Totowa, New Jersey, 07512

Library of Congress Cataloging in Publication Data

Wells, Robin Headlam.
Spenser's Faerie queene and the cult of Elizabeth.
Bibliography: p.
1. Spenser, Edmund, 1552?-1599. Faerie queene.
2. Spenser, Edmund, 1552?-1599 – Religion and ethics.
3. Rhetoric – 1500-1800. 4. Typology (Theology) in literature.
I. Title.
PR2358.W4 1982 821'.3 82-11568

ISBN 0-389-20324-6

Printed and bound in Great Britain by
Biddles Ltd, Guildford and King's Lynn

# CONTENTS

TO THE MEMORY OF
HENRY HEADLAM WELLS
1972-81

All looks be pale, harts cold as stone.
For *Hally* now is dead, and gone,
*Hally*, in whose sight,
Most sweet sight,
All the earth late tooke delight.
Ev'ry eye, weepe with mee,
Joyes drown'd in teares must be.

His Iv'ry skin, his comely hayre,
His Rosie cheekes, so cleare and faire,
Eyes that once did grace
His bright face,
Now in him all want their place.
Eyes and hearts, weepe with mee,
For who so kinde as hee?

His youth was like an *Aprill* flowre,
Adorn'd with beauty, love, and powre;
Glory strow'd his way,
Whose wreaths gay
Now are all turn'd to decay.
Then again weepe with mee,
None feele more cause then wee.

No more may his wisht sight returne,
His golden Lampe no more can burne;
Quencht is all his flame,
His hop't fame
Now hath left him nought but name.
For him all weepe with mee,
Since more him none shall see.

Thomas Campion, Elegy on the Death of Henry,
Prince of Wales, d. 1612

# PREFACE

The Renaissance inherited from the Middle Ages a theory of allegory which distinguished four senses or levels of meaning: the *sensus litteralis*; the *sensus allegoricus*, or historical allegory; the *sensus tropologicus*, or moral allegory; and the *sensus anagogicus*, or mystical allegory. In practice, of course, no Renaissance poem will respond satisfactorily to the systematic application of an exegetical method which was originally evolved as part of the medieval science of biblical hermeneutics. Nevertheless, as an allegorical poem *The Faerie Queene* does have, broadly speaking, an historical, a moral and a mystical significance. The different levels on which the poem works are reflected in the rather clearly demarcated areas on which criticism has chosen to concentrate. While the principal emphasis of modern Spenser scholarship has been on the moral allegory, there have also been a number of outstanding studies of the historical and archetypal aspects of the poem.

Scholarly specialization has resulted in an enormous enrichment of our understanding both of *The Faerie Queene* and of the age which produced it. As a consequence few modern critics would still wish to claim that Spenser did not fully understand the form he had chosen to use. But although the view that the moral and political elements of the poem are at cross purposes is no longer current, there have been few convincing attempts to show how they complement one another. While the historian usually has little to tell us about the way the moral allegory works, the critic whose main concern is with the heroes as people seldom relates his analysis of their moral struggles to the poem's religio-political framework. The present study will attempt to show that these two aspects of the poem – the moral and the political – are parts of a continuous pattern of meaning. This is not to say that every incident in the poem has a topical significance, indeed the merely topical will form no part of my discussion; rather that the moral allegory is informed at every point, and not just in the obvious cameo portraits of the Queen in Books II and V, by the object of glorifying Elizabeth as the ideal Renaissance prince. The Renaissance believed, with Donatus, that in order to understand the *Aeneid* the reader must be familiar with Virgil's epideictic intention. I shall argue that the idea of praise is similarly fundamental to the conception of *The Faerie Queene* as a didactic poem: it is the unifying principle which binds together its different levels of meaning.

# *Preface*

No student of Spenser can hope to acknowledge all his debts (the bibliography on pp. 162-73 lists only works which have been cited in footnotes and does not claim adequately to represent the wealth of Renaissance scholarship available to the modern student). Equally, however, no one professionally interested in the cult of Elizabeth can emphasize too strongly his special debt to the pioneering scholarship of the 1930s and 1940s. It was Greenlaw, who, in his posthumous *Studies in Spenser's Historical Allegory* (1932), first demonstrated the true importance of national myth in Elizabethan literature when he showed that *The Faerie Queene* was intended primarily as a glorification both of Elizabeth's ancestry and of her person. Greenlaw's ideas exercised a far-reaching influence on scholarship devoted to the Elizabethan period. Not least among the studies which owe their inspiration to Greenlaw is Yates's extensive article 'Queen Elizabeth as Astraea' (1947). This seminal study of Elizabethan imperial propaganda depended heavily for its illustrative material on another outstanding work of scholarship. To describe Wilson's *England's Eliza* (1939) as no more than an anthology of literature in praise of the Queen would be to give a false impression of a survey so encyclopaedic that it still forms an invaluable source book for the modern student of Elizabethan panegyric.

If it has long been recognized that *The Faerie Queene* is primarily a poem of praise, it is only comparatively recently, since the publication of Hardison's *The Enduring Monument* (1962), that it has been possible to set Elizabethan panegyric within the context of a well-defined Renaissance theory of epideictic literature. Yet despite the stimulus afforded by this exemplary study of the idea of praise in the Renaissance, there has been only one attempt to re-examine *The Faerie Queene* in the light of Hardison's research. Cain's *Praise in 'The Faerie Queene'* (1978) appeared when the bulk of the present study was complete. It will be clear, however, that despite our mutual interest in Spenser as an epideictic poet, our paths seldom cross. Where Cain places the main emphasis of his discussion on the formal, or 'iconic', representations of Elizabeth in *The Faerie Queene*, and disregards, for the most part, the moral allegory, my own concern, as I shall explain in the introductory chapter, has been to try to show that panegyric is not an aspect of the poem which may be considered in isolation from the moral allegory, but is essentially a determinant of it.

Acknowledgement of another kind is due to my colleagues Tom McAlindon and Peter McClure, whose expertise in medieval and Renaissance matters is matched only by their generosity: from them I received more help than an author has a right to expect from his friends. I am grateful, also, to A.C. Hamilton for finding time to make valuable comments on my manuscript at what, for him, was a particularly busy period. Finally, I should like to thank Dick Jenkinson of the Department of Classics, Hull University, who generously helped me with the sometimes elliptical syntax of the Elizabethan Latin poets. Where the name of a translator is not given in the footnotes, the translation is his.

Parts of Chapters 1, 6 and 7 have appeared in a different form in *Anglia*, *English Studies*, *Comparison* and *Modern Language Review*. Section 4 of the introduction is based on a paper written in collaboration with Peter McClure and read at the 1982 conference of the International Society for the History of Rhetoric in Edinburgh.

# LIST OF ABBREVIATIONS

| | |
|---|---|
| BIHR | Bulletin of the Institute of Historical Research |
| BJRL | Bulletin of the John Rylands Library |
| CritS | The Critical Survey |
| CQ | Classical Quarterly |
| ELH | Journal of English Literary History |
| ELN | English Language Notes |
| ELR | English Literary Renaissance |
| ES | English Studies |
| HACB | Humanities Association of Canada Bulletin |
| HLQ | Huntington Library Quarterly |
| JEGP | Journal of English and Germanic Philology |
| JMRS | Journal of Medieval and Renaissance Studies |
| JWCI | Journal of the Warburg and Courtauld Institutes |
| MLN | Modern Language Notes |
| MLR | Modern Language Review |
| MP | Modern Philology |
| NQ | Notes and Queries |
| PMLA | Publications of the Modern Language Association of America |
| PQ | Philological Quarterly |
| RenD | Renaissance Drama |
| RES | Review of English Studies |
| SEL | Studies in English Literature |
| SixCT | The Sixteenth Century Journal |
| SP | Studies in Philology |
| TCAS | Transactions of the Connecticut Academy of Arts and Sciences |
| UTQ | University of Toronto Quarterly |

# TO SOUND HER PRAISES: INTRODUCTION

## 1. The Poetry of Praise

Great wrong I doe, I can it not deny,
to that most sacred Empresse my dear dred,
not finishing her Queene of faery,
that mote enlarge her liuing prayses dead.
(*Amoretti*, XXXIII)[1]

Spenser had completed six books of *The Faerie Queene* when he published the *Amoretti* in 1595. The apologetic tone of sonnet no. 33 suggests that he probably knew that his original plans for a poem consisting of twelve books devoted to the 'priuate morall vertues', to be followed by another twelve devoted to the 'pollliticke vertues',[2] would never be realized. But more important than what this sonnet tells us of Spenser's state of mind is what it says concerning the purpose of his epic. As a poetic tribute to Elizabeth, *The Faerie Queene* was intended to 'enlarge her prayses'.

Renaissance criticism, following a tradition going back at least as far as Plato, accorded a special status to the poetry of praise.[3] Puttenham, in his defence of the dignity of poetry, claims that, second only to poetry written in praise of the immortal gods, is that which honours 'the worthy gests of noble Princes'.[4] However humble his own position might be, the poet could lay claim to a unique office, since he alone was able to offer the glory of immortality through verse. As Spenser himself remarks in a sonnet addressed to the Earl of Northumberland:

The sacred Muses haue made alwaies clame
To be the Nourses of nobility,
And Registres of euerlasting fame.[5]

In the Renaissance it was believed that the highest poetic kind was the epic, and most critics were agreed that the function of epic was essentially epideictic, that is, to display the virtues of some great man as a pattern for emulation.[6] The poem which was universally held to be the supreme example of its genre was the *Aeneid*. Donatus, writing in the fourth century, claimed that 'If anyone wants to measure Virgil's genius, his morality, the nature of his speech, his knowledge, character, and skill in rhetoric, he must first learn whom he undertakes to praise in his poem.'[7] This view of the *Aeneid* is repeated in Fulgentius's *De Contentia Virgiliana* (c. sixth century), a work which has been described as 'the most characteristic monument we possess of Vergil's celebrity during the times of Christian barbarism'.[8] Although Fulgentius's commentary turns the *Aeneid* into something akin to a medieval allegory of Everyman in which epic combats are seen as psychomachia, the underlying conception of the poem as 'panegyrical biography'[9] is one which formed the basis of most Renaissance interpretations of Virgil. As late as 1715 it was argued that

> the whole *Aeneis* of Virgil may be said to be an allegory, if we consider Aeneas as representing Augustus Caesar and his conducting the remains of his countrymen from the ruins of Troy to a new settlement in Italy as emblematical of Augustus' modelling a new government out of the ruins of the aristocracy and establishing the Romans, after the confusion of the civil war, in a peaceable and flourishing condition.[10]

Such a view of the *Aeneid* is also substantially Spenser's. Indeed it has been claimed that 'Of all sixteenth-century epics, none better illustrates the continuity of the Fulgentius tradition than Edmund Spenser's *Faerie Queene*.'[11] That Spenser himself wished *The Faerie Queene* to be identified with this tradition is apparent from the way he deliberately modelled his own poetic career on Virgil's example. Already in the 'October' eclogue of *The Shepheardes Calender* we find him alluding to the passage in the third book of the *Georgics* (10-30) where Virgil speaks of the heroic poem he intends to write in honour of Augustus. To Piers's suggestion that he turn from lesser matters and honour 'fayre Elisa' by singing 'of bloody Mars, of wars, of giusts', Cuddie replies that he has indeed heard of how 'Romish Tityrus'

> left his Oaten reede,
> Whereon he earst had taught his flocks to feede,
> And laboured lands to yield the timely eare,
> And eft did sing of warres and deadly drede,
> So as the Heauens did quake his verse to here.
> ('October', 56-60)

If Spenser's choice of the pastoral mode for his apprentice work is clearly based on Virgil's example, it is well known also that he closely identified the epic poem he was anticipating in these lines with the *Aeneid*.[12]

To describe *The Faerie Queene* as a poem of praise belonging to a long tradition of epideictic poetry is not, of course, to say anything new. Many critics have asserted what Spenser himself tells us in his letter to Ralegh, namely that *The Faerie Queene* was designed as a glorification of Elizabeth and the British nation.[13] However, although Cain is right in saying that 'Spenser's great poem exists to praise Elizabeth',[14] this does not mean that it is merely an elaborate vehicle for flattery. The purpose of epideictic poetry is essentially moral. The special nature of the responsibilities assumed by the panegyrist is perhaps best explained by Erasmus writing in 1504:

> Those who believe panegyrics are nothing but flattery seem to be unaware of the purpose and aim of the extremely far-sighted men who invented this kind of composition, which consists in presenting princes with a pattern of goodness, in such a way as to reform bad rulers, improve the good, educate the boorish, reprove the erring, arouse the indolent, and cause even the hopelessly vicious to feel some inward stirrings of shame.[15]

In proclaiming the moral function of praise Erasmus is rehearsing a commonplace of classical and Renaissance poetics;[16] he is also anticipating the treatise which he presented to his own patron twelve years later on the occasion of his appointment as counsellor to Charles V (then Archduke of Burgundy). As a *speculum principis*, *The Education of a Christian Prince* belongs to an ancient tradition of hortatory treatises on the subject of kingship.[17] Although Erasmus characterizes his book as a work of praise,[18] his object is an ethical one. Underlying his portrait of the Christian ruler are two principles which are also fundamental to the conception of *The Faerie Queene* as a mirror for Elizabeth: first, that the prince, as God's deputy on earth, is to be seen as performing a function in the hierarchy of the state analogous to that performed by God in the universal order of things (pp. 158-9), and second, that upon the moral character of the prince depends the well being of the state (p. 157) By defining the characteristics of the ideal prince and comparing these with an image of the corrupt ruler, Erasmus is in effect creating a pattern of Christian conduct to which all men should aspire. Informing the whole book is the humanist belief in the moral value of learning. As Spenser says in *The Teares of the Muses*,

By knowledge wee do learne our selues to knowe,
And what to man, and what to God wee owe.

From hence wee mount aloft vnto the skie,
And looke into the Christall firmament . . .
(503-6)

*The Faerie Queene* does not offer the reader a scheme of practical education; nevertheless, as a moral poem which undertakes to instruct the reader in the nature of virtue, it testifies to the belief – central to Erasmus's thought, and indeed to the humanist movement as a whole – that knowledge brings us nearer to God. As one recent critic has said, the various books of the poem trace 'a sequence displaying the dignity of man, a progression of learning for the reader'.[19]

In so far as he is presenting his reader with an image of princely magnificence in the figure of Arthur, Spenser may be seen to be writing within a clearly defined tradition of treatises on kingship. But when he announces his intention of fashioning 'a gentleman or noble person in vertuous and gentle discipline',[20] it is the courtesy book rather than the prince's mirror with which his poem may best be compared.[21] Many scholars have written on Spenser's debt to the courtesy tradition and to Castiglione in particular.[22] Whereas the *speculum* concerns itself with the virtues of the ideal prince and offers advice on the art of government, the courtesy book is less specialized in its subject matter and deals with the education and accomplishments of noblemen and courtiers. In their most elementary form Renaissance courtesy books were little more than manuals of self-improvement. However, the more serious writers of the period are unanimous in their insistence that the courtier's accomplishments are worth nothing if they are not devoted to the cause of realizing what Sir Thomas Elyot terms the 'iuste publike weale'.[23] Castiglione's claim that the courtier must employ his accomplishments as a means of gaining the goodwill and favour of his prince and that he should use the influence he wins in this way to supply the prince with virtuous counsel,[24] is a favourite maxim among Renaissance humanists.

The close similarities between the *speculum principis* and the courtesy book are illustrated in the work of Castiglione's most celebrated English imitator.[25] Addressed to Henry VIII, *The Boke Named the Governour* is both a manual on the art of government which offers its dedicatee a portrait of the ideal ruler, and at the same time a handbook of education for the sons of English gentlemen. Of the vast number of pedagogic treaties which appeared in the sixteenth century, Elyot's book is arguably the most important so far as Spenser is concerned. Indeed it has been claimed that *The Governour* and *The Faerie Queene* 'have almost identical aims'.[26] Although this is an exaggeration, it is true that Spenser, like Elyot, does combine elements of the *speculum principis* with certain features of the courtesy book. That Spenser saw these two functions of his poem as aspects of a single meaning is clear from his statement in the letter to Ralegh of his intentions regarding the character of Prince Arthur. As Virgil had combined features of Homer's Agamemnon and his Ulysses in the single figure of Aeneas, says Spenser, so Arthur is to be seen as a composite figure representing 'a good gouernour and a vertuous man'.[27]

Spenser's general intention may be summed up, then, as being to praise Elizabeth by presenting her with a portrait of the ideal ruler – a portrait which she would recognize as her own, but which would at the same time serve as a pattern of conduct for her courtiers. Summarized in this way *The Faerie Queene* sounds not unlike a versification of *The Governour*. What this account does not recognize is the political dimension of Spenser's poem. In addition to its pedagogic aspect, *The Faerie Queene* is a national epic whose purpose is to celebrate Queen Elizabeth as the predestined ruler of an elect nation. In this respect it has more in common with the *Aeneid* than with *The Governour*. In celebrating a national ideal Spenser, like Virgil, employs one of the favourite *topoi* of the epideictic poet and constructs a genealogy – part mythical and part historical – in which he traces his prince's ancestry to its supposedly divine origins. Since it is sometimes claimed that the Elizabethans were quite uncritical in their appetite for literature dealing with the mythical history of their country (see Appendix), it is important to consider the status of Spenser's genealogical material, particularly with regard to his use of typology as a means of proclaiming the predestinate nature of Elizabeth's rule.

## 2. Allegory and Typology

In one of the commendatory verses annexed to *The Faerie Queene* (chosen, no doubt, for the aptness of its sentiments rather than its poetic merit) explicit comparison is made between Spenser and Virgil:

> Graue Muses march in triumph and with prayses,
> Our Goddesse here hath giuen you leaue to land:

And biddes this rare dispenser of your graces
Bow downe his brow vnto her sacred hand.
Desertes findes dew in that most princely doome,
In whose sweete brest are all the Muses bredde:
So did that great *Augustus* erst in Roome
With leaues of fame adorne his Poets hedde.
Faire be the guerdon of your *Faery Queene*,
Euen of the fairest that the world hath seene.[28]

Although Spenser never won the royal patronage which the author of these verses anticipates, his poem has much in common with Virgil's. Indeed the similarities between the *Aeneid* and *The Faerie Queene* would have appeared far more striking to the Renaissance reader than they do to us. The modern student, familiar with the idea that *The Faerie Queene* has a number of different levels of meaning, might possibly be surprised to be told that the *Aeneid* had a similar fourfold significance. But in the Middle Ages and the Renaissance it was commonly accepted that, in addition to its literal significance, Virgil's narrative embodied certain moral and political meanings. Boccaccio, for example, tells us that 'concealed within the veil' ('sub velamento latet poetico') of the story of Aeneas's abandonment of Dido are three ulterior purposes: first, to offer a universal moral truth concerning the need to subdue the destructive passions; second, to glorify Augustus by praising Aeneas's steadfast devotion to his political destiny; and third to celebrate the martial successes of the Roman people in terms of the events which prefigured these triumphs.[29]

Boccaccio's interpretation of Virgil is clearly based on the analogy of contemporary scriptural exegesis. But although he speaks of the poet's fourfold purpose, his method cannot properly be compared with that of a true allegorist like Aquinas. For, of the three levels of meaning which Boccaccio finds in addition to the literal significance of Virgil's narrative, it is only the first which is, strictly speaking, allegorical (in this case, tropological); the latter two are typological. The distinction is important. Where moral allegory is usually timeless and characteristically involves the use of signs – more or less arbitrary in themselves – to point to moral or spiritual truths which have a universal applicability, typology reveals a pattern in the course of history by establishing connections between events or persons which have a historical reality.[30] For Boccaccio there was no more need to explain the difference between allegory and typology than there was for Spenser, writing some 300 years later. However, such a way of reading literature belongs essentially to a pre-modern culture; and the twentieth-century critic must spell out distinctions which would have been self-evident to Boccaccio's and Spenser's readers.

The literary use of typology is familiar enough to students of medieval drama.[31] However, unlike the medieval writer, who is dramatizing events which – so far as he is concerned – have a historical reality, Spenser creates an imaginary world. In establishing parallels between the fictional characters who inhabit this world and the real historical person whom they prefigure, Spenser is attributing a providential significance to contemporary events in much the same way that the New Testament writer sees in the past a series of figures prognosticating Christ. But the analogy is not a true one. Where the New Testament writer concerns himself only with historical realities, Spenser creates characters which are, for the most part, purely fictional. This mingling of the fictional and the real presents critical problems of a very different nature from those associated with the miracle play. Because these problems have received scant critical attention and because, as a consequence, there is some confusion about what we mean when we speak of typology in *The Faerie Queene*,[32] it is necessary to rehearse a subject whose general principles are by now well established.[33]

As an exegetical method typology originates in St Paul and other New Testament writers who interpreted certain events and persons in the Old Testament as τύποι, or prefigurations of Christ; as a method of composition, however, typology antedates the Christian era. Medieval and Renaissance commentators on the *Aeneid* were fully aware, as we have seen, of the way Virgil links events widely separated in time in order to show that they form steps in an historical progression culminating in the reign of Augustus.[34] If the patterns of recurrence and prefiguration we find in the *Aeneid* bear similarities to those in the Bible, this is because they are the product of a similar view of history. Typology is essentially the product of a theory of history which sees events not simply as sequence, but as significant elements of a divine plan. Such a providential view of history is not, of course, unique to Christendom.

In praising his sovereign, Spenser, like Virgil, used typology to suggest that her reign had been anticipated or foreshadowed by events in the ancient past. Whether Virgil intended the allegorical meanings his medieval commentators found in the *Aeneid* we shall probably never know; with Spenser we are on surer ground. We know that, in addition to its historical aspect, *The Faerie Queene* is a 'continued Allegory, or darke conceit' designed to illustrate a humanist ideal of moral conduct.

This mixing of allegory and typology is one of the characteristic features of the poem. On the one hand there are purely allegorical characters such as Furor, or Malbecco, who clearly have no typological significance; on the other hand there are characters like Belphoebe, whose significance is primarily typological and who tell us very little about the nature of the virtue which they supposedly represent. Between these two extremes are those characters such as Mercilla or Britomart who are both 'historical' types foreshadowing their antitype, Queen Elizabeth, and also allegorical symbols of the virtues which form the subjects of the books in which they appear.

We must be clear, however, exactly what is implied by describing a character like Britomart as a type of Queen Elizabeth. *The Faerie Queene* is a poem which makes extensive use of prophecy and historical parallelism. But these do not in themselves necessarily involve typology. For example, in the final stanza of the proem to Book V Spenser invokes his muse:

Dread Souerayne Goddesse, that doest highest sit
In seate of iudgement, in th'Almighties stead,
And with magnificke might and wondrous wit
Doest to thy people righteous doome aread,
That furthest Nations filles with awfull dread,
Pardon the boldnesse of thy basest thrall,
That dare discourse of so diuine a read,
As thy great iustice praysed ouer all:
The instrument whereof loe here thy ***Artegall***.

The terms in which Spenser addresses his 'Souerayne Goddesse' make it impossible to say whether he is speaking to Astraea or Queen Elizabeth. In fact, of course, he is doing both. Behind the familiar Elizabethan identification of the Queen with the goddess of justice lies the prophetic annunciation of Virgil's fourth Eclogue: 'iam redit et Virgo, redeunt Saturnia regna'. It was to these famous words that chroniclers like Richard Nicols were alluding when they hailed Elizabeth's reign as a return to the golden age:

No sooner did this Empires royall crowne
Begirt the temples of her princelie hed;
But that *Iove*-borne *Astraea* straight came downe
From highest heauen againe, to which in dread
Of earths unpietie before shee fled:

> Well did shee know, *Elizaes* happie reigne
> Would then renew the golden age againe.[35]

But if Spenser, like so many of his contemporaries, is suggesting that Elizabeth represents the fulfilment of Virgilian prophecy, that she is indeed Astraea *rediviva*, this does not mean that the relationship is typological. For an antitype is not a reincarnation of the type by which it has been anticipated, but a fulfilment of its hidden meaning. In a truly typological relationship type and antitype always retain their separate identities. It would be improper, therefore, to describe as typological that form of prophetic recurrence which is in fact a recapitulation, though, as we shall see, prophecy does not exclude typology.

It may help to clarify the unique relationship between type and antitype if we consider another form of reiterative relationship in *The Faerie Queene* which is, nevertheless, not typological. When Paridell abducts Malbecco's wife Hellenore (III, x, 1 ff.) in a crude re-enactment of the tale he had been telling Britomart the previous evening (III, ix, 33-7), we scarcely need to be told by the narrator that his lover is 'a second *Hellene*' (13), or that the firing of Malbecco's castle recalls the sack of Troy (12). But although Paridell and Hellenore are clearly linked both by name and temperament with their notorious forbears, they are not their antitypes. In no sense can they be said to reveal the true significance of the past. Paridell the seducer and Hellenore the faithless wife are human stereotypes who tell us no more about their originals than Paris and Helen tell us about them. The relationship is simply analogical. By investing this allegory of concupiscence, infidelity and jealousy with historical echoes, Spenser is doing no more than reminding his reader that human nature is the same in all ages, and that what was capable of bringing about chaos in the past is still capable of doing so now.

Paridell, Hellenore and Malbecco are personifications of the moral evils against which Britomart is pledged to fight; as the champion of fidelity she is the allegorical antithesis of everything they represent. But when Spenser describes this 'Magnificke Virgin' (V, vii, 21) in terms which evoke her illustrious descendant, Queen Elizabeth, he is writing not as an allegorist, but as a typologist. For it is only in the distant future when another 'royall virgin' celebrated, like Britomart, for her chastity – shall come to rule a divided world, that the true meaning of Britomart's 'perillous emprize' will be revealed (III, iii, 48-9). Although her reign has been prophesied by Merlin, Elizabeth is not a reincarnation of Britomart, but a fulfilment of the divine historical plan foreshadowed in the deeds of her heroic ancestress.

It would be wrong to suggest that *The Faerie Queene* cannot be understood without making these distinctions. Nevertheless, they are ones which Spenser's contemporaries regarded as significant,[36] and some awareness of them may sharpen our understanding of the kind of poem *The Faerie Queene* is. If Spenser treats characters like Britomart, now as types of Elizabeth, now as allegorical symbols, we may reasonably assume that this is not because he was as confused as a good many of his twentieth-century readers are about the difference between typology and allegory, but because such a technique was to some extent dictated by his 'whole intention' in writing *The Faerie Queene*. As an epideictic poet he is attempting both to define an abstract ideal of 'vertuous and gentle discipline' as a pattern for emulation, and also to praise Queen Elizabeth as predestined ruler of a chosen people. To accomplish this latter purpose Spenser made use of two quite separate typological traditions: a classical tradition and a Christian tradition. The body of classical legend which forms part of the mythical background of *The Faerie Queene* is well known and need not detain us long; the Christian material, though familiar to Spenserians in principle, is deployed in a more extensive and systematic fashion than is generally recognized. In the remaining sections of this introduction I shall try to show how Spenser combines this heterogeneous material to reveal the providential nature of Elizabeth's reign.

### 3. The Myth of Troy

Although she is referred to only through the medium of prophecy, and then not by her own name, Queen Elizabeth nevertheless dominates *The Faerie Queene* in much the same way that Augustus's presence can be felt throughout the *Aeneid*, in spite of the fact that he never actually appears in the poem. As protagonists *in absentia* Augustus and Elizabeth have much in common: each is portrayed as the instrument of a providential purpose, a peace-bringer descended from the gods, who is at the same time a dispenser of ruthless justice. To enforce the parallel Spenser begins *The Faerie Queene* with a direct allusion to the *Aeneid*.[37] But undue emphasis should not be given to this initial echoing of Virgil, for in the poem as a whole there is little explicit verbal parallelism. Although certain incidents, such as Duessa's journey to the underworld in Book I, canto v, for example, are loosely based on passages in the *Aeneid*, these parallels are not always of thematic significance, and in form the poem owes more to Ariosto and Tasso than it does to Virgil.

Spenser does, however, link his poem with the *Aeneid* in a more radical way. Just as Virgil, by connecting Roman history with its legendary past, had shown Augustus to be the instrument of a providential plan, so Spenser employs ancient myth to glorify Queen Elizabeth. It is, moreover, the same myth which Virgil had used to claim divine ancestry for Augustus, that Spenser uses in *The Faerie Queene*. In Book III, canto iii, Britomart visits the cave of Merlin where it is revealed that from her

a famous Progenie
Shall spring, out of the auncient *Troian* blood,
Which shall reuiue the *sleeping* memorie
Of those same antique Peres the heauens brood,
Which *Greeke* and *Asian* riuers stained with their blood.
(III, iii, 22)

The passage is a direct imitation of the third canto of the *Orlando Furioso* where Bradamante similarly learns of her Trojan ancestry and is told by Merlin of the glorious deeds of her descendants. Spenser, like Ariosto, is deliberately inviting comparison between his poem and the *Aeneid*. Later, in Book III, canto ix, we discover that Britomart, herself an ancestor of Elizabeth, is 'lineally extract' from Brutus, great-grandson of Aeneas and founder of Troynovaunt, or London. Elizabeth is thus shown to be, like Augustus, a direct descendant of the gods through Aeneas, and her reign to be the fulfilment of a divine plan.

As it is told in *The Faerie Queene* the Troy story is a complex one, for instead of presenting its events in chronological order, Spenser divides his narrative into four main parts. The first part of the story dealing with the flight of Aeneas from Troy and the founding by Ascanius of a new Troy in Alba Longa, is told by Paridell to Britomart in Malbecco's castle (III, ix, 40-3). When Britomart mentions the building of a third Troy by descendants of Aeneas, Paridell recalls the details, which he had until then forgotten, of Brutus's accidental parricide, his years of self-imposed exile and his eventual conquest of Albion. For the second part of the story, dealing with Brutus's descendants, we have to turn back to Book II, canto x, where Prince Arthur reads a chronicle of British kings from Brutus to his own father Uther Pendragon. The continuation of this chronicle, beginning with Arthur's grandson and tracing the descent as far as Cadwallader, last of the British kings, is related in the form of a prophecy by Merlin in Book III, canto iii. With the coming of the Saxons and the death of Cadwallader the succession of British kings is finally broken. But Merlin prophesies that in due time the British line will be restored, that the country will be united, and that a royal virgin will reign in glorious peace. This final part of the story, dealing with the Tudor dynasty, is then retold in Book III, canto x, in the form of a history of Faeryland.

Spenser's reason for presenting the story in such a disjointed form was principally chronological: since the action of *The Faerie Queene* is presumed to have taken place before Arthur's accession, all later events would necessarily have to take the form of prophecy. Such, however, was the popularity in Elizabethan England of the Trojan myth that Spenser could afford to distort his narrative without risk of losing his readers.[38] This popularity is not difficult to account for. By tracing his nation's ancestry to ancient Troy, the chronicler was able to show that his people were not barbarians, but had been marked out by providence for a special purpose. Since national pride is a commodity of no great rarity, it is not surprising to find that in medieval Western Europe the Trojan myth was 'everybody's game';[39] as early as the seventh century, Frankish legend had spoken of a Trojan national ancestry, while closer to Spenser's own time we find Ariosto employing the same myth in his glorification of the House of Este.

In England the Trojan myth owed its currency to Geoffrey of Monmouth. Drawing on fragmentary literary sources and orally transmitted material, Geoffrey created in his *Historia Regum Britanniae* (c. 1135) a masterpiece of imaginative literature which dominated antiquarian thought for centuries to come: 'within fifteen years of its publication not to have read it was a matter of reproach; it became a respected text-book of the Middle Ages; it was incorporated in chronicle after chronicle; it was turned into poetry; it swept away opposition with the ruthless force of a great epic . . .'[40] Geoffrey's chronicle of ancient British kings from Brutus to Cadwallader became the most important single source not only for medieval chroniclers, but also for apologists of the Tudor right to accession. Of especial significance was Geoffrey's portrayal of Brutus as a man marked out by divine prophecy as the founder of a universal empire. When Brutus petitions the gods to reveal his destiny he is told to seek an island beyond France where giants once lived but which is now uninhabited. There he would find a land fit for his descendants, where another Troy would be built and kings would be born to whom the whole world would bow.[41]

The idea of the British nation as one destined for world-wide sovereignty reappears in popular Tudor literature. Among the stories added by John Higgins to the *Mirror for Magistrates*, for example, is the *Tale of Albanact* (one of Brutus's three sons), in which, following Geoffrey, the poet relates how Diana appeared to Brutus in a dream prophesying that he would establish a new kingdom in an island beyond France where he would build 'an other stately Troye':

> Here of thy progenye and stocke, shall mighty kinges descende:
> And vnto them as subiecte, all the worlde shall bowe and bende.[42]

Such a myth had its obvious political uses. It was revived by Henry VII on his accession as a way of justifying his claim to the throne. Hall records how, claiming to be able to trace his ancestry back to Cadwallader, Henry encouraged the idea that he represented a fulfilment of the ancient prophecy that a British king would return to rule the land.[43] The myth was revived for similar reasons during Elizabeth's reign and became a familiar feature of the patriotic minor literature which flourished in the 1580s and 1590s.[44] Chroniclers from Geoffrey onwards had kept the Trojan myth alive, and it now found expression in pageants, narrative poems and plays celebrating the glory of England's Queen and tracing her ancestry back to Brutus.

When we speak of the popularity of the Trojan myth in Elizabethan England we must be clear that no historiographer worthy of the title ever accorded it the status of historical fact.[45] It was antiquarians such as Leland and Churchyard and poets such as Baldwin, Peele, Warner, Nicols and of course Spenser himself who popularised the myth. In doing so they were continuing a medieval chronicle tradition in which moral utility was the writer's chief concern. Unlike the historiographer, the poet was considered to be free to adapt his historical material to suit his moral purpose. One of the most memorable passages in Sidney's *Defence of Poetry* deals with precisely this distinction. Where the historiographer is bound to record only 'what men have done' the poet,

> Disdaining to be tied to any such subjection, lifted up with the vigour of his own invention, doth grow in effect another nature, in making things either better than nature bringeth forth, or, quite anew, forms such as never were in nature, as the Heroes, Demigods, Cyclops, Chimeras, Furies, and such like: so as he goeth hand in hand with nature, not enclosed within the narrow warrant of her gifts, but freely ranging only within the zodiac of his own wit.[46]

The poet imitates not an imperfect sensible world, but an ideal world. It is by 'feigning notable images' of virtue or vice that he is able to 'lead and draw us to as high a perfection, as our degenerate souls, made worse by their clayey lodgings, can be capable of'. It would be naive, Sidney tells us, to suppose that there ever existed so perfect a prince as Xenophon's Cyrus or so excellent a man as Virgil's Aeneas. Yet by taking the idealized heroes of mythology and literature as models of our own conduct we encourage the growth of the virtues they embody.[47]

When Spenser incorporated the Trojan myth in *The Faerie Queene* he did not wish to suggest that the British were in a literal sense descended from Troy; indeed elsewhere he speaks with scorn of those 'vaine *Englishmen*' who claimed that Brutus 'first conquered and inhabited this Land, it being . . . impossible to proove, that there was ever any such *Brutus* of *England* . . .'[48] The relationship is typological: in showing that the events of Elizabeth's reign have been foreshadowed by events in the ancient world Spenser is suggesting that they are to be seen as part of a divine historical plan. Though the Troy story is dealt with only in Books II and III of *The Faerie Queene*, it forms an essential part of the mythico-historical background of the whole poem. Rightly to understand the historic significance that Spenser attributed to Elizabeth we must see her, like Virgil's Augustus, as a descendant of the gods, born to bring peace to a divided world.

## 4. Marian Iconography

Virgil's praise of Augustus in terms of the legendary ancestor by whom he is shown to have been prefigured provided a typological model for Renaissance epideictic poets. The fact that Virgil was a pagan writer did not matter. A long tradition of interpreting the enigmatic fourth Eclogue as unconscious Christian prophecy[49] offered justification for regarding the empire foretold by Anchises (*Aeneid*, VI, 756 ff.) as preparatory for the coming of Christ, while, conversely, the birth of Christ was spoken of as heralding the return of the golden age.[50] In this way Virgilian myth was assimilated to a Christian view of world history. Thus when Spenser gives his reader the sequel to the Troy story in Books II and III of *The Faerie Queene* and traces, in the form of prophecy, its future events as far as Elizabeth's England he is in effect extending the Christian providential view of history back into the ancient world and forward into the present. What the Trojan myth could not suggest, however, was Elizabeth's specifically Protestant destiny. To convey the idea that the British were in a particular religious sense a 'chosen and peculier people'[51] Spenser drew on a popular tradition of biblical typology.

In tracing Britomart's descent from 'auncient Troian blood' (III, iii, 22), Spenser links his heroine with a familiar body of classical legend. But when he describes her genealogical tree as a

> worthy stock, from which the branches sprong,
> That in late yeares so faire a blossome bare,
> As thee, O Queene, the matter of my song.
> (III, iv, 3)

it is to a Christian typological tradition that he is alluding. The prophetic blossoming tree whose branches stretch to heaven's height (III, iii, 22) echoes the familiar image of the *Virga Iesse* in Isaiah, XI. Owing, perhaps, to the verbal similarity of *virga* (rod) and *virgo* (virgin), the Tree of Jesse came to be identified in the Middle Ages as a type of the Virgin Mary.[52] Indeed so habitual in medieval and Renaissance iconography was this interpretation of Isaiah, that to employ such a familiar image in a sixteenth-century poem was to guarantee the evocation of Marian associations. Since Britomart is herself a type of Queen Elizabeth this means that Spenser is establishing a typological connection between Elizabeth and the Virgin Mary.

It may at first seem strange to find an Elizabethan poet drawing parallels between his prince and the Catholic Queen of Heaven, more particularly since the Reformed Church of which she was Supreme Governor had been zealous to abolish what it saw as the idolatrous, Romish and hence unpatriotic veneration and invocation of the saints, especially that of the Virgin Mary. However, Spenser was not alone in making this comparison. Secularized versions of the Tree of Jesse are not uncommon in Elizabethan patriotic literature. In *The Misfortunes of Arthur* the ghost of Gorlois addresses the queen as

> That vertuous *Virgo* borne for *Brytaines* blisse:
> That piereless braunch of *Brute*: that sweete remaine
> Of *Priam's* state: that hope of springing *Troy*:
> Which time to come, and many ages hence
> Shall of all warres compound eternall peace.[53]

Virgilian and Christian traditions are here combined to express the idea of Elizabeth's role as predestined inaugurator of a new golden age of 'Religion, ease and health'.

The most explicit identification of Elizabeth with the Virgin of the Tree of Jesse is the illustration on the title page of Stow's *Annals* where the traditional iconography of the *Virga Iesse* has been adapted to a Tudor genealogy with Queen Elizabeth as the royal flower 'enraced', like the Blessed Virgin, in 'stocke of earthly flesh' (*FQ*, III, v, 52).[54]

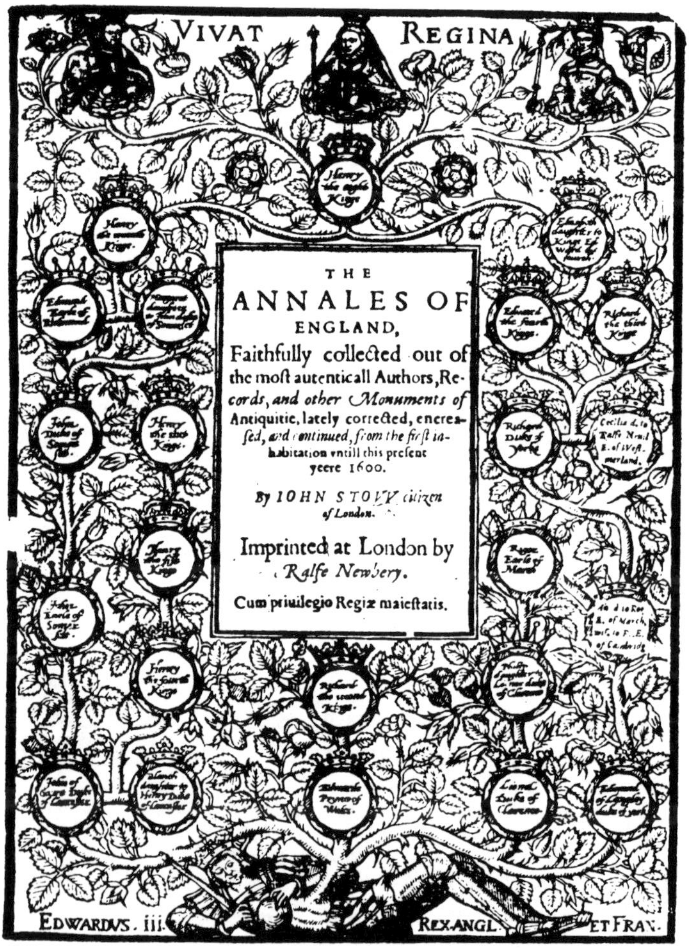

VIVAT REGINA

THE ANNALES OF ENGLAND,

Faithfully collected out of the moſt autenticall Authors, Records, and other *Monuments* of Antiquitie, lately corrected, encreaſed, and *continued, from the firſt in*habitation vntill this preſent yeere 1600.

By IOHN STOVV citizen of London.

Imprinted at London by *Ralfe Newbery.*

Cum priuilegio Regiæ maieſtatis.

EDWARDVS. iii. REX ANGL. ET FRA.

That identification of the Queen with the Virgin Mary was a central feature of the cult of Elizabeth is well known.[55] What is not widely understood is the way in which Spenser systematically exploits this typology in his characterization of most of the important regal female figures in *The Faerie Queene*. A review of the more important aspects of the cult of the Virgin Mary and the ascription to Elizabeth of Marian attributes will serve to show how perfectly suited this material was to Spenser's purpose.

From the time of the early Church Fathers Mary was revered in her own person as Mother of God,[56] and in symbol as the Church in its true faith.[57] By the end of the Middle Ages the cult of her person had grown to enormous proportions, emphasizing her quasi-divine powers and privileges as predestined Queen of heaven and hell,[58] co-redeeming vanquisher of death and the devil,[59] mystical bride of Christ,[60] miraculous protectress, and merciful intercessor for all mankind, both in this world and at the Day of Judgement.[61] Her feast days were highly popular, not least the day of her Nativity and the day of her Assumption into heaven. It was from these special powers, privileges and devotions that the Virgin Mary was firmly divested by the Church reformers in their zeal to return to the orthodoxy of the primitive Church.

The abolition of such deep-rooted beliefs could hardly be accomplished without leaving an emotional and intellectual gap in the life of Christendom. As Wilson has remarked, 'Human devotion changes more slowly than its objects shift. From 1558 to 1603 the virgin queen of England was the object of a love not dissimilar in quality from that which for centuries had warmed English hearts that looked to the virgin Queen of Heaven for all grace.'[62] However, it is important to realize that the adaptation of Marian imagery to the praise of Elizabeth was rare until the mid-1570s,[63] and that when it did become current its purpose was more than sentimental or merely metaphoric. Rather it is to be seen as a later extension of the very earliest attempts to identify Elizabeth as a predestined champion of the Protestant cause; as such it had a precise historical and apocalyptic function.

As soon as Elizabeth acceded to the throne she was greeted as a godly prince providentially appointed to deliver a chosen people from Antichrist. 'Let us daily call to God with lifted up hearts and hands for her preservation and long life', wrote John Aylmer in 1559 in reply to Knox's *Monstrous Regiment of Women*, 'that she may many years carry the sword of our defence, and therewith cut off the head of that Hydra, the Antichrist of Rome, in such sort that it may never grow again in this realm of England.'[64] With the publication of Jewel's *Apology of the Church of England* in 1562 and of the English version of Foxe's *Acts and Monuments* in the following year, the predestinate nature of the role the new queen was to play – already firmly implanted in the popular mind through civic pageantry[65] – received the confirmation of a seemingly overwhelming weight of historical evidence. As Haller has shown, the great achievement of the *Acts and Monuments* was to demonstrate that 'by all the signs to be found in scripture and history the will of God was about to be fulfilled in England by a prince perfect in her obedience to her vocation . . .'[66]

What was not apparent in the early years of Elizabeth's reign was the apocalyptic significance of her virginity. Quite apart from the consideration that to be ruled by a woman ran counter to natural law, there was much pressure on her to marry for the sake of ensuring the succession.[67] But the longer Elizabeth reigned, miraculously impregnable to Catholic plots and presumptive husbands, the greater was the tendency for Protestant Elizabethans to see the adulation of their Virgin Queen as a precise and proper substitute for the cult of the Virgin Mary. '*Vivat ELIZA!* for an *Ave MARI!*' sings Dowland,[68] while Dekker (born c. 1570) declares that his own generation 'never shouted any other *Aue* than her name . . .'[69] As her reign wore on the pious hopes expressed in the allegorical pageantry of the accession-day festivities were naturally transformed into confident tributes to Elizabeth's godly statesmanship. By the 1580s it was a common belief that 'the whole course of hir Maiesties life is myraculous'.[70] November 17 was fervently kept as a day of patriotic rejoicing, 'in the forme of an Holy-day',[71] to celebrate the date of 'saint' Elizabeth's accession to the throne. Another day of celebration which gave particular offence to English Catholics was Elizabeth's birthday, for September 7 was also the feast of the Nativity of the Blessed Virgin Mary. Thomas Holland, in a sermon for 17 November 1599, adverts to the complaint that Protestants contemptuously ignored the Virgin's nativity and 'insteede thereof, most solemnly doe celebrate the birth-day of Q. Elizabeth', even to the extent that in St Paul's Cathedral

> That Antiphone or Himne that was accustomably in the end of the service song by the Quier in the honor of the blessed Virgin, is now converted (as it is reported by common fame) to the laude and honor of Queene Elizabeth, thereby to sounde her praises.[72]

The transference to Elizabeth of certain deep-rooted devotional habits no doubt filled an important emotional gap in the lives of her subjects. But it would be misleading to suggest that the reasons for this phenomenon were purely intuitive: the celebration, in the later years of her reign, of Elizabeth as a post-figuration of the Virgin Mary is an important but neglected ramification of the nationalistic propaganda whose essential features had been definitively established in the *Acts and Monuments*. From the first year of her reign, some time before Marian comparisons had begun to be made, Elizabeth was likened to the biblical Deborah who saved God's chosen race from the idolatrous heathen.[73] But later in her reign, in the mid-1570s, other Old Testament analogies became popular. From that time onwards Elizabeth is frequently likened to Judith and Esther,[74] both of whom were formerly types of the Virgin Mary in her conquest of the Devil;[75] she is compared with the Queen of Sheba[76] (another type of Mary), whose homage to Solomon symbolized the faith and worship of the true Church;[77] she is seen as a daughter of King David, a virgin begotten of the Lord and espoused to God's only son to rule over Sion;[78] her people are a second Israel,[79] her country a second Canaan, the promised land flowing with milk and honey.[80]

The motive behind these comparisons is not sentimental but political. In drawing parallels between his Queen and certain Old Testament figures who are themselves types of the Virgin Mary, the panegyrist is implying that Elizabeth's royal virginity signifies the fulfilment of God's special will for his chosen people. Though the promise contained in these Old Testament figures was fulfilled in the Blessed Virgin, her life does not represent a consummation of the historical process of which it forms a part. For the antitype itself contains the promise of a future event and looks forward to the end of time and the establishment of God's kingdom on earth.[81] As a post-figuration of the Virgin Mary, Elizabeth performs a crucial role in this millenial plan. For if Mary is, above all, a type of the Church, then Elizabeth's triumph over popery could be seen as the defeat of Antichrist prophesied in the Apocalypse, and the institution over which she presided as indubitably the one true Church.[82]

It is not surprising, therefore, that the coincidence of Elizabeth's own nativity with Mary's should have been regarded as more than a happy accident of fate. To the Protestant Elizabethan it seemed to be a divine omen, whose full import – that the entire reign of the Virgin Queen and her Anglican Church had been authorized, miraculously sustained and sanctified by divine providence – was indisputably confirmed by the date of Elizabeth's death, 24 March 1603. The fact that 'This Maiden Queen Elizabeth came into this world the Eve of the Nativity of the blessed Virgin Mary; and died on the Eve of the Annunciation of the Virgin Mary'[83] was a clear sign of predestination. Dekker wrote:

Shee came in with the falle of the leafe, and went away in the Spring:

> her life (which was dedicated to Virginitie,) both beginning & closing vp a miraculous Mayden circle: for she was borne vpon a Lady Eue, and died vpon a Lady Eue.[84]

When Elizabeth was addressed as queen of heaven and hell,[85] vanquisher of death and the devil,[86] mystical bride of Christ,[87] miraculous protectress and merciful intercessor,[88] few educated Elizabethans would have failed to recognize the apocalyptic significance of such appellations: it was as if she had, by providential design, attained a symbolic kinship with the Virgin Mary, and so, without any impropriety, could be venerated by Protestant patriots in the terms and images reserved for the honour of the Queen of Heaven.

Nowhere is the belief that the resemblances between Elizabeth and Mary were the coherent revelations of a divine purpose clearer than in the English and Latin verses composed in commemoration of Elizabeth's death. Here we find not only quasi-Marian litanies of her titles and epithets, but also the most direct and explicit comparisons between the two women. 'Do you wish to know the reason why it was on the Eve of Lady Day that the holy Eliza ascended into heaven?' asked the anonymous author of one Latin elegy. His answer was simple:

> being on the point of death she chose that day for herself because in their lives these two were as one. Mary was a Virgin, she, Elizabeth, was also; Mary was blessed; Beta was blessed among the race of women. Mary's heir was a prince, Elizabeth was the heir of a prince. Mary bore God in her womb, but Elizabeth bore God in her heart. Although in all other respects they are like twins, it is in this latter respect alone that they are not of equal rank.[89]

For an Elizabethan poet undertaking to vindicate his prince's claim to be the restorer of the one true Church the tradition of veneration which culminates in these memorial verses provided a vehicle of praise which was uniquely suited to his purpose. If Elizabeth's sex created serious problems for an epideictic poet writing in the heroic mode, at the same time it made available to him a form of praise which no poet had been able to use before. The reason why Spenser's use of these techniques has, on the whole, gone unnoticed is probably the fact that he often combines Marian and classical imagery in describing the same character. Belphoebe in Book II and Cynthia in the 'Mutabilitie' fragment are the most notable examples of this fusion of the Christian with the pagan. However, it is important that we distinguish between the purely metaphoric significance of the latter – the stock in trade of the epideictic poet – and the typological significance of the former. When Spenser compares Elizabeth with a classical goddess like Cynthia he is writing figuratively: he wishes to persuade us that Elizabeth possesses those virtues of which Cynthia is a personification. But when he uses Marian imagery to describe the same character he is implying that the relationship between Elizabeth and the Virgin Mary is not just an imaginary one, but a kinship of character and of providential function between two historical figures. The resemblances between them – too complete to be explained as mere coincidence – appeared to confirm the fact that Elizabeth was no ordinary ruler, but indeed a 'Prince of peace from heauen blest' (*FQ*, IV, proem, 4).

Marian typology thus complements the Trojan myth; together they form the background of a poem which can, in the fullest sense of the term, be described as a work of Christian humanism. Allusion to these two bodies of mythico-historical matter is by no means continuous throughout *The Faerie Queene*: as Virgil allows his reader occasionally to catch, as it were, a glimpse of Augustus, without his ever appearing in the *Aeneid* in person, so Spenser reminds his reader, at certain dramatic moments in the narrative, that the events which he is witnessing have a significance beyond their literal, or indeed their allegorical meaning – a significance which can only be perceived in its entirety within the context of a Christian humanist view of world history.

In addressing his poem to Queen Elizabeth and telling her that she may trace her own 'great auncestry' in its 'antique Image' (II, proem, 4), Spenser set himself a twofold task – a task which is perhaps best summed up by Erasmus when he claims that the purpose of the epideictic writer is to present his prince with an image of virtue, both as a pattern for emulation and as a warning against the dereliction of his sacred responsibility. The virtues which form the subjects of the six completed books of *The Faerie Queene* are to be understood, then, not simply as facets of a Renaissance ideal of human conduct, but as attributes of Queen Elizabeth. In the chapters which follow I shall try to show how each is defined in such a way as to reveal Elizabeth's unique qualification for the role of Christian prince.

## Notes

1. All quotations from Spenser are from *The Poetical Works of Edmund Spenser*, edited by J.C. Smith and E. de Selincourt, one vol. edn (Oxford, 1924).

2. Letter to Ralegh, Smith and de Selincourt, p. 407.

3. The best modern account of the theory of praise in Renaissance literature is O.B. Hardison, Jr., *The Enduring Monument: A Study of the Idea of Praise in Renaissance Literary Theory and Practice* (Westport, Conn., 1962). See also Theodore Burgess, *Epideictic Literature* (Chicago, 1902); A. Leigh De Neef, 'Epideictic Rhetoric and the Renaissance Lyric', *JMRS*, 3 (1973), 203-31; Barbara Kiefer Lewalski, *Donne's 'Anniversaries' and the Poetry of Praise: The Creation of a Symbolic Mode* (Princeton, 1973), pp. 15-41; James D. Garrison, *Dryden and the Tradition of Panegyric* (Berkeley, Los Angeles and London, 1975), pp. 1-82; Thomas H. Cain, *Praise in 'The Faerie Queene'* (Lincoln, Nebr., 1978), pp. 1-10; John W. O'Malley, *Praise and Blame in Renaissance Rome: Rhetoric, Doctrine, and Reform in the Sacred Orators of the Papal Court, c. 1450-1521* (Durham, N.C., 1979), pp. 36-76; Richard S. Peterson, *Imitation and Praise in the Poems of Ben Jonson* (New Haven, Conn. and London, 1981), pp. 1-43.

4. George Puttenham, *The Arte of English Poesie*, edited by Gladys Doidge Willcock and Alice Walker (Cambridge, 1936), p. 24.

5. Smith and de Selincourt, p. 411.

6. Epideictic poetry (from Gr. ἐπιδείκνυμι) means literally poetry of display. On the analogy of epideictic oratory it normally signifies poetry of praise. (Epideictic oratory is one of the three classical divisions of rhetoric; see Aristotle, *Rhetoric*, I, iii, 3; [Cicero?] *Rhetorica ad Herennium*, I, ii, 2; Cicero, *De Inventione*, I, v, 7; *De Oratore*, I, xxxi, 141; Quintilian, *Institutio Oratore*, III, iv; Menander Rhetor, I, i, 1-14.)

7. *Donati interpretationes Virgilianae*, quoted by Hardison, p. 33 (Hardison's translation). Servius (c. fourth-fifth century) likewise claimed that Virgil's intention was 'to imitate Homer and to praise Augustus in terms of his ancestors' (Introduction to *P. Vergilii Carmina Commentarii*, quoted by D.L. Drew, *The Allegory of the 'Aeneid'* (Oxford, 1927), p. 98 (my translation)). On Servius as an interpreter of Virgil, see also Michael O'Connell, *Mirror and Veil: The Historical Dimension of Spenser's 'Faerie Queene'* (Chapel Hill, N.C., 1977), pp. 25-31. As O'Connell writes: 'Servius held a position of unique authority and honor in sixteenth-century editions of Vergil. Indeed his commentary was practically inescapable by Renaissance readers of Vergil . . .' (pp. 25-6).

8. Domenico Comparetti, *Vergil in the Middle Ages*, translated by E.F.M. Benecke (London, 1895), p. 108.

9. Hardison, p. 78.

10. John Hughes, 'An Essay on Allegorical Poetry' (1715) rpt. in *Edmund Spenser: A Critical Anthology*, edited by Paul J. Alpers (Harmondsworth, 1969), p. 82. Cf. Dryden: 'Virgil . . . designed to form a perfect prince, and would insinuate that Augustus, whom he calls Aeneas in his poem, was truly such . . .', 'Dedication of the Aeneis', *Essays of John Dryden*, edited by W.P. Ker, 2 vols (New York, 1961), II, 179.

11. Hardison, p. 80.

12. Many scholars have written on Spenser's debt to Virgil. See in particular Merritt Y. Hughes, *Virgil and Spenser* (New York, 1929); Wm. Stanford Webb, 'Vergil in Spenser's Epic Theory', *ELH*, 4 (1937), 62-84; Josephine Waters Bennett, *The Evolution of 'The Faerie Queene'* (New York, 1942), pp. 6 ff.; William Nelson, *The Poetry of Edmund Spenser* (New York and London, 1963), pp. 117 ff.; O'Connell, pp. 23-30.

13. 'In that Faery Queene I meane glory in my generall intention, but in my particular I conceiue the most excellent and glorious person of our soueraine the Queene, and her kingdome in Faery land' (Letter to Ralegh, Smith and de Selincourt, p. 407). See Edwin Greenlaw, *Studies in Spenser's Historical Allegory*, Johns Hopkins Monographs in Literary History, II (Baltimore, 1932); Frances

Yates, 'Queen Elizabeth as Astraea', *JWCI*, 10 (1947), 27-82; Hardison, pp. 80-4; Frank Kermode, '*The Faerie Queene*, I and V', *BJRL*, 47 (1964), rpt. in *Shakespeare, Spenser, Donne: Renaissance Essays* (London, 1971), p. 40; Cain, *Praise in 'The Faerie Queene'*, passim.

14. *Praise in 'The Faerie Queene'*, p. 1.

15. Letter to Jean Desmarez, *The Correspondence of Erasmus*, translated by R.A.B. Mynors and D.F.S. Thomson, 2 vols (Toronto, 1975), II, 81.

16. See Hardison, pp. 27-42.

17. For discussions of the *speculum principis* tradition see John E. Mason, *Gentlefolk in the Making: Studies in the History of English Courtesy Literature and Related Topics from 1531-1774* (Philadelphia, 1935), pp. 10-11; Lester K. Born, introduction to a translated edition of Erasmus's *Education of a Christian Prince*, Columbia University Records of Civilisation, XXVII (New York, 1936), pp. 44-130.

18. Dedicatory Epistle to *The Education of a Christian Prince*, edited by Born, pp. 135-6.

19. Helena Shire, *A Preface to Spenser* (London, 1978), p. 84.

20. Letter to Ralegh, Smith and de Selincourt, p. 407.

21. The standard works on the Renaissance courtesy book are Ruth Kelso, *The Doctrine of the English Gentleman in the Sixteenth Century*, University of Illinois Studies in Language and Literature, XIV (Urbana, Ill., 1929) and Mason, *Gentlefolk in the Making*.

22. See in particular Mohinimohan Bhattacherje, *Studies in Spenser* (Calcutta, 1929) extract rpt. in *The Works of Edmund Spenser*, Variorum edition, edited by Edwin Greenlaw, Charles Grosvenor Osgood, Frederick Morgan Padelford and Ray Heffner, 10 vols (Baltimore, 1932-49), Books VI and VII, 328-33; H.S.V. Jones, *A Spenser Handbook* (New York, 1930), pp. 287-92; A.C. Judson, 'Spenser's Theory of Courtesy', *PMLA*, 47 (1932), 122-36; Fritz Caspari, *Humanism and the Social Order in Tudor England* (Chicago, 1954), pp. 176-80.

23. 'Proheme' to *The Boke Named the Governor* (1531), edited by Foster Watson, Everyman edition (London, 1907), p. xxxi. For further discussion of this point see Robin Headlam Wells, 'Spenser and the Courtesy Tradition: Form and Meaning in the Sixth Book of *The Faerie Queene*', *ES*, 58 (1977), 226-8.

24. *The Book of the Courtier*, translated by Sir Thomas Hoby, Everyman edition (1928; rpt. London, 1966), pp. 260-1.

25. On Elyot's debt to Castiglione and the differences as well as similarities between *The Courtier* and *The Governour* see John M. Major, *Sir Thomas Elyot and Renaissance Humanism* (Lincoln, Nebr., 1964), pp. 61-76.

26. Caspari, p. 183.

27. Smith and de Selincourt, p. 407.

28. Smith and de Selincourt, p. 409.

29. *Genealogie Deorum Gentilium Libri*, edited by Vincenzo Romano, *Opere*, 7 vols (Bari, 1928-51), VII, 721-3. On Boccaccio's influence in Renaissance England see Charles G. Osgood (ed.), *Boccaccio on Poetry: Being the Preface and the Fourteenth and Fifteenth Books of Boccaccio's* 'Genealogie Deorum Gentilium' (1930; rpt. Indianapolis, 1956), p. xliv.

30. It was the arbitrary nature of much medieval interpretation of the Bible which led to the condemnation of this form of hermeneutics by Reformation exegetes. For the Protestant seeking the one true sense of Scripture, allegorists of the school of Philo were held in deep suspicion because they dealt with arcana. The typologist, on the other hand, sought only to reveal an aspect of the literal meaning of sacred texts. (See Lewalski, pp. 150-6. See also Philip Rollinson, *Classical Theories of Allegory and Christian Culture* (Pittsburg and Brighton, 1981), pp. 29-86.)

31. See V.A. Kolve, *The Play Called Corpus Christi* (London, 1966), pp. 63 ff.

32. In one of the fullest of the rare discussions of typology in *The Faerie Queene* Angus Fletcher consistently and wrongly equates typology not only with prophecy, but with parody and literary parallelism of the most general kind (*The Prophetic Moment: An Essay on Spenser* (Chicago, 1971), pp. 57-132). To say that 'Insofar as Book II seems grossly analogous to Book I it has always been read in a typological way . . .' (p. 84) or that the names of the rivers attending the marriage of the Thames and the Medway in Book IV 'Come from the matrix of Ovidian typology' (p. 96) does more to obscure the meaning of typology than to clarify it.

33. The most scholarly modern discussion of typology is still Erich Auerbach's 'Figura' in *Scenes from the Drama of European Literature* (New York, 1959), pp. 11-76. See also Auerbach, *Mimesis: The Representation of Reality in Western Literature* (1946; rpt. New York, 1953), pp. 13-14; 42-3; 64-6; Austin Farrer, 'Typology', *The Expository Times*, 67 (1956), 228-31; K.J. Woollcombe, 'The Biblical Origins and Patristic Development of Typology' in *Essays on Typology*, edited by G.W.H. Lampe and K.J. Woollcombe (London, 1957), pp. 39-75; Jean Danielou S. J., *From Shadows to Reality: Studies in the Biblical Typology of the Fathers*, translated by Dom Wulstan Hibberd (London, 1960), pp. 1-7 and passim; Thomas M. Davis, 'The Tradition of Puritan Typology', *Early American Literature*, 5 (1970), 1-50, rpt. in *Typology and Early American Literature*, edited by Sacvan Bercovitch (Amherst, Mass., 1972), pp. 11-45; John MacQueen, *Allegory* (London, 1970), pp. 18-23; Karlfried Froehlich, '"Always to keep to the Literal Sense in Holy Scripture Means to kill One's Soul": The State of Biblical Hermeneutics at the Beginning of the Fifteenth Century' in *Literary Uses of Typology from the Late Middle Ages to the Present*, edited by Earl Miner (Princeton, 1977), pp. 20-48; Mason I. Lowance, Jr., *The Language of Canaan: Metaphor and Symbol in New England from the Puritans to the Transcendentalists* (Cambridge, Mass. and London, 1980), pp. 13-27.

In recent years there have appeared some outstanding studies of typology in literature. See in particular A.C. Charity, *Events and their Afterlife: The Dialectics of Christian Typology in the Bible and Dante* (Cambridge, 1966); Stephen Manning, 'Scriptural Exegesis and the Literary Critic', *Early American Literature*, 5 (1970), 51-73 rpt. in Bercovitch, pp. 47-66; Lewalski, *Donne's 'Anniversaries'*, pp. 149-58; Robert Hollander, 'Typology and Secular Literature: Some Medieval Problems and Examples' in Miner, pp. 3-19; Steven N. Zwicker, 'Politics and Panegyric: The Figural Mode from Marvell to Pope' in Miner, pp. 115-46.

34. The first modern critic to draw attention to this aspect of the *Aeneid* is Drew, *The Allegory of the 'Aeneid'*, p. 4. See also Hollander, 'Typology and Secular Literature', p. 6.

35. Richard Nicols, *Englands Eliza: or The Victoriovs and Trivmphant Reigne of that Virgin Empresse of Sacred Memorie, ELIZABETH* . . . printed in *A Mirovr for Magistrates*, edited by John Higgins (London, 1610), p. 784.

36. See Lewalski, pp. 150-8.

37. Spenser's edition, like all Renaissance editions of the *Aeneid*, began, as Nelson reminds us (p. 117), not with the words 'Arma virumque cano . . .' but:

Ille ego qui quondam gracili modulatus avena
Carmen, et egressus silvis, vicina coegi
Ut quamvis avido parerent arva colono
Gratum opus agricolis: at nunc horrentia Martis
Arma virumque cano . . .

38. For discussions of the Trojan myth from a literary point of view see

A.E. Parsons, 'The Trojan Legend in England', *MLR*, 24 (1929), 253-64, 394-408 and Greenlaw, *Studies in Spenser's Historical Allegory*, pp. 1-58. T.D. Kenrick (*British Antiquity* (London, 1950), passim), and F.J. Levy (*Tudor Historical Thought* (San Marino, 1967), pp. 65-6) consider the myth from the points of view of the Tudor antiquarian and historian respectively.

39. Kenrick, p. 3.

40. Kenrick, p. 7.

41.

Brute sub occasu solistrans gallica regna.
Insula in occeano est habitata gigantibus olim.
Nunc deserta quidem gentibus apta tuis.
Illa tibi fietque tuis locus aptus aeuum.
Hec erit & natis attera troia tuis.
Hie de prole tua reges nascentur & ipsis.
Totius terrae subditus orbis erit.

(*The* Historia Regum Britanniae *of Geoffrey of Monmouth*, edited by Acton Griscom (London, 1929), p. 239.)

42. *Parts Added to The Mirror for Magistrates*, edited by Lily B. Campbell (Cambridge, 1946), p. 55.

43. *The Union of the Two Noble and Illustre Famelies of Lancastre & Yorke, Beeyng, Long in Continual Discension for the Crowne of this Noble Realme, with all the Actes Done in Bothe the Tymes of the Princes* . . . (1548; rpt. London, 1809), p. 423.

44. The myth was also revived on James I's accession. See Charles Bowie Millican, *Spenser and The Table Round*, Harvard Studies in Comparative Literature, VIII (Cambridge, Mass., 1932), pp. 127-41 and Glynne Wickham, *Shakespeare's Dramatic Heritage* (London, 1969), pp. 250-8.

45. See Appendix, 'Polydore Vergil and English Historiography'.

46. *A Defence of Poetry*, *Miscellaneous Prose of Sir Philip Sidney*, edited by Katherine Duncan-Jones and Jan Van Dorsten (Oxford, 1973), p. 78.

47. Sidney, p. 79.

48. *A View of the Present State of Ireland*, *Variorum Spenser*, *The Prose Works* (1949), edited by Rudolf Gottfried, p. 82.

49. See Comparetti, *Vergil in the Middle Ages*, pp. 99-101; Yates, 'Queen Elizabeth as Astraea', pp. 32-3; Marina Warner, *Alone of All Her Sex: The Myth and the Cult of the Virgin Mary* (London, 1976), pp. 264-5.

50. Lydgate, for example, writes, 'Sythe [Christ] is borne with so fayre a face, /The golden worlde makying to retourne,/The worlde of pece, the kyngdome of Satourne . . .' (*Life of Our Lady*, edited by Joseph A. Lauritis, Ralph A. Klinefelter and Vernon F. Gallagher, Duquesne Studies in Philosophy, II (Pittsburg, 1961), p. 533).

51. John Lyly, *Euphues' Glass for Europe*, *The Complete Works of John Lyly*, edited by R. Warwick Bond, 3 vols (Oxford, 1902), II, 205.

52. See Arthur Watson, *The Early Iconography of the Tree of Jesse* (Oxford, 1934). In medieval Marian literature the Virgin Mary is sometimes compared, as empress, with the most illustrious pagan rulers of the ancient world and her royal lineage with theirs. See, for example, *The Myroure of oure Ladye*, edited by John Henry Blunt, Early English Text Society (London, 1873), pp. 216, 258-9, John Lydgate, *Life of Our Lady*, pp. 252-3. In constructing a mythical genealogy for Queen Elizabeth, Spenser conflates the pagan with the Christian.

53. Quoted by Elkin Calhoun Wilson, *England's Eliza*, Harvard Studies in English, XX (1939; rpt. London, 1966), p. 103. Elizabeth is similarly described as a 'matchlesse flower' springing from 'the Royall Garden of a King' in Bacon's prophecy from Greene's *Friar Bacon and Friar Bungay* (see Wilson, pp. 103-4).

54. The same illustration is used in the 1580 edition of the *Annals*, entitled *The Chronicles of England*.

55. See Yates, 'Queen Elizabeth as Astraea', pp. 74-5; John Buxton, *Elizabethan Taste* (London, 1963), p. 50; Jean Wilson, *Entertainments for Elizabeth I* (Woodbridge, 1980), pp. 21-2.

56. See the *New Catholic Encyclopaedia* (Washington, D.C., 1967) under 'Mother of God'.

57. See Warner, pp. 104-5.

58. See Émile Mâle, *Religious Art in France: XIII Century*, translated by Dora Nussey (London, 1913), p. 235.

59. See Mirella Levi D'Ancona, *The Iconography of the Immaculate Conception in the Middles Ages and Early Renaissance*, Monographs on Archaeology and Fine Arts sponsored by the Archaeological Institute of America and the College Art Association of America, VII (New York, 1957), pp. 20-8, 32-3 and Rosemary Woolf, *The English Religious Lyric in the Middle Ages* (Oxford, 1968), pp. 121-3.

60. See Warner, pp. 121-33, 247. The imagery is drawn from the Canticles and the Apocalypse, XXI, 2.

61. See D'Ancona, pp. 34-5; Mâle, pp. 23-66; Woolf, pp. 123-4.

62. Wilson, *England's Eliza*, p. 215. Much of the illustrative material contained in the following paragraphs is taken from Wilson's invaluable compilation of Elizabethan panegyric. Although Wilson discusses the Elizabethan habit of comparing the Queen with the Virgin Mary in a chapter somewhat obliquely entitled 'Diana', many Marian analogies are to be found in other chapters, often in a form whose significance was apparently not recognised by him.

63. See Wilson, passim.

64. *An Harborowe for faithfull and true subjectes* (1559), quoted by William Haller, *Foxe's Book of Martyrs and the Elect Nation* (London, 1963), p. 88.

65. At the royal entry of 1558 Elizabeth was represented as Deborah, judge and restorer of Israel, 'sent/From Heaven, a long comfort to us thy subjectes all'. See *The Progresses and Public Processions of Queen Elizabeth*, edited by John Nichols, 3 vols (1788-1805; rpt. London, 1823), I, 56.

66. Haller, p. 225.

67. See J.E. Neale, *Queen Elizabeth* (London, 1934), Chs. V, XV.

68. *The Second Book of Airs* (1600) (quoted by Wilson, p. 206).

69. Thomas Dekker, *The Wonderfull Yeare* (1603) (quoted by Wilson, p. 393).

70. Henri Estienne, *The Stage of Popish toyes* (1581) (quoted by Wilson, p. 225). Cf. also Thomas Bentley, *The monument of matrones*, 'The first Chapter of the HEAST', reproduced by Wilson in a plate facing p. 220: God has 'miraculouslie deliuered [Elizabeth] out of so manie & so great dangers . . .' In her ageless virginity, too, she is 'Heauens miracle' (*Histriomastix* (c. 1589), quoted by Wilson, p. 109). For the Virgin Mary's agelessness see Warner, p. 95.

71. Thomas Holland, *A sermon preached at Pauls in London* (1599) (quoted by Wilson, p. 223, n. 100).

72. Quoted by Wilson, pp. 221-2.

73. See above, note 65.

74. Cf. Thomas Deloney, *The ouerthrow of proud Holofornes, and the triumph of vertuous Queene Iudith* (1588): 'How often hath our Iudith sau'd,/ and kept vs from decay:/Gainst Holofernes, Deuill and Pope . . .' (quoted by Wilson, p. 44). For other examples of Elizabeth as Judith see Wilson, pp. 36, 81, 185, 372, 380. As with Judith, analogies between Elizabeth and Esther, who preserved her people against the plots of Haman, were especially popular after the defeat of the Armada. For examples see Wilson, pp. 81, 101 n. 27, 185, 376, 380.

75. See Woolf, p. 285.

76. Thomas Holland's sermon for 17 November 1599 compares Elizabeth

('*Regia Virgo*') with the Queen of Sheba (see Wilson, p. 223, n. 100).

77. See Mâle, p. 157.

78. In Thomas Bentley's *The monument of matrones* God addresses Elizabeth in the following words: 'Elizabeth, thou Virgin mine, the KINGS Daughter, and fairest among women; most full of beautie and maiestie: attend a litle to my Heast, and marke what I shall say. Thou art my Daughter in deede, this daie haue I begotten thee, and espoused thee to thy king CHRIST, my Sonne; crowned thee with my gifts, and appointed thee QVEENE, to reigne vpon my holie mount Zion' (reproduced by Wilson in a plate facing p. 220).

79. In *The monument of matrones* God declares to Elizabeth: '[I have] annointed thee with holie oile, to be the Queene, the Mother, and the Nursse of my people in Israel . . .' (Wilson, plate facing p. 220). Lyly speaks of England as 'a new *Israel*' in *Euphues' Glass for Europe*, p. 205.

80. See the poems extracted by Wilson, pp. 376, 387.

81. Isabel Rivers is misleading when she writes: 'the antitype once and for all fulfils the type and the meaning hidden in it' (*Classical and Christian Ideas in English Renaissance Poetry* (London, 1979), p. 149). As Auerbach argues, both type and antitype 'have something provisional and incomplete about them; they point to one another and both point to something in the future, something still to come, which will be the actual, real, and definitive event' ('Figura', p. 58).

82. Interpretations of the Apocalypse as an allegorical prophecy of the struggle between the English Protestants and their persecutors were common in the sixteenth century. See below, Chapter 1.

83. Memorial inscription in Westminster Abbey cited by Buxton, p. 51. Buxton notes that the 'Lady Chapels which their grandfathers had built on to the east end of English churches were now replaced by . . . secular shrines for their devotion to the Queen' (p. 50).

84. *The Wonderfull Yeare* (quoted by Wilson, pp. 220-1).

85. In Dekker's *Old Fortunatus* (1599) it is claimed of Eliza that 'heau'n and hell her power obey' (quoted by Wilson, p. 116).

86. In *Idea the Shepheards Garland* (1593) Drayton depicts Elizabeth as the Marian composite of the Second Eve, trampling the serpent of Eden under her heel (Genesis, III, 15), and the woman of the Apocalypse threatened by the beast or dragon with seven heads (Revelation, XII, 3-4) when he writes 'And thy large empyre stretch her armes from east unto the west,/And thou under thy feet mayst tread, that foule seven-headed beast' (quoted by Wilson, p. 146). The seven-headed beast is to be interpreted in regular Protestant fashion as the papacy. See, for example Bale's *Image of Both Churches*. In his paraphrase of Revelation, XII, 3 Bale writes, 'this is the very papacy here in Europe, which is the general antichrist of all the whole world almost' (*Select Works of John Bale*, edited by Henry Christmas, Parker Society Reprints (Cambridge, 1849), p. 407). On the traditional conflation of Genesis, III, 15 with Revelation, XII, 3-4 see Warner, pp. 244-6.

87. See above, note 78.

88. In a ballad of 1584 celebrating her triumph over Catholic plots, Elizabeth, the 'pearle of princes' and 'renowned virgin queen' is represented as a protector of her loyal followers from the rod of God's vengeance for sin (see Wilson, pp. 32-4). On the Virgin Mary as protecting intercessor see Louis Réau, *Iconographie De L'Art Chrétien*, 6 vols (Paris, 1955-9), III (1957), 116-17.

89.

Scire cupis causam pridie cur, sacra, diei
*Virginis*, ad superas scandit *Elisa* domus?
Disce brevi: moritura diem sibi legerat istum,
Caetera quod paribus, par sit vtrisq; dies.

Virgo *Maria* fuit, fuit *illa*: beata *Maria*,
Inter foemineum *Beta* beata genus.
Haeres *huic* princeps fuit, *altera* principis haeres,
*Haec* vtero gessit, corde sed *illa* Deum.
Caetera cum similes, cum caetera poeme gemellae,
Hoc vno parilem non habuere statum . . .

Lines from an anthology of Latin funeral verses published by Oxford University in 1603 (quoted by Wilson, p. 382).

# 1 PRINCE OF PEACE FROM HEAVEN BLEST

It is well known to modern scholars that the first book of *The Faerie Queene* is 'a celebration in image and allegory of the Foxian version of history . . .'[1] The romance story of the royal virgin whose rightful inheritance is restored to her by her faithful knight is the story of Elizabeth as a divinely appointed ruler authorized by providence to restore the Christian religion to its original purity. Holiness may be seen as the definitive attribute of the godly prince.

But if Book I is a 'Tudor Apocalypse',[2] it is also an allegory of Christian salvation. When Spenser tells us in the letter to Ralegh that Gloriana is intended as a portrait of Elizabeth, he explains that she may be considered under two aspects, or 'persons': 'the one of a most royall Queene or Empresse, the other of a most vertuous and beautifull Lady . . .'[3] In his characterization of the first of the Queen's 'two persons' Spenser followed a well-documented tradition of humanist thought; however, his portrayal of the individual's struggle to realize an ideal of spiritual perfection presents a more difficult problem for the critic. For in defining the nature of holiness Spenser engaged in a theological debate which deeply divided the sixteenth century and which continues to divide Spenserians in the twentieth century. In this chapter I shall argue that, in portraying an ideal of holiness, Spenser's object was not so much accurately to reflect Elizabeth's own religious beliefs, as to illustrate the characteristics – official and personal – of the ideal Christian prince, partly as a tribute to her achievements, but more importantly as a pattern for emulation.

Spenser was heir to a long tradition of humanist thought on the subject of the character and responsibilities of the Christian prince, a tradition which regarded the true prince as an imperial figure with a divine mission to restore the Christian religion to its primitive state. The concept of the prince, as it was promulgated by such Tudor moralists as Starkey and Elyot, owes much to the Oxford humanist movement, and to Erasmus in particular.[4] According to Erasmus,

> no prince is so seculer, but that he hath to doe with the profession of the gospell, the Emperours are anoynted & sacred for this very purpose, that they may eyther maynteyne or restore, or elles enlarge and sprede abrode the religion of the gospel.[5]

The Christian prince is thus closely associated with the humanist appeal for a return to original scriptural sources. In applying philological principles to the study of sacred texts humanists like Colet and Erasmus provided a theoretical basis for the Elizabethan Church's claim to authenticity. When Foxe and Jewel defended secession from Rome it was on the grounds that the reformed Church of England represented a restoration of the true Catholic Church. In the exordium to the *Acts and Monuments* Foxe argued that the

> form, usage, and institution of this our present reformed church, are not the beginning of any new church of our own, but the renewing of the old ancient church of Christ; and that they are not any swerving from the church of Rome, but rather a reducing to the church of Rome. Whereas contrary, the church of Rome which now is, is nothing but a swerving from the church of Rome which then was . . .[6]

Jewel similarly claimed that the Elizabethan Church marked a return to the purity of the early church:

> we are come, as near as we possibly could, to the church of the apostles and of the old catholic bishops and fathers, which church we know hath hitherunto been sound and perfect and, as Tertullian termeth it, a pure virgin, spotted as yet with no idolatry nor with any foul or shameful fault . . .[7]

Yates and other scholars have shown how, in justifying royal governorship of the Church, Elizabethan historians appealed to a tradition of sacred empire.[8] Foxe regarded the early Christian empire as the golden age of the Church. In his view Constantine was the perfect godly ruler. In recounting the life of the first Christian emperor it was Foxe's hope that

> the divine disposition and singular gentle nature of this meek and religious Constantine might more notoriously appear to all princes, for them to learn by his example what zeal and care they might bear toward the church of Christ, and how gently to govern, and how to be beneficial to the same.[9]

If the first Christian emperor was the true pattern of a godly ruler, the Governor of a reformed church could be seen as a second Constantine bringing peace to a divided world. 'Let Constantinus be never so great', wrote Foxe in his dedication to Elizabeth, 'yet wherein is your noble grace to him inferior?'[10]

When Foxe compares his queen with an idealized image of the Christian prince, his purpose, like Spenser's, is, as Haller has rightly said, to instruct Elizabeth in the way she should conduct her affairs by praising her for already having done so.[11] The characteristics of the godly ruler, as they are presented to us in *The Faerie Queene*, have much in common with Foxe's portrait of Constantine. One cannot point to a particular stanza or even canto for a summary of these characteristics. Although Spenser tells us in the letter to Ralegh that the Faery Queen is a personification of glory and that Arthur is a portrait of princely magnificence, neither of these types of Elizabeth is fully characterized in the poem. Instead, Spenser builds up a composite image using a number of different figures to represent different facets of the Christian prince's character and office.

The character who is most obviously intended to 'shadow' Elizabeth is Una. As Jewel had spoken of the primitive church as an unspotted virgin, so Spenser employs the figure of a 'royall virgin' (I, ii, 7; I, iii, 5; I, viii, 26) 'withoutten spot' (I, xii, 22) and descended from 'ancient Kings and Queenes' (I, i, 5) to represent the Supreme Governor of the Elizabethan Church. Una is based, in part, on the 'woman clothed with the sun' from St John's Revelation (XII, 1).[12] The Apocalypse provided an ideal vehicle for Spenser's purpose, for here was a ready-made allegory of the Protestant Reformation. Identification of the Pope with the Antichrist of Revelation had been made as early as 1378 by Wyclif after the Great Schism; by the second decade of the sixteenth century commentaries which interpreted the drama of the Apocalypse as a prophecy of the war between Protestantism and Popery were legion.[13] The gloss to the Geneva Bible explains that, while the 'great whore' of Chapter XVII represents 'the Papistrie, whose crueltie and blood sheding is declared by skarlat' (Sig. GGgiv),[14] the woman clothed with the sun who is threatened by a dragon signifies 'how ye Church which is compassed about with Iesus Christ the Sonne of righteousnes, is persecuted of Antichrist' (Sig. GGgiiv). Like the bride of the lamb (Rev. XXI, 9) and the bride without spot of the Canticles (IV, 7), the woman clothed with the sun is a type of 'the Church, which is maried to Christ by faith' (Sig. HHhiv).

It has been shown that the name of Una was firmly linked in the popular mind with Queen Elizabeth.[15] However, even without this link it is unlikely that the contemporary reader would fail to make the comparison between Elizabeth and the royal virgin of Book I. For the bride of the Canticles and the woman clothed with the sun are well-known types of the Virgin Mary. As Mary was represented in medieval literature as the 'blossum and bud of all oure glorye' descended from the royal stock of David,[16] so Una is described as 'the chastest flowre, that ay did spring/On earthly braunch, the daughter of a king' (I, i, 48). For an Elizabethan poet undertaking to defend his prince's claim to be the chosen instrument of providence, the popular identification of Elizabeth with the Virgin Mary provided an invaluable repertory of rhetorical techniques.

But Una represents only one facet of Elizabeth's character – her official one. (Though Una's most salient moral quality – her fidelity – is, of course, partly symbolic of Elizabeth's own steadfast devotion to her sacred responsibility, it stands principally for the one true faith of which the Queen is, *ex officio*, defender.) To amplify our portrait of the Christian prince we must turn to other characters. One of Spenser's most typical devices in *The Faerie Queene* is the definition of a virtue or an idea by its contrary. Thus in canto iv we are presented with a parody of the godly ruler.

It has been suggested that Lucifera is based on a biblical image of corrupt womanhood drawn partly from Isaiah XLVII and partly from Revelation XVII.[17] While the alleged parallels with Isaiah's 'daughter of Babylon' must remain a matter of conjecture, those with the 'great whore' are undeniable: they form part of a well-documented pattern of allusion to St John. However, what would be most likely to strike a contemporary reader in a stanza such as the following, is not its biblical echoes, but its striking similarity with popular evocations of Queen Elizabeth:

High aboue all a cloth of State was spred,
  And a rich throne, as bright as sunny day,
  On which there sate most braue embellished
  With royall robes and gorgeous array,
  A mayden Queene, that shone as *Titans* ray,
  In glistring gold, and peerelesse pretious stone:
  Yet her bright blazing beautie did assay
  To dim the brightnesse of her glorious throne,
As enuying her selfe, that too exceeding shone.
(I, iv, 8)

The elevated throne, the robes of office, the precious stones and the blazing beauty of this 'mayden Queene' are all standard features of Elizabethan royal portraiture, whether visual or poetic.[18] In one example – an illustrated capital from the *Acts and Monuments* – Elizabeth is represented in the character, as it were, of a second Eve, trampling under foot a figure which is at once the serpent of Eden and also the Antichrist of Rome.[19] Lucifera is similarly depicted with a hideous dragon 'vnderneath her scornefull feete' (10). However, unlike Una/Elizabeth with her ancient royal lineage, this maiden queen lacks the 'heritage of natiue soueraintie', but has usurped 'with wrong and tyrannie/Vpon the scepter, which she now did hold' (12). Lucifera is clearly not only a symbol of Antichrist, as Protestant reformers interpreted this figure, but also a demonic parody of Elizabeth.

Although Spenser emphasizes the sumptuousness of the spectacle Lucifera creates as she progresses in her golden car (16 ff.), her pomp is not condemned in itself. Indeed it is precisely in this respect that she most resembles Elizabeth. What does condemn her is her pride, symbolized by the mirror 'Wherein her face she often vewed fayne,/And in her self-lou'd semblance tooke delight' (10) and by her doorkeeper, Vanitie. By contrast, the name of the porter in the House of Holiness is Humilitá (I, x, 5). As Foxe suggests in his portrait of Constantine, the ideal Christian prince is not an ascetic who abjures all worldly glory, but one who tempers magnificence with humility.[20] Perhaps the most succinct statement of this ideal is contained in some lines which Spenser wrote in quite another context:

> In that proud port, which her so goodly graceth,
>   whiles her faire face she reares vp to the skie:
>   and to the ground her eie lids low embaseth,
>   most goodly temperature ye may descry,
> Myld humblesse mixt with awfull maiesty.
>
> (Amoretti, XIII)[21]

It is 'goodly temperature', above all, which characterizes the figure of Arthur, the epitome of princely magnificence. For all the cruel ferocity of his dismemberment of Orgoglio, it is an essentially compassionate man who, in canto vii, comforts the weeping Una, distraught by the fall of her champion.

If we describe Spenser's characterization of the first of the Queen's 'two persons' as that of a holy prince who tempers magnificence with humility, we are on reasonably safe ground. We are on much less sure ground when we attempt to define holiness as an aspect of the second of her two 'persons'. The scholarly controversy generated by Spenser's allegory of salvation is due in part to the apparently contradictory nature of the evidence with which he provides us.

Much of the appeal of Book I lies in the fact that spiritual trials are presented through the vehicle of romance – in this case a story of love, jealousy, betrayal and eventual reunion. And it is a measure of Spenser's skill as an allegorist that the *sensus tropologicus* is combined so harmoniously with the wider aspects of his subject. When Una mourns the Redcrosse Knight's defeat by Orgoglio (I, vii, 22-3) it is in language whose eloquence expresses not only a slighted lover's anguish, but a mind overwhelmed by the burden of human sin. But although Spenser emphasizes, as he does in each of the subsequent books of *The Faerie Queene*, that 'blisse may not abide in state of mortall men' (I, viii, 44), his view of man seems to be one of tolerant compassion rather than contempt for human iniquity. It is true that the Redcrosse Knight is quickly parted from the woman to whom he has sworn fidelity; but we should recall that even Una, the personification of truth itself, is paradoxically deceived by false appearances. In his account of the hero's rehabilitation after his ordeal in the Cave of Despair Spenser devotes only four stanzas to his mortification: for the rest, the House of Holiness is unequivocally a place of joy where the weary traveller is kindly and hospitably nursed back to spiritual health.

It is all the more surprising, therefore, that canto x should begin with what looks very much like an assertion of the total depravity of human nature:

> What man is he, that boasts of fleshly might,
> And vaine assurance of mortality,
> Which all so soone, as it doth come to fight,
> Against spirituall foes, yeelds by and by,
> Or from the field most cowardly doth fly?
> Ne let the man ascribe it to his skill,
> That thorough grace hath gained victory.
> If any strength we haue, it is to ill,
> But all the good is Gods, both power and eke will.

Such a view of man seems more in keeping with orthodox Calvinist Protestantism than Fidelia's 'celestiall discipline' (I, x, 18) or Arthur's 'Faire feeling words' and 'goodly reason' (I, vii, 38, 42). Behind the apparent antinomies of Book I is a debate which exercised a powerful hold on the sixteenth-century mind – a debate which concerned itself with the essential nature of man. Rightly to understand Spenser's position in this controversy we must briefly rehearse its terms.

In 1574, when Spenser was probably still in Cambridge,[22] Peter Baro, Lady Margaret Professor of Greek and Theology, began lecturing on Christian salvation.[23] His programme was of a very different character from that of his unfortunate and more famous predecessor (Thomas Cartwright was expelled from Cambridge in 1570). Baro spoke of the harmony between nature and grace and argued that God's reason was reflected in man's own powers of reason. His claim that salvation was essentially a matter of co-operation between divine grace and human effort led to his denunciation by more orthodox Protestant opinion as a 'new Pelagian'.[24] The controversy which Baro precipitated in Cambridge was part of a long tradition of debate on salvation which goes back to Augustine and the Pelagians and which lies at the heart of the theological conflicts of the sixteenth century.

Baro's standpoint in this debate may best be described as that of a Christian humanist.[25] Whether Catholic or Protestant (Baro was a Protestant refugee from Paris), the Christian humanist adopted a Catholic position on the question of the Fall and the freedom of the will.[26] While he accepts the fact of fallen man's moral weakness and acknowledges his propensity to err from the path of virtue, the Christian humanist asserts, at the same time, the potential dignity of man and claims that, with divine assistance, he is capable of realizing an ideal of perfection through virtuous self-discipline. Before the publication of Hooker's *Laws of Ecclesiastical Polity*, the most complete statement by an Englishman of the central tenets of Christian humanist thought was Thomas Starkey's *Dialogue between Pole and Lupset*.[27] One of the fundamental principles underlying Starkey's analysis of the just society is the Platonic belief that ignorance is the 'fountayn of al yl, vyce, and mysery, as wel in euery priuate mannys lyfe as in euery commynalty' (p. 31). Provided that a man possesses knowledge of the good he will never choose to abandon it (p. 30), for God has implanted in him 'a sparkyl of his owne dyuynyte, – that ys to say, ryght reson, – wherby he schold gouerne hymselfe in cyuyle lyfe and gud pollycy, accordyng to hys excellent nature and dygnyte' (p. 165). Starkey does not deny the effect of the passions, but claims that 'dylygent instructyon and wyse conseyl may at the lest in long tyme restore the wyl out of such captyuyte, and bryng hyt agayne to the old lyberty' (pp. 30-1). By imitating Christ and steadfastly devoting himself to a life of virtue man may be assured of salvation (p. 213) and enjoy 'suche end and perfectyon as, by the prouydence of God, ys ordeynyd to the excellent nature and dygnyte of man' (p. 65).

Starkey's eloquent defence of the 'excellent nature and dygnyte of man' offers a complete contrast to the view of human nature expressed in the official theology of the Elizabethan Church. Where Starkey's conception of man is an optimistic one, the Protestant theologian emphasizes the depravity of the natural man. The keystone of Reformation theology was the doctrine of free grace. But the security afforded by the knowledge that man is justified by faith alone, regardless of merit or good works, depended upon an admission of the inefficacy of all human effort. For if salvation is due entirely to divine grace, nothing can be due to man. The Protestant believes that the consequences of the Fall were so damaging that without divine assistance man is incapable of making any effort towards good, much less of effecting his own salvation. Although good works after justification may be acceptable to God, this does not mean that they are meritorious in themselves. Grace may be given to those who strive for holiness; however, this gift is in no way due to man's striving, but to God's infinite graciousness alone.

It is this Calvinist view of human nature which is enshrined in the Thirty-nine Articles approved by Convocation in 1562 and ratified by Parliament in 1571. Article X states that 'The condition of man after the Fall of Adam is such that he cannot turn and prepare himself by his own natural strength and good works, to faith and calling upon God: Wherefore we have no power to do good works, pleasant and acceptable to God, without the grace of God by Christ preventing us . . .' John Jewel rehearses the Calvinist doctrine that salvation is due entirely to divine grace in his *Apology of the Church of England* (1562, revised 1564): 'we have no meed at all by our own works and deeds, but appoint all the means of our salvation to be in Christ alone . . .'[28] The same view is reflected by the Protestant pulpit of the later sixteenth century. George and George in their survey of Protestant opinion in this period conclude that 'English Protestantism clearly affirms . . . that, since all men are by nature sinful and are therefore justly damned, the saved owe their salvation entirely to God's grace and arbitrary choice.'[29] The reaction of Baro and the Cambridge humanists was thus a response to an official theology which was Calvinist in its fundamental doctrines.

Modern commentators are divided on the question of Spenser's position in this debate, some critics arguing that his entire view of man was coloured by his Calvinism,[30] others claiming that he rejected Calvin's fundamental teachings and 'accepted the humanist view of man's capacities which descended from the classics to medieval Christianity'.[31] One of the most influential proponents of the former view is Padelford. In a series of articles written in the early years of this century Padelford argued that Book I illustrates all the fundamental principles of Calvinism.[32] In support of his claim he compares the first stanza of canto x (quoted above) with the following passage from Calvin's *Institutes of the Christian Religion*:

> Everything good in the will is entirely the result of grace . . . All the fruits of good works are originally and immediately from God . . . nothing good can proceed from our will, until it be formed again, and . . . after it is formed again, in so far as it is good, it is of God, and not of us.[33]

The parallel is persuasive: like Calvin, Spenser appears categorically to deny man's ability in any way to effect his own salvation. Such a reading of Book I seems, in one sense, reasonable enough: if Spenser's poem is designed to praise the Supreme Governor of the Elizabethan Church, then it would seem entirely appropriate for its theology to accord with the official doctrines of that church. However, reasonable as such a conclusion may sound, it is open to some rather serious objections.

It may be argued that there are signal differences between Calvin's and Spenser's positions on certain important philosophical questions such as the nature of providence and fortune and the meaning of natural law.[34] However, these are not central issues in Book I; what is most difficult to reconcile with Calvin's theology is the fundamental conception of *The Faerie Queene* as an epideictic poem. Indeed the very notion of celebrating an ideal of princely magnificence is one which is alien to his view of man. While Calvin allows that the divine image in which man was formed was not wholly obliterated by the Fall and concedes that man is still capable of exercising reason in practical affairs, he insists on his impotence in spiritual matters (*Institutes*, II, ii, 13-26). The depravity of human nature is the theme to which he repeatedly returns in the *Institutes*. It is because the work of grace cannot begin until man has acknowledged his own corruption that Calvin condemns the humanist doctrine of the excellence of man's nature. By teaching man to place confidence in his own abilities, says Calvin, this philosophy 'does nothing more than fascinate by its sweetness, and . . . so delude as to drown in perdition all who assent to it'.[35] Yet fundamental to Spenser's poem as a pedagogic treatise is the principle of 'reason's due regality' (*FQ*, II, i, 57), or right reason – the belief that God has implanted in man (in Starkey's words) 'a sparkle of his own divinity whereby he should govern himself in civil life and good policy, according to his excellent nature and dignity'.

The humanist aspect of Spenser's thought is perhaps best illustrated in the following stanza from Book II:

Of all Gods workes, which do this world adorne,
There is no one more faire and excellent,
Then is mans body both for powre and forme,
Whiles it is kept in sober gouernment;
But none then it, more fowle and indecent,
Distempred through misrule and passions bace:
It growes a Monster, and incontinent
Doth loose his dignitie and natiue grace.
(II, ix, 1).

Where Book I speaks, apparently, of the depravity of the natural man, Book II praises his 'dignitie and natiue grace'.

This disparity between Calvinist and humanist elements in *The Faerie Queene* is the subject of an important and influential article by Woodhouse. Woodhouse takes as his premise the assumption that Book I presents a Calvinist theory of salvation: 'Padelford's demonstration is conclusive', he writes, 'that holiness is a purely Christian virtue, and that the *Institutes* of Calvin furnishes a relevant gloss, while the *Ethics* of Aristotle does not.'[36] He goes on to offer the hypothesis that Spenser was consciously differentiating between the order of grace and the order of nature with the intention of synthesizing these two levels of existence in a projected twelfth book. Woodhouse's hypothesis is a persuasive one and provides us with a valuable way of approaching *The Faerie Queene*. But it is open to the objections which must be made to any Calvinist interpretation of Book I.

It is not true to say, as Woodhouse does, that the supporting imagery of Book I is drawn almost entirely from the Bible with little reference to the pagan classics.[37] Not only is much of the incidental imagery of Book I drawn from classical sources (Duessa's journey to the underworld in canto v, for example, owes much to Virgil's account of Aeneas's descent into Hades), but pagan and Christian images are actually combined at certain stages in the narrative. The description of Una at I, iii, 4 is an allusion to the woman clothed with the sun, but in canto vi, the satyrs mistake her for Venus; the Hill of Contemplation, in canto x, is compared to the Mount of Olives *and* to Parnassus; the Redcrosse Knight's three-day battle with the dragon, in canto xi, alludes to Christ's harrowing of Hell *and* to the labours of Hercules.

The central motif of Book I – the destruction of a tyrannizing dragon – is taken from Revelation. But this quest is presented in such a way as to form a continuous allusion not only to the Bible, but also to Plato.[38] The Redcrosse Knight's first adventure takes place in the Cave of Errour; later when he emerges from Orgoglio's dungeon, his eyes, like those of Plato's philosopher, are at first unable to endure the sun's light (I, viii, 41); and when, finally, he receives the divine vision, he, like the philosopher, is reluctant to return to the mundane world, and experiences difficulty in adjusting his vision to earthly things:

> adowne he looked to the ground,
> To haue returnd, but dazed were his eyne,
> Through passing brightnesse, which did quite confound
> His feeble sence, and too exceeding shyne.
> So darke are earthly things compard to things diuine.
> (I, x, 67)[39]

The images of light and darkness which recur throughout Book I are part of an overall pattern whose significance transcends the exclusively Christian. It has been shown, moreover, that the poem's very structure is based upon a system of number symbolism which is not Christian, but Pythagorean.[40]

In harmony with these pagan elements in Book I are the repeated references to the humanist virtue of rational stoicism. The Redcrosse Knight's hasty and emotional reaction to apparent misfortune, in canto ii, is contrasted with Una's stoical reception of ill tidings, in canto vii: 'She heard with patience all vnto the end,/And stroue to maister sorrowfull assay' (I, vii, 27). When Una does succumb to feelings of despondency Prince Arthur tells her that reason can repair the injuries of passion (I, vii, 41). Arthur himself is a model of temperance (I, viii, 34), and, in canto viii, advises the Redcrosse Knight to meet adversity with patience (45).

Prince Arthur's stoicism gives to Book I a moral tone which is alien to the spirit of Calvinism. Medieval and Renaissance Christian writers drew freely upon Stoic thought,[41] and no Calvinist would deny that it is the Christian's duty to endure suffering with patience and humility. But to speak, as Prince Arthur does, of the rehabilitative powers of reason is, for the Calvinist, to fall into the sin of spiritual pride. Indeed when Arthur tells Una that 'will to might giues greatest aid' (I, vii, 41), he is apparently contradicting one of the most fundamental principles of Calvin's teaching. For Calvin the doctrine of original sin entails an absolute denial of the freedom of the will. Since the Fall, every man's will is 'bound by the fetters of sin',[42] and 'when the will is enchained as the slave of sin, it cannot make a movement towards goodness, far less steadily pursue it'.[43] Yet in the House of Holiness the Redcrosse Knight learns 'of God, of grace, of iustice' *and* 'of free will' (I, x, 19).

Calvin strenuously opposed the Pelagian belief that man's will is such that, though corrupted, it is still capable of co-operating with divine grace.[44] In his view the human will was so radically corrupted by the Fall that salvation could only be won by an equally radical conversion, the credit for which is God's alone. But on this fundamental point of Reformist teaching Spenser seems to adopt the very position which Calvin is at pains to demolish. When the Redcrosse Knight has at last defeated the dragon, at the end of canto xi, Una gives thanks to God for victory. But she also praises the Knight for his strength in overcoming the enemy: 'Then God she praysd, and thankt her faithfull knight,/That had atchieu'd so great a conquest by his might' (I, xi, 55). Although she uses an ambiguous pronoun, it is clear from the context of Una's remark that she attributes victory to the combined effects of divine grace and human will. As an orthodox Protestant she would have been bound to give the credit to God alone, for, as Calvin urges, 'we must not entertain any opinion whatever of our own strength, if we would enjoy the favour of God . . .'[45] Central to the Protestant doctrine of salvation is a belief in the inefficacy of the human will. Yet Book I seems to imply that salvation involves the co-operation of divine grace and human effort.

It may seem surprising that a poem which undertakes to define holiness as an attribute of the Supreme Governor of the Church of England should apparently contradict that church's official doctrine. But it should be emphasized that 'the story of the theology of the Elizabethan Church of England was that of a debate, and not of an unchallenged Calvinist oration'.[46] The Thirty-nine Articles were essentially a compromise measure designed, above all, to safeguard the royal supremacy. The fact that Elizabeth, after some demur, finally approved them in 1571 does not, of course, mean that the theological questions upon which they pronounced were settled once and for all. In particular it should not be assumed that the Edwardian theology of Cranmer's articles on grace and election necessarily reflects the views of an Elizabethan poet writing in the 1580s (in Parker's revision of the Forty-two Articles of 1553, articles IX, X and XVII remained virtually unchanged). In seeking an answer to our problem we must once again consider the historical character of the person whom Spenser's poem was designed to praise.

We have already discussed the general character of the godly prince and the public virtues to which he should aspire. Concerning the nature and meaning of holiness as a personal virtue we can scarcely do better than follow Starkey's advice[47] and consult the most famous lay sermon of the age, that is Erasmus's *Enchiridion Militis Christiani*, or, to use the title of Tyndale's translation, *The Manual of the Christian Knight*.[48] For here, in a portrait which in some ways anticipates the *Institutio Principis Christiani*, Erasmus sets out the 'opinions meete' for a Christian prince.

*The Manual of the Christian Knight* is one of the most important documents in the history of the northern humanist movement. It may be described as a truly seminal work, for it was the views that Erasmus put forward in this book which provoked the celebrated quarrel with Luther on the subject of grace and free will, a topic which, as we have seen, continued to divide theologians until the end of the century and beyond. Erasmus intended his book to be a guide to the 'certayne craft of vertuous liuing' (Sig. Di). It is divided into two parts. The first describes the nature of the Christian warfare and lays the basis for the second part, which consists of a set of rules designed to promote a life of spiritual piety.

Erasmus begins by stressing the need for moral vigilance in a world where the majority of mankind is deceived as if by a subtle magician (Sig. Di$^{v}$). He emphasizes that the Christian's battle is not like a physical encounter whose reward is a reputation for bravery, but rather a spiritual battle in which the warrior is never entirely free from danger. Indeed it is precisely when he feels most sure of victory that he is in greatest peril. Idleness and a false sense of security are above all what he must guard against. However the odds are not hopeless, for in his battle against Satan, who is for ever waiting to entrap us, like a serpent 'lurking in caues' (Sig. Dii$^{v}$), the Christian Knight is provided with a 'sure and impenetrabel shield of faith', and it is only by the use of this shield that he can hope to avoid defeat (Sig. Dii).

It is thus in the imagery of St Paul that Erasmus begins his book. But as he goes on to describe the weapons of the Christian warfare he impresses on the reader the importance of a familiarity not only with the Bible but also with the pagan classics. 'Pyke and chose out of the bookes of the gentyles, of euery thynge the best', he writes, and, echoing Seneca, tells his readers, 'if thou by the example of the Bee, fleying rounde aboute by the gardynes of oulde authors, shalt sucke out only the holsome and swete iuce . . . thy mynde shalbe better apparayled . . .' (Sig. Fiii$^{v}$).[49]

Erasmus's sermon is a truly Christian humanist work. Although its object is the inculcation of Christian piety, it is a humanist ideal of rational conduct which forms the core of the book. Erasmus's prince owes more to Cicero than he does to the Christian Fathers. What disturbed Luther, however, was not the pagan and secular elements in Erasmus's book so much as his teaching on the question of grace and free will. Erasmus's position on this point is substantially the same as that of Spenser's contemporary, Hooker. The Catholic reformer and the Elizabethan Protestant both adopt a Thomist view of the Fall. Neither denies that man's reason was impaired by the Fall; yet both affirm that, with the assistance of divine grace, reason is capable of directing the will to virtue.

Although there are certain obvious similarities between Erasmus's Christian Knight and Spenser's hero, these may possibly be coincidental. For the image of warfare is so widespread in Christian literature that it might almost be said to spring inevitably from the Protestant conception of man as a divided being, lacking in grace, and for ever at war with himself. But the metaphor can be used in different ways to express radically different views of man. The parallels between *The Manual of the Christian Knight* and the first book of *The Faerie Queene* are instructive, not in the crude sense of suggesting a possible source for the Redcrosse Knight, but because they may help us more precisely to define Spenser's methods and intentions.

What would be immediately apparent to the contemporary reader with an interest in theological matters is that Erasmus uses the metaphor of Christian warfare in a way which is, in certain important respects, inimical to the spirit of orthodox Elizabethan Protestantism.[50] For the Protestant the warfare between flesh and spirit signifies a battle between the corrupt, unregenerate man and the new, regenerate man. But for Erasmus the Christian warfare means not so much man's struggle against sin in the sense of a wilful surrender to evil, as the war against the passions which disfigure the moral character. In thus concerning himself with an ideal of *humanitas* Erasmus lays himself open to the charge of spiritual pride: for to minimize, by implication, the importance of salvation is, for the Calvinist, tantamount to a denial of man's absolute dependence on divine grace.

John Downame, in a work entitled *The Christian Warfare* (1634), makes precisely this point when he distinguishes between the way the Protestant interprets this image and the error committed by the Catholic when he takes the flesh to mean 'the body, and the sensuall facultie' and the spirit to mean 'the intellectual faculties, the minde, reason . . .' According to the Papist, the Christian warfare means 'the fight between the flesh and spirit, when as the body and sensitive parts doe rebell . . . against the understanding and reason . . .'[51] In Downame's view the flesh signifies not merely the sensual part of man's nature, but 'those reliques of corruption, which after regeneration, doe still remaine in us . . . or that part of a Christian which is unregenerate and continually fighteth against the spirit'. Spirit, he believes, signifies 'the new man, or the regenerate part of the Christian . . . the whole man renewed unto God's image'.[52] When the Protestant speaks of the corruption of man's natural faculties he does so in order to emphasize that total submission of the will is the essential precondition for the gift of divine grace. But the key to Erasmus's conception of holiness lies not in a violent suppression of the will, but in its discipline. Though he is insistent in warning his reader of the dangers of pride, his ideal might more properly be described as one of *humanitas* than *humilitas*.[53]

Comparison of Erasmus's imagery with Spenser's suggests that both writers are using the metaphor of Christian warfare in essentially the same way. Like Erasmus, Spenser begins by establishing the principal theme of his book as the need for moral vigilance. As the Redcrosse Knight approaches the Cave of Errour Una tells him to beware -

> Least suddaine mischiefe ye too rash prouoke:
> The danger hid, the place vnknowne and wilde,
> Breedes dreadfull doubts.

She then offers him a piece of proverbial wisdom followed by a further caution against rash action:

> Oft fire is without smoke,
> And perill without show: therefore your stroke
> Sir knight with-hold, till further triall made.
> (I, i, 12)

At this stage 'dreadful doubts' are what seem to be furthest from the Redcrosse Knight's mind, and so, ignoring Una's advice, he plunges into Errour's cave, does battle with the monster, and eventually defeats it. Confident at his first success he then rides off looking for new adventures. Very quickly, however, he falls prey to the deceptions of Archimago, and, as we see him tricked into doubting Una's fidelity, the significance of her advice becomes clear. It becomes clear that when she had warned him of the deceptive nature of appearances, she was referring not simply to this particular manifestation of evil, but to the nature of error as a universal phenomenon.

If, as is sometimes objected, Spenser's characterization of Errour seems to be lacking in subtlety,[54] this is for the very simple reason that the dragon represents evil in its least subtle form. What the Redcrosse Knight has to learn, as Erasmus's Christian Knight must learn, is first, that evil and temptation can occur in a variety of different ways: sometimes in a crude and grossly physical shape, sometimes in much subtler forms; and second, that 'he which loueth peryls is [in Erasmus's words] worthye in them to peryshe'.[55] In reality, of course, error cannot be defeated once and for all like an ugly dragon, a truth which Spenser hints at in his punning account of the battle. As the monster winds its tail about the Knight's body the narrator comments: 'God helpe the man so wrapt in *Errours* endlesse traine' (I, i, 18). Errour, like most of the allegorical figures in Book I, is a personification not of an abstract metaphysical principle, but of a human weakness, and the Redcrosse Knight's encounter with the monster establishes the dominant theme of the whole book. In each case his lapses into sin are brought about by a failure of judgement rather than by a wilful rejection of grace. Moral vigilance, then, is the key-note which is repeatedly sounded throughout Book I (notably at I, iv, 1; I, vii, 1; and I, viii, 44) as it is in *The Manual of the Christian Knight*. The fact that Spenser, like Erasmus, characterizes the Christian life in terms of a battle is in itself without significance. However, the way in which he defines this image is important. Not only does he place great emphasis on the individual's ability to control his spiritual destiny through self-knowledge and self-discipline, but he sets the drama of Christian salvation in the wider context of a humanist ideal of moral excellence. After instruction in the nature of good works the Redcrosse Knight attains to such perfection,

> That from the first vnto the last degree,
> His mortall life he learned had to frame
> In holy righteousnesse, without rebuke or blame.
> (I, x, 45)

The final stage in the Redcrosse Knight's sanctification is his vision of the new Jerusalem. Overwhelmed by his experience, the Knight is tempted by the attractions of a life of contemplation. But his mentor reminds him that his destiny lies not in a life of solitary prayer, but in heroic service of the Faery Queen (I, x, 63). It is Spenser's humanist emphasis on the active life of public service together with his leaning towards the Catholic view of good works[56] that sets him apart from the more orthodox Calvinist Protestant.

If Spenser's emphatic assertion at I, x, 1 of man's spiritual bankruptcy seems to contradict his humanist belief in man's 'dignity and native grace', it is probably wisest to accept this for the anomaly it is. Spenser's intention, after all, was not to write a theological treatise, but to praise his prince by presenting her with an ideal of human conduct while at the same time celebrating the Protestant cause of which she was champion. If this involved him in what appear to be certain theological inconsistencies, these are not such as to trouble the contemporary Christian humanist. Indeed it is precisely the same combination of apparently contradictory elements that we find in Sidney's well-known claim concerning the power of learning 'to lead and draw us to as high a perfection as our degenerate souls, made worse by their clayey lodgings, can be capable of'. The Elizabethan Christian humanist who combines a belief in the corruption of human nature with a faith in man's god-like powers of reason owes much to Erasmus. In the *De Libero Arbitrio* Erasmus writes:

> To those who maintain that man can do nothing without the help of the grace of God, and conclude that therefore no works of man are good – to these we shall oppose a thesis to me much more probable, that there is nothing that man cannot do with the help of the grace of God, and that therefore all the works of man can be good.[57]

However, even Erasmus acknowledges the fact of man's total dependence on divine grace. In *The Manual of the Christian Knight* he admits that 'Whatsoeuer [the Christian] hath, whatsoeuer he is, that altogether let him ascribe not to him selfe, but vnto god the author thereof . . .' (Sig. Kii$^{v}$). In warning his reader against arrogating merit to himself Erasmus is not denying altogether the efficacy of human will; he is merely arguing the need for a due sense of humility.[58]

Spenser similarly cautions the reader against pride. In his presumption, the Redcrosse Knight on two occasions ignores the advice he is given and deliberately courts danger in the mistaken belief that he is proof against any form of evil (I, i, 12 and I, ix, 31). From pride he then falls to the opposite extreme: despair. Holiness, Spenser is saying, can only be achieved by avoiding both these extremes and following a middle path: believing that divine grace will assist us in the battle against evil, while at the same time retaining a due sense of humility; recognizing that 'all the good is God's, both power and eke will', but at the same time acknowledging that 'will to might gives greatest aid'. The point is summarized by Erasmus in the rules to be observed by the Christian prince:

> Thou must kepe a meane course, as it were betwene Scilla, and Charibdis, that neyther trustinge to mutche, and bearyng the ouer bolde upon the grace of God, thou be carelesse and reachles, neyther yet so mistrustinge in thy selfe, feared with the difficulties of the war: doe cast from thee courage, boldnes or confidence of minde . . . (Sig. Ci$^{v}$)

Holiness, then, as Spenser portrays it, signifies an ideal of spiritual perfection which may be achieved through virtuous self-discipline assisted by divine grace. Although Spenser could not have known this, it is an ideal which is actually summed up by the Queen herself in her book of private devotions. 'In the exercise of my government', she wrote, 'let soul so rule flesh; reason, soul; faith, reason; and thy grace, faith; that nothing may please me that displeaseth thee.'[59] In emphasizing the primacy of grace in the Christian life Elizabeth is acknowledging what neither Catholic nor Protestant would deny: the corruption of the natural man. However, this is not to derogate the rational faculties; merely to place them in their true perspective. Indeed it would be strange if a Renaissance prince, educated by one of the great humanist pedagogues of the age, were to deny altogether the power of right reason to co-operate with grace in the work of sanctification. Such is the Christian humanist view of man's spiritual life, and it is this Christian philosophy which informs not only Book I, but the whole of *The Faerie Queene*.

There is no Renaissance poet who takes a keener interest in theological matters than Spenser. However, his ultimate concern as Protestant and humanist is not so much the salvation of the individual soul, as the realizing of the true Christian state. Unlike Bunyan's hero, Spenser's Christian Knight is not a solitary pilgrim of eternity, but a heroic champion of the English Protestant cause. To summarize: the ideal prince is one who tempers the magnificence which is an essential feature of his office with the humility which becomes the servant of God; in his virtue he must be a pattern and example of the Christian life for his subjects to follow; above all he must remain true to his mission as divinely appointed ruler of a chosen people. Idealized though this composite portrait may be, it is nevertheless one whose lineaments Elizabeth would have had little trouble in recognizing as her own. For, just as the name Una was a popular pseudonym for the Queen, so St George, adopted saint of Tudor princes,[60] was identified with Elizabeth in her capacity as protector of the kingdom against Antichrist. One contemporary writer argued that

> whereas vnder the person of the noble champion Saint GEORGE our Sauiour Christ was prefigured, deliuering the Virgin (which did signifie the sinfull soules of Christians) from the dragon or diuels power: So her most excellent Maiesty by aduancing the pure doctrine of CHRIST IESVS in all truth and sincerity, hath (as an instrument appointed by diuine prouidence) bene vsed to performe the part of a valiant champion . . .[61]

The historical counterpart of the Redcrosse Knight's rebirth through sanctifying grace is the restoration of the true Catholic Church under a 'heauenly borne' prince (I, x, 59).

Incorporating, as it does, a defence of the reformed Church of England, the political allegory of Book I is more detailed and more complex than that of the subsequent books of *The Faerie Queene*. Nevertheless, in its general outlines Book I is typical of the poem in so far as it shows that the way Spenser defines the virtue which gives each book its title is essentially determined by his epideictic purpose. Spenser begins with holiness because, in the curriculum of the Christian prince, religion is paramount.[62] As the theological premise of Book I is amplified in the succeeding books, *The Faerie Queene* unfolds the most comprehensive poetic statement we have of the principles of Elizabethan Christian humanism. But while Spenser subscribes to a humanist tradition of belief in man's 'dignity and native grace', he never allows us to forget that the Christian prince has been appointed to rule a fallen world. Indeed it is precisely because the world has lost its natural 'temper' that the prince must cultivate the virtue which forms the subject of the second book of *The Faerie Queene*.

## Notes

1. Kermode, '*The Faerie Queene*, I and V', p. 41.
2. Kermode, 'Spenser and the Allegorists', The British Academy Warton Lecture (1962), rpt. in *Shakespeare, Spenser, Donne*, p. 14.
3. Smith and de Selincourt, p. 407.

4. On the general character and responsibilities of the Christian prince see Edward O. Smith, Jr., 'The Elizabethan Doctrine of the Prince as Reflected in the Sermons of the Episcopacy, 1559-1603', *HLQ*, 28 (1964), 1-17.

5. *Paraphrase of Erasmus upon the Newe Testamente*, translated by N. Udall (London, 1548), Sig. Cvi$^{v}$.

6. *The Acts and Monuments of John Foxe*, edited by George Townsend, 8 vols (London, 1843-9), I, 9.

7. John Jewel, *An Apology of the Church of England*, edited by J.E. Booty, Folger Documents of Tudor and Stuart Civilization (New York, 1963), p. 121.

8. Yates, 'Queen Elizabeth as Astraea', pp. 32 ff.; Roy C. Strong, 'The Popular Celebration of the Accession Day of Queen Elizabeth I', *JWCI*, 21 (1958), 97 ff.; Kermode, '*The Faerie Queene*, I and V', pp. 17 ff. See also Richard Koebner, '"The Imperial Crown of this Realm"; Henry VIII, Constantine the Great, and Polydore Vergil', *BIHR*, 26 (1953), 29-52.

9. *Acts and Monuments*, p. 298.

10. Quoted by Yates, p. 41.

11. *Foxe's Book of Martyrs and the Elect Nation*, p. 125.

12. The parallels between Book I and St John's Revelation have been extensively documented. See, in particular, Bennett, *The Evolution of 'The Faerie Queene'*, pp. 109-15; John E. Hankins, 'Spenser and the Revelation of St. John', *PMLA*, 60 (1945), 364-81; S.K. Heninger, Jr., 'The Orgoglio Episode in *The Faerie Queene*', *ELH*, 26 (1959), 171-87.

13. See Bennett, pp. 110-11.

14. *The Geneva Bible*, facsimile of the 1560 edition with an introduction by Lloyd E. Berry (Madison, Wis., 1969). All quotations from the Bible are from this edition.

15. Lawrence Rosinger, 'Spenser's Una and Queen Elizabeth', *ELN*, 6 (1968-9), 12-17. See also Ray Heffner, 'Spenser's Allegory in Book I of the *Faerie Queene*', *SP*, 27 (1930), 142-61 and C. Bowie Millican, 'Spenser's and Drant's Poetic Names for Elizabeth: Tanaquil, Gloria, and Una', *HLQ*, 2 (1938-9), 251-63.

16. John Lydgate, 'Ballade at the Reverence of our Lady', *The Minor Poems of John Lydgate*, edited by Henry Noble MacCracken, Early English Text Society, 2 vols (London, 1911 and 1934), I, 259.

17. See Hankins, pp. 366-8.

18. See Roy Strong, *The Cult of Elizabeth: Elizabethan Portraiture and Pageantry* (London, 1977). See also Wilson, *England's Eliza*, especially Ch. VI.

19. Reproduced by Yates in a plate facing p. 42. The same figure is used by John Dee in his *General and rare memorials* (1577) (reproduced by Yates opposite p. 43). On the Virgin Mary as second Eve see Warner, pp. 59-61.

20. This traditional image of the prince is reflected in Tudor drama. In Skelton's *Magnyfycence*, for example, it is claimed that 'Where Measure is mayster, Plenty dothe none offence' (I, iii, 121). It is only when the prince, having abandoned Measure, becomes inflated with pride that he falls prey to the blandishments of Courtly Abusyon and eventually brings about his own downfall.

21. In view of the prevalence of such imagery in the *Amoretti*, the currently unfashionable suggestion of George Chalmers that the sonnets were addressed to Queen Elizabeth may well have some truth in it (*A Supplemental Apology for the Believers in the Shakespeare-Papers* (London, 1799), pp. 31-7). If Chalmers is right, Spenser was by no means alone in addressing love sonnets to the Queen (see Wilson, pp. 230-72; see also Ralegh's commendatory sonnet on *The Faerie Queene*, Smith and de Selincourt, p. 409).

22. Spenser graduated in 1573. He was awarded his MA three years later in 1576. It is not known if he actually remained in Cambridge during this interval.

23. See H.C. Porter, *Reformation and Reaction in Tudor Cambridge*

(Cambridge, 1958), p. 281. See also Virgil K. Whitaker, *The Religious Basis of Spenser's Thought* (1950; rpt. New York, 1966), pp. 60-3.

24. Porter, p. 388.

25. This is not the place to attempt a survey of the Christian humanist movement. The following are standard accounts of the subject: Douglas Bush, *The Renaissance and English Humanism* (1939; rpt. Toronto, 1958), pp. 69-100; Herschel Baker, *The Image of Man: A Study of the Idea of Human Dignity in Classical Antiquity, The Middle Ages, and the Renaissance* (1947; rpt. New York, 1961), pp. 258-74; Hiram Haydn, *The Counter-Renaissance* (New York, 1950), pp. 30-67; Myron P. Gilmore, *The World of Humanism, 1453-1517* (1952; rpt. New York, 1962), pp. 204-28; Caspari, *Humanism and the Social Order in Tudor England*, pp. 37-49; E.H. Harbison, *The Christian Scholar in the Age of the Reformation* (New York, 1956), passim; Robert Hoopes, *Right Reason in the English Renaissance* (Cambridge, Mass., 1962), pp. 59 ff.

26. Haydn, *The Counter-Renaissance*, p. 59.

27. Unpublished in Starkey' lifetime, the *Dialogue* was first edited by J.M. Cowper for the Early English Text Society in 1878 under the title *England in the Reign of King Henry the Eighth*. All quotations from Starkey are from the second edition of 1927.

28. Jewel, p. 39.

29. Charles H. and Katherine George, *The Protestant Mind of the English Reformation 1570-1640* (Princeton, 1961), p. 55. See also A.G. Dickens, *The English Reformation* (London, 1964), p. 314.

30. Paul N. Siegel, 'Spenser and the Calvinist View of Life', *SP*, 41 (1944), 201.

31. Whitaker, p. 58, cf. William H. Marshall, 'Calvin, Spenser, and the Major Sacraments', *MLN*, 74 (1959), 97-101. Marshall argues that Spenser's use of sacramental symbols suggests a rejection of 'the very heart of Calvin's . . . theological system' (p. 99).

32. F.M. Padelford, 'Spenser and the Puritan Propaganda', *MP*, 11 (1913-14), 85-106; 'Spenser and the Theology of Calvin', *MP*, 12 (1914-15), 1-18; 'Spenser and the Spirit of Puritanism', *MP*, 14 (1916-17), 31-44; 'The Spiritual Allegory of *The Faerie Queene*, Book One', *JEGP*, 22 (1923), 1-17.

33. Quoted by Padelford, 'Spenser and the Theology of Calvin', p. 12 (I have abbreviated Padelford's quotation).

34. An important aspect of Calvin's doctrine of salvation is his theory of providence. Calvin argues that all events in the world are so regulated by God that nothing can be said to happen fortuitously (*Institutes*, I, xvi, 4-5). Yet, as many writers have noticed, the unpredictability of fate is a major theme in *The Faerie Queene*, particularly in Book VI, where the Boethian figure of Meliboe counsels rational indifference to the vicissitudes of fortune. In Book V it is the principle of natural law as something 'investigable by Reason, without the help of Revelation supernatural and divine' (Hooker, *Of the Laws of Ecclesiastical Polity*, edited by Ronald Bayne, 2 vols (1907; rpt. London, 1925), I, 182) which forms the basis of Spenser's theory of justice (see below, Chapter 5). But for Calvin natural law confirms man, not, as Hooker asserts, in his powers of reason, but in his imbecility (*Institutes*, II, viii, 1).

35. *Institutes of the Christian Religion*, II, i, 2 (translated by Henry Beveridge, 2 vols (London, 1949), I, 211).

36. A.S.P. Woodhouse, 'Nature and Grace in *The Faerie Queene*', *ELH*, 16 (1949), 201.

37. Woodhouse, p. 208.

38. Cf. Ernst Cassirer: 'We have [in the Redcrosse Knight's adventures] in a poetic setting an account of the ascent of the human soul to that source of beauty

which is also the source of all wisdom and of all religious knowledge. When Una finally reveals herself to the hero, it is as the highest truth, the highest beauty, and the highest form of love' (*The Platonic Renaissance in England*, translated by James P. Pettegrove (London, 1953), pp. 112-13).

39. Nelson suggests (p. 170) that I, x, 63, may be an allusion to Cicero's *Somnium Scipionis*. I find a closer parallel with Plato, *Republic*, VII, iii.

40. Fowler, passim.

41. See Hoopes, pp. 132-3 and 142.

42. *Institutes*, II, ii, 7, Beveridge, I, 229.

43. *Institutes*, II, iii, 5, Beveridge, I, 253.

44. In the *Institutes*, II, iii, 7, Calvin refutes the view that the will, when prepared or prevented by grace, acquires merit in the performance of good works. To take Augustine's description of human will as the 'handmaid of grace' to mean that will accompanies preventing grace as a voluntary attendant is quite erroneous, Calvin argues. Augustine's purpose was not to assign to human will a co-operative role in the performance of good works, but to refute the pestilential Pelagian view that merit is the first cause of salvation. When Augustine says that God 'prevents the unwilling in order to make him willing' his intention, says Calvin, is to make it clear that God is the 'sole author of good works' (Beveridge, I, 257). As Calvin himself repeatedly insists, 'everything good in the will is entirely the result of grace' (II, iii, 6, Beveridge, I, 256).

45. *Institutes*, I, ii, 10, Beveridge, I, 232.

46. Porter, *Reformation and Reaction in Tudor Cambridge*, p. 287.

47. *Dialogue between Pole and Lupset*, p. 211.

48. *A booke called in Latyn* Enchiridion militis christiani *and in englyssche the manuell of the christen knyght* (London, 1533). All quotations are from the tenth edition of 1576.

49. Cf. Seneca, *Ad Lucilium Epistulae Morales*, LXXXIV.

50. The immense popularity of the *Enchiridion* among sixteenth-century Protestants must be attributed to a tendency to interpret the book simply as a call to a life of piety based on a personal reading of holy scripture and to disregard its polemical theology. John Gough, for example, in introducing an abridged version of Erasmus's book, wrote: it is 'evident that the right life of a Christian consisteth not either in multitude of people, prescription of time, forefathers, nor outward ceremonies, but only in virtuousness of life, leaving our own dreams and inventions, and in following the sacred and holy Scriptures . . . as our only lodestar to follow, and touchstone to try all doctrine by' ('Prologue to an Abridged Edition of Erasmus's *Enchiridion*' (1561) in *Elizabethan Puritanism*, edited by Leonard J. Trinterud (New York, 1971), p. 38).

51. Quoted by George and George, p. 36.

52. Ibid.

53. Caspari, p. 38.

54. See, for example, Yvor Winters, *The Function of Criticism* (Denver, 1957), p. 44.

55. *The Manual of the Christian Knight*, Sig. Xv.

56. See Whitaker, p. 47. Of the character Enuie in the House of Pride, Spenser says, 'He hated all good workes and vertuous deeds' (I, iv, 32).

57. *De Libero Arbitrio*, translated and edited by E. Gordon Rupp in collaboration with A.N. Marlow in *Luther and Erasmus: Free Will and Salvation*, The Library of Christian Classics, XVII (London, 1969), p. 85.

58. Erasmus explains the point at greater length in the *De Libero Arbitrio*: 'Nor . . . does our will achieve nothing, although it does not attain the things that it seeks without the help of grace. But since our efforts are so puny, the whole is ascribed to God . . . Since human labor does nothing except when divine favor is

also present, the whole is ascribed to the divine beneficence' (p. 79).

59. Quoted by William P. Haugaard, 'Elizabeth Tudor's *Book of Devotions*: A Neglected Clue to the Queen's Life and Character', *SixCT*, 12 (1981), 89.

60. On St George as patron of the Tudors see Strong, *The Cult of Elizabeth*, p. 181.

61. Gerrard De Malynes, *Saint George For England, Allegorically Described* (London, 1610), Sigs. Aii$^{v}$-Aiii.

62. Lodowick Bryskett, *A Discovrse of Civill Life* (London, 1606), p. 85.

# 2 SWEET SISTER TEMPERANCE

Book I has been denominated the Book of the Sun.[1] Complementing the heroic evocation of Queen Elizabeth as St George, champion of holiness and conqueror of Antichrist, is the 'sunshyny' figure of Una (I, xii, 23). With her complex biblical ancestry Una forms part of an elaborate system of solar symbolism[2] whose function is to suggest, in part, the sun-like glory of that

> Great Lady of the greatest Isle, whose light
> Like *Phoebus* lampe throughout the world doth shine,
> (I, proem, 4)

In Book II it is as a moon goddess that Elizabeth is evoked. Belphoebe, Spenser tells Ralegh, represents Elizabeth in the character of 'a most vertuous and beautifull Lady'.[3] Fowler is undoubtedly correct in suggesting that this 'queen and huntress chaste and fair' is intended mythologically to suggest the moon-goddess Phoebe.[4] But her classical name and foster-parentage should not disguise for us her Christian associations. Her identification with the moon; the roses and lilies with which her complexion is compared (II, iii, 22); her ambrosial fragrance (ibid.); and above all her immaculate conception (III, vi, 6-8) all serve unambiguously to identify her with the Virgin Mary.[5]

The parallels between Una and the Virgin in Book I are familiar enough to modern Spenserians; what has not been noticed is that, despite its predominantly classical tone, Book II is equally rich in Marian imagery. Indeed it is with a parody of one of the most familiar of all Marian symbols – the enclosed garden – that Book II concludes. So deeply imbedded in the corporate mind was the traditional stock of images to which this symbol belongs, that when Spenser hails his queen as a 'flowre of grace and chastitie' whose 'glory shineth as the morning starre' (II, ix, 4), there could be no question of a contemporary reader failing to catch so conspicuous an allusion to the virgin Queen of Heaven.[6]

The function of these Marian images is rhetorical: they serve both to remind the reader that the poem is a 'mirrhour' designed to reflect the glory of England's virgin queen, and at the same time to reveal the historic significance of Guyon's quest. Many critics have noticed that

Books I and II are structurally and thematically complementary. As the presiding deity of Book II, Belphoebe is the counterpart of Una. In their symbolic aspects as lunar and solar principles they suggest the idea of Elizabeth's 'imperiall powre' (II, ix, 3): just as the Virgin Mary was compared with the sun and the moon in her sovereignty of heaven and earth, so Una and Belphoebe, as types of Elizabeth, symbolize the goddess-like powers of the 'mighty Queene of *Faerie*' whose 'light the earth enlumines cleare' (II, ix, 4).[7] As the reader follows the adventures of Sir Guyon he is repeatedly reminded by symbolic means that the virtue of which this hero is champion is not simply an abstract ideal to be cultivated for its own sake, but second among the attributes of a queen who was affectionately known as 'sweet Sister Temperance'.[8]

Unlike holiness, temperance is not problematic in itself. Whereas Protestant and humanist took radically opposed views of the nature of holiness, there is no debate in the sixteenth century on the essential meaning of temperance. Guyon's definition of this virtue at II, i, 57-8 does not differ in any significant way from such standard sixteenth-century formulations as that of Sir Thomas Elyot, who says that to be temperate is 'nat to excede the boundes of medyocritye, and to kepe desyre under the yocke of reason';[9] or of La Primaudaye, who defines temperance as the 'stedfast and moderate rule of reason ouer concupiscence, and ouer other vehement motions of the mind'.[10] What Guyon, as servant of the Faery Queene, must learn is not so much a question of how to be temperate, as why this virtue is important. It is for this reason that his two most significant educational adventures take the form of a court visit – the royal court of Philotime in canto vii and Alma's court in cantos ix and x.

Philotime's court forms the symbolic centrepiece of the Cave of Mammon. As many critics have rightly insisted, our interpretation of this episode must affect our reading of the whole book. The journey to the underworld has a long history in mythological literature[11] and the imaginative appeal of this episode is reflected in the volume of scholarly attention it has received. Much of the criticism which has dealt with the Cave of Mammon has taken the form of an attempt to define the nature of Guyon's virtue by reference to the authorities upon which Spenser appears to be drawing. While older critics tended to look to the classical moralists, more recent writers have focused attention on the Christian elements in Guyon's ordeal.[12] But even where critics concur in seeing Guyon as an essentially Christian hero, there is little agreement on the precise significance of his experience. Kermode has assembled an impressive body of Christian doctrine in support of his claim that what

Guyon undergoes in the cave is a three-fold temptation parallel to that of Christ in the wilderness, and that the purpose of this initiatory ordeal is to prepare him for his assault on the Bower of Bliss.[13] Other critics, however, argue that the whole episode serves to demonstrate not the impregnability of the hero's virtue, but his sin in succumbing to the temptation of *curiositas*.[14] Confronted with such contradictory interpretations it is an understandable response to conclude that there is no correct answer and that 'the reading, like the virtue, is not on the page but in the air around us'.[15] It is true that no reading of a syncretic poem like *The Faerie Queene* can ever claim finality; but we negate the very principle of epideictic literature if we suggest that the poet is unwilling to commit himself to a consistent moral statement. If the Cave of Mammon appears to yield contradictory answers to our questions, then it seems probable that we are asking the wrong questions. Although the significance of some details will perhaps inevitably remain hidden from a twentieth-century reader, the episode is, nevertheless, clear in its general moral purpose. But it is important that we appreciate that this purpose does not concern the essential nature of temperance, for Guyon has already shown that he fully understands the meaning of this virtue and can define it as well as any sixteenth-century moralist. While his ordeal is certainly reminiscent of Christ's temptation in the wilderness, it is, as Tonkin notes,[16] nothing more than this, and we should recall that Spenser's major literary source for this episode is the sixth book of the *Aeneid*. For Spenser's hero, as for Virgil's, the journey to the underworld serves an illustrative as much as a probative function.

The first clue to the symbolic significance of the cave is contained in the debate on the use of riches which takes place before Guyon and Mammon make their descent into the nether regions. While Mammon claims that wealth is the true source of glory and renown (II, vii, 11), Guyon argues that it is the 'roote of all disquietnesse' (12). When he is challenged to account for the fact that man should strive for what is evil, Guyon replies with an historical argument. He explains that in the infancy of time man enjoyed a life of innocent plenty, but that in succeeding ages he lost his former contentment and violated the principle of natural proportion. To satisfy his newly awakened greed man began to mine the earth for precious metals:

> The antique world, in his first flowring youth,
> Found no defect in his Creatours grace,
> But with glad thankes, and vnreproued truth,
> The gifts of soueraigne bountie did embrace:

> Like Angels life was then mens happy cace;
> But later ages pride, like corn-fed steed,
> Abusd her plenty, and fat swolne encreace
> To all licentious lust, and gan exceed
> The measure of her meane, and naturell first need.
>
> Then gan a cursed hand the quiet wombe
> Of his great Grandmother with steele to wound,
> And the hid treasures in her sacred tombe,
> With Sacriledge to dig. Therein he found
> Fountaines of gold and siluer to abound,
> Of which the matter of his huge desire
> And pompous pride eftsoones he did compound;
> Then auarice gan through his veines inspire
> His greedy flames, and kindled life-deuouring fire.
>
> (II, vii, 16-17)

Guyon's account of man's fall from his golden-age state of grace is, of course, a conflation of ideas which were commonplace in classical and medieval literature.[17] They were available, even to the reader with small Latin and less Greek, in one of the several sixteenth-century translations of Boethius, or, more importantly, in Golding's translation of Ovid. For the Renaissance Ovid's account in the first book of the *Metamorphoses* of the early history of the world was the *locus classicus* for ideas about the consequences of man's fall from his golden-age state of innocence: its phrases are repeated countless times in the literature of the sixteenth, seventeenth and eighteenth centuries. We may note that of all the activities traditionally associated with the Fall – that is, shipbuilding, land enclosure, agriculture, mining and warfare – it is mining alone which Guyon mentions in his account of the passing of the golden age. Since the subject of their debate is wealth, the reason for this is obvious. But Guyon's argument is important in preparing the reader for the discovery that Mammon is himself the proprietor of a gold mine. In the most memorable (for Keats, at least) lines of the canto, we are told that Mammon's Cave is

> hewne out of rocky clift,
> From whose rough vaut the ragged breaches hong,
> Embost with massy gold of glorious gift,
> And with rich metall loaded euery rift.
>
> (II, vii, 28)

The function of the debate which takes place outside the cave is to set Mammon's mine firmly within a mythico-historical context. Having given the reader a narrative account of the Fall, Spenser then provides him with a concrete symbol of that fact.[18]

Many of the details of Mammon's Cave which commentators have found problematic are perfectly intelligible as constituents of this complex symbol of a fallen world. The Garden of Proserpina, for example, has been described by one critic as 'the most puzzling aspect of Mammon's realm'.[19] Whether Spenser's source for these stanzas (51-6) was Claudian[20] or Dante[21] or Palingenius[22] is immaterial; the important thing is the symbolic truth they embody. If we recall that the golden age was the time when the earth produced food in natural abundance, then Proserpina's Garden may be seen for what it is: a grotesque parody of nature's uncorrupted fertility. Ovid describes how in the golden age 'The fertile earth as yet was free, untoucht of spade or plough,/And yet it yeelded of it selfe of every things inough'.[23] But the herbs and fruits which flourish in Proserpina's Garden are

> Not such, as earth out of her fruitfull woomb
> Throwes forth to men, sweet and well sauoured,
> But direfull deadly blacke both leafe and bloom,
> Fit to adorne the dead, and decke the drery toombe.
> (II, vii, 51)

For man one of the chief consequences of a fallen nature was the necessity for work. By a nice irony the substance for which the denizens of Mammon's Cave are seen to be labouring ('And euery one did swincke, and euery one did sweat' (36)) is gold. The paradox is similar to that which informs the opening scene of *Volpone*. In a world which has lost its golden-age innocence, it is gold which has ironically become the measure of all things. As Volpone claims that his gold is 'virtue, fame,/Honour and all things else' so Mammon's wealth is 'the fountaine of the worldes good' (38). But Mammon's argument is, of course, a false one. Gold generates not happiness but discord, as the notorious golden apples in the Garden of Proserpina remind us.

As a symbol of a fallen world the Cave of Mammon is, as Fowler notes, a place of 'aggressive and laborious competition'.[24] At its centre is the corrupt court of Philotime, where the chain of cosmic concord, which unites all the disparate parts of the universe in one hierarchical and harmonious order,[25] has been transformed into its opposite: an image of universal strife:

There, as in glistring glory she did sit,
She held a great gold chaine ylincked well,
Whose vpper end to highest heauen was knit,
And lower part did reach to lowest Hell;
And all that preace did round about her swell,
And catchen hold of that long chaine, thereby
To clime aloft, and others to excell:
That was *Ambition*, rash desire to sty,
And euery lincke thereof a step of dignity.

Some thought to raise themselues to high degree,
By riches and vnrighteous reward,
Some by close shouldring, some by flatteree;
Others through friends, others for base regard;
And all by wrong wayes for themselues prepard.
Those that were vp themselues, kept others low,
Those that were low themselues, held others hard,
Ne suffred them to rise or greater grow,
But euery one did striue his fellow downe to throw.
(II, vii, 46-7)

The corrupt court of Philotime is clearly a parody of Elizabeth's own court. But in representing its ruler as a woman of 'Soueraigne maiestye' controlling the cosmic golden chain, Spenser may possibly have been parodying some lines by Lydgate in which it is the Virgin Mary who superintends the golden chain. In his *Life of Our Lady* Lydgate addresses Mary as 'souerayne lady . . . bothe of londe and see,/And of the axtre bytwene the polez tweyne/And all the enbrasyng of the golden cheyne . . .'[26] Whether or not Spenser was deliberately parodying these lines is not important, for it is clear that, intentionally or unintentionally, Philotime is the antithesis of everything which Lydgate's image symbolizes. Epitomizing, as they do, the 'horrour and deformitie' of Mammon's 'darksome neather world' (II, vii, 49), Philotime and her court serve as a visionary warning to Guyon of the excesses to which man's fallen nature may lead him if he is not subject to a wise and temperate rule.

Having defined good 'by paragone/Of euill' (III, ix, 2), Spenser then gives us an image of the temperate court in canto ix. Like Medina, whose *ménage* is an allegory of the Elizabethan Church and its policy of 'mediocrity',[27] Alma is a portrait of Elizabeth: she herself has never felt the effects of '*Cupides* wanton rage', though, like her real-life counterpart, she has been 'woo'd of many a gentle knight' (II, ix, 18).

Her description in stanzas 18-19, as with that of so many of the virtuous female characters in *The Faerie Queene*, draws upon a conventional stock of imagery habitually employed in Elizabethan panegyric, imagery which, in its turn, either consciously or unconsciously echoes the language of Marian homage. The function of such phrases as 'virgin bright' and 'flowre . . . of grace' together with the emblematic description of her dress is typological. By identifying Alma with an historical image of quasi-divine virtue, Spenser is hinting at the providential nature of Elizabeth's rule.

Alma's castle (the castle is itself a standard Marian symbol in medieval literature[28]) has been described as 'an over-literal allegory – which would be intolerably tedious were it not for the absurdity and quaint humour of much of its detail – of the human soul and body under constant siege by a rabble of knaves representing evil desires, vices, temptations, and the senses and the passions which, uncontrolled or put to ill use, continually threaten the virtuous man'.[29] Though it would be difficult to improve on so admirably succinct a summary, it should be recalled that, fundamental to Elizabethan political thought, was the principle of analogy. Since man himself is 'an abstract or model, or briefe Storie of the Vniuersall',[30] it means that a 'publike weale' is in effect a kind of 'body lyuyng, compacte or made of sondry astates and degrees of men . . . gouerned by the rule and moderation of reason'.[31] It is upon this universally accepted axiom that the well-known principle of the 'king's two bodies' depends. In a frequently quoted passage Edmund Plowden explains that a prince may be seen both as a private individual, or 'body natural', and also as a symbolic representative of the 'body politic' he serves.[32] Though these two 'bodies' are quite separate and independent of one another, they are, in a mystical sense, identical. When Spenser tells us in the letter to Ralegh that Elizabeth 'beareth two persons, the one of a most royall Queene or Empresse, the other of a most vertuous and beautifull Lady . . .'[33] he is appealing to a political doctrine which was familiar to every educated Elizabethan.

No less familiar is the architectural conceit which Spenser employs in this allegory of the Queen's 'body natural'.[34] Indeed the house is one of the most ancient and universal symbols of man.[35] But since man himself is a little world made cunningly of elements, it follows that any symbolic representation of his body is almost certain to suggest macrocosmic analogies to the Renaissance mind. Thus the author of a treatise entitled *The Mirrovr of Policie* (1599) writes:

> In all Disciplines, if wee list well to consider it, we find that we beginne with the meanest parts thereof . . . Why then should not wee,

> speaking of a ciuile Societie . . . begin with the least parts thereof, namely, the parts of a house . . .[36]

That Spenser undoubtedly intended his readers to interpret Alma's castle as a symbol of the relationship between microcosm and macrocosm is confirmed by the geometric imagery of stanza 22:

> The frame thereof seemd partly circulare,
> And part triangulare, O worke diuine;
> Those two the first and last proportions are,
> The one imperfect, mortall, foeminine;
> Th'other immortall, perfect, masculine,
> And twixt them both a quadrate was the base,
> Proportioned equally by seuen and nine;
> Nine was the circle set in heauens place,
> All which compacted made a goodly diapase.

The numerical symbolism of canto ix has been the subject of careful and informed scrutiny;[37] but it has not been noted that the geometry of Alma's castle suggests the simple, but very important truth that the individual is an aspect of the universal. For it can surely be no coincidence that the three figures upon which the castle is founded – the square, the circle and the triangle – also form the basis of both Eastern and European schematic representations of the universe.[38] Like a three-dimensional cosmographer's diagram, the castle of Alma symbolizes the interrelation of microcosm and macrocosm, or, to use Spenser's own terms, the Queen's 'two persons'. In praising Elizabeth's body politic in terms of her body natural, Spenser reminds us that the 'temper' of the commonweal depends upon the 'temper' of its prince.

Spenser's point can be seen in graphic form in a well-known illustration from John Case's *Sphaera Civitatis* (1588). On a typical Renaissance diagram of the cosmos have been inscribed not only the usual symbols of the sun, the moon and the six planets, but also the moral virtues of Queen Elizabeth, *Primum Mobile* of the state.[39] As the cosmos is informed by the wisdom and justice of providence, so the various spheres of the body politic are united in harmonious equilibrium by their prime mover.

> Above all things is the sphere whose name is *Primum Mobile* and which unites the whole network [of interrelated phenomena] in its embrace. Thou, Virgin, Mighty Queen, thou *Primum Mobile,*

Elizabeth, doest inspire thy people to noble deeds. Thus with thy daily motion doest thou render impotent the recalcitrant and rebellious spirit and regulate matters of highest import.[40]

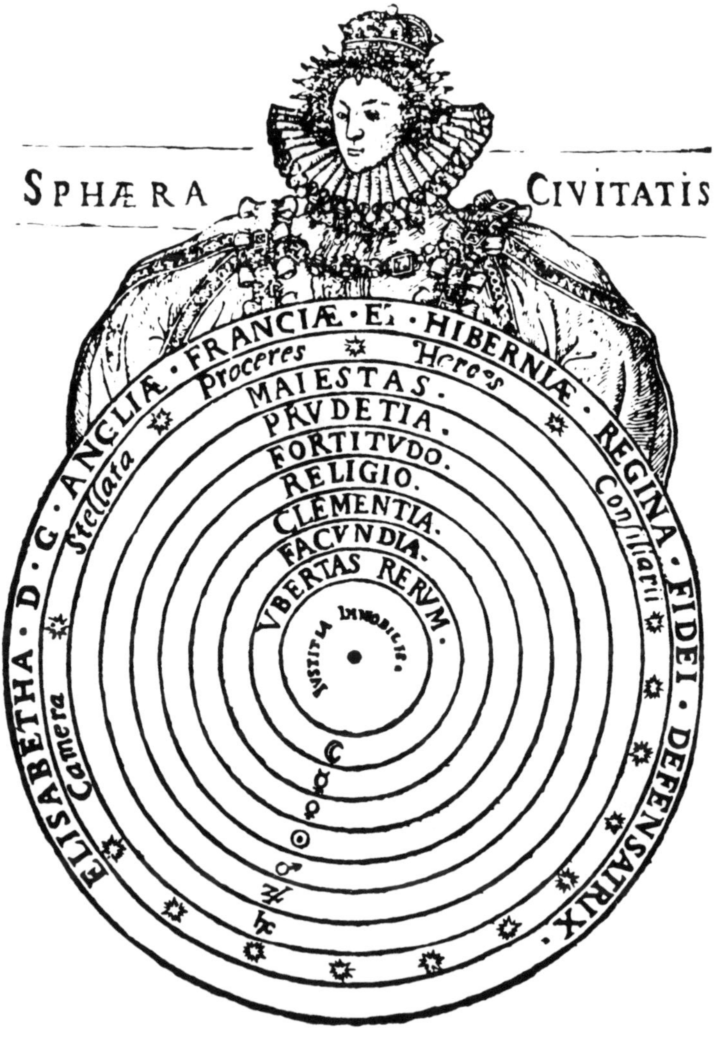


The claim which Case is making in these lines from the gloss accompanying his diagram is no more than a reflection of the universal belief that a prince's office is analogous to that of the God whose vicar he is on earth.[41] In one respect, however, the analogy is an imperfect one.

Case goes on to warn his reader that, unlike its celestial counterpart, the *sphaera civitatis* is subject to mutability:

> Such is the order of things: thus are the affairs of the world and of the state united in harmony. Yet the latter differs from the former in this respect alone: its stability cannot be guaranteed for all times, as that of the former is.[42]

Spenser offers a similar warning when he prefaces his account of Alma's castle with a description of the rebel forces which for seven years have been besieging it (12-16). No matter how 'faire and excellent' the body politic may be, if its 'sober gouernment' is allowed to become 'Distempred through misrule and passions bace', it will become corrupted in the same way that the intemperate individual loses his 'dignitie and natiue grace' (II, ix, 1).

It is because temperance is not just a private virtue, but also 'necessary in euery politicke gouernment',[43] that Guyon's instruction in Alma's castle takes the form, not of a discourse on the nature of this particular virtue, but of a history lesson.[44] That the story which he and Arthur read in Alma's chronicles is one which has its beginnings in Troy is doubly significant. For an Elizabethan, as for a Roman poet, the sack of Troy was quite simply the most important event in the legendary history of the ancient world. Since the achievements of Elizabeth, like those of Augustus, were foreshadowed in the story of Aeneas, any attempt rightly to interpret the significance of the present must begin with its prefigurations in the past. Thus from one point of view Troy could be regarded as the inevitable starting point for a history of Rome (as it was for Livy) and consequently for Britain (as it was for Camden). By tracing the ancestry of the British people to its ancient origins, Alma's chronicles serve to reveal the significance of the present as part of a divine historical plan.

But from another point of view the story of Troy could be seen as embodying an important moral lesson. If providence had ordained that from this calamity there would follow a long train of events leading ultimately to the founding of two great civilizations, it was believed that their establishment was only made possible through the subjection of passion by the rule of reason. The lesson of Troy, as Golding succinctly explains in his commentary on Ovid's *Metamorphoses*, was the dangers of sensuality:

> The seege of Troy, the death of men, the razing of the citie,

> And slaughter of king Priams stock without remors of pitie,
> Which in the xii. and xiii. bookes bee written doo declare
> How heynous wilfull perjurie and filthie whoredome are
> In syght of God.
>
> (Dedicatory Epistle, 242-6)

The sack of Troy was the supreme example of a state overthrown by lust. As Ralegh laconically puts it in his *History of the World*: 'All writers consent with *Homer*, that the rape of *Helen* by *Paris* the son of *Priamus*, was the cause of taking arms . . .'[45] If history is morally valuable in holding up a mirror to the present,[46] the lesson it teaches is the primacy of temperance among the civic virtues.

The allegory of Alma's court is thus both a compliment to Elizabeth and a warning. Though the poet, to adapt Sidney's words, 'maketh us know what perfection is', at the same time he reminds us that in a fallen world 'our infected will keepeth us from reaching unto it'.[47] As an educational experience, the purpose of Guyon's visit to Alma's castle is to teach him that, though the prince whom he serves may be 'the flowre of grace and chastitie/Throughout the world renowmed far and neare' (II, ix, 4), nevertheless she rules in a fallen world. The corollary is unequivocal: since the rebellious passions which continually threaten the body natural are one and the same as the dissident elements which seek to destroy the equilibrium of the body politic, the servant of the temperate state may never abrogate his civic responsibilities. For Guyon the supreme test of his virtue occurs in the final canto of Book II. The Bower of Bliss is one of Spenser's greatest imaginative symbols. Its purpose is twofold: to sum up the lesson concerning the need to suppress that which history has shown to be the most potent threat to civilized order; and at the same time to reveal the true significance of the artifice for which Elizabeth's own court was renowned.

Fundamental to Book II is, of course, the debate on the question of active virtue versus private pleasure. When Mammon invites Guyon to share his wealth it is clear to the champion of temperance that his duty lies 'in armes, and in atchieuements braue', not in seeking satisfaction of personal desires (II, vii, 33). The debate is first introduced when Braggadocchio meets Belphoebe in canto iii. Recognizing that Belphoebe is no ordinary country girl,[48] Braggadocchio asks her why she prefers a life of sylvan obscurity to the pleasures of the court. Belphoebe replies with a paradox, telling him that a courtly existence which is devoted simply to pleasure is in reality a life of obscurity:

Who so in pompe of proud estate (quoth she)
Does swim, and bathes himselfe in courtly blis,
Does waste his dayes in darke obscuritee,
And in obliuion euer buried is:
(II, iii, 40)

Her point is that the important choice confronting the virtuous knight is not between rural obscurity and courtly sociability, but between active virtue and private pleasure. Belphoebe is about to enlarge on the nature of the royal court when her discourse is interrupted by a crude display of violent passion on the part of Braggadocchio. Though her argument is lost on Braggadocchio, it is one which Guyon is keenly aware of. That Guyon never actually meets Braggadocchio may be taken to signify the fact that the cruder forms of intemperance such as boastfulness or physical violence do not present a serious temptation to the hero of Book II. As the narrator remarks in the first stanza of canto vi:

A harder lesson, to learne Continence
In ioyous pleasure, then in grieuous paine:
For sweetnesse doth allure the weaker sence
So strongly, that vneathes it can refraine
From that, which feeble nature couets faine;
But griefe and wrath, that be her enemies,
And foes of life, she better can restraine;
Yet vertue vauntes in both their victories,
And *Guyon* in them all shewes goodly maisteries.

It is when sexual temptation is combined with an invitation to relinquish his courtly mission that Guyon is most vulnerable. This happens on two occasions: first when Phaedria seeks to persuade him to relinquish his 'thought of warlike enterprize' (II, vi, 25), and second when the mermaids in the final canto of Book II invite him to find refuge in their 'Port of rest from troublous toyle' (32). Though Guyon is successful in subduing his 'fond desire', his decision is complicated in both instances by the fact that nature appears to give support to the arguments of his temptresses. Though the point which Spenser is making by means of this seeming paradox is, in essence, a simple one, it has been so widely misinterpreted by modern commentators, that we must devote some space to unravelling it.

When Guyon arrives at Phaedria's island he is enchanted by the natural beauty of the scene:

The fields did laugh, the flowres did freshly spring,
The trees did bud, and earely blossomes bore,
And all the quire of birds did sweetly sing,
And told that gardins pleasures in their caroling.
(II, vi, 24)

Phaedria's own voice seems to harmonize perfectly with this consort of natural music:

And she more sweet, then any bird on bough,
Would oftentimes emongst them beare a part,
And striue to passe (as she could well enough)
Their natiue musicke by her skilfull art:
(25)

The same musical metaphor occurs in canto xii. As the mermaids sing of a life of ease and tranquillity, the sea and the winds provide a natural accompaniment to their beguiling song in what must be the most beautiful stanza of the book:

With that the rolling sea resounding soft,
In his big base them fitly answered,
And on the rocke the waues breaking aloft,
A solemne Meane vnto them measured,
The whiles sweet *Zephirus* lowd whisteled
His treble, a straunge kinde of harmony;
Which *Guyons* senses softly tickeled,
That he the boateman bad row easily,
And let him heare some part of their rare melody.
(II, xii, 33)

When the image is repeated a third time we may be sure that it embodies some important truth. As Guyon and his Palmer approach the object of their quest they are met with the most beautiful sounds:

Eftsoones they heard a most melodious sound,
Of all that mote delight a daintie eare,
Such as attonce might not on liuing ground,
Saue in this Paradise, be heard elswhere:
Right hard it was, for wight, which did it heare,
To read, what manner musicke that mote bee:

For all that pleasing is to liuing eare,
Was there consorted in one harmonee,
Birdes, voyces, instruments, windes, waters, all agree.

The ioyous birdes shrouded in chearefull shade,
Their notes vnto the voyce attempred sweet;
Th'Angelicall soft trembling voyces made
To th'instruments diuine respondence meet:
The siluer sounding instruments did meet
With the base murmure of the waters fall:
The waters fall with difference discreet,
Now soft, now loud, vnto the wind did call:
The gentle warbling wind low answered to all.
(II, xii, 70-1)

Once again natural music provides an accompaniment to a song of temptation. This seeming paradox is one aspect of a problem which has disturbed many readers since Lewis made his penetrating and provocative analysis of the Bower of Bliss. Lewis argued that in contrast with the natural virtue of the Garden of Adonis, the patently evil bower was characterized by its artificiality: 'the one is artifice, sterility, death: the other, nature, fecundity, life'.[49] The problem with such an interpretation is that nature, instead of being set in antithesis to the artificial elements of Acrasia's island, appears to mingle with them.

Other critics have suggested that the key to the significance of the bower lies not in a simple antithesis between nature and art, but in some form of 'improper rivalry'[50] or 'war'[51] between the two. It is true that stanza 59 tells us that

nature had for wantonesse ensude
Art, and that Art at nature did repine;
So striuing each th'other to vndermine.

However, if the relationship is judged by its effects, it would appear to be more in the nature of a conspiracy than a feud. Stanza 59 continues:

Each did the others worke more beautifie;
So diff'ring both in willes, agreed in fine:
So all agreed through sweet diuersitie,
This Gardin to adorne with all varietie.

Far from opposing the work of the island's artificer, nature provides an accompaniment to her false music. As the deceptive (and notably artificial[52]) song in imitation of Tasso concludes its seductive invitation to intemperance, nature seems to voice her approval:

> He ceast, and then gan all the quire of birdes
> Their diuerse notes t'attune vnto his lay,
> As in approuance of his pleasing words.
> (76)

In so far as it was capable of soothing the passions, music was believed to be morally beneficial.[53] But if the natural harmony of birds and of the elements lends support to Acrasia's evil purpose, then it would appear that Spenser is denying music its traditional meliorative function. However, this is not the anomaly it may at first sight appear to be, for Spenser is attacking not art itself, but its misuse. Acrasia's song is an ironic parody of the 'sweete Musicke' which is heard at the betrothal ceremony in the corresponding canto of Book I.[54] Una's song, like Acrasia's, elicits a sympathetic echo:

> And all the while sweete Musicke did apply
> Her curious skill, the warbling notes to play,
> To driue away the dull Melancholy;
> The whiles one sung a song of loue and iollity.
>
> During the which there was an heauenly noise
> Heard sound through all the Pallace pleasantly,
> Like as it had bene many an Angels voice,
> Singing before th'eternall maiesty,
> In their trinall triplicities on hye;
> Yet wist no creature, whence that heauenly sweet
> Proceeded, yet each one felt secretly
> Himselfe thereby reft of his sences meet,
> And rauished with rare impression in his sprite.
> (I, xii, 38-9)

But the sound which echoes Una's song is not the music of 'wanton' nature (II, xii, 59); it is the 'heauenly noise' of the spheres. Music is morally valuable in so far as it aspires to the condition of this perfect harmony.[55] Acrasia's music is evil because it imitates not the perfect harmony of the spheres, but the 'base' music of nature: instead of subduing the natural passions, it seeks to enflame them.[56]

Spenser's pun in stanza 71 on nature's 'base' music warns us that nature is not the wholly beneficent principle she is often assumed to be.[57] But this should not cause surprise. Spenser was no cultural primitivist. Indeed the primary function of the Cave of Mammon was to remind us that we inhabit a fallen world. While the gold mine itself symbolizes the depravity of fallen man, the Garden of Proserpina is an equally vivid reminder of the fact that nature fell with man. As a consequence 'Nature giveth not vertue; it is an art to be made good'.[58] It is because nature is herself corrupted since the Fall that Acrasia is able to find in her so compliant an ally. Indeed the appeal to nature is a standard argument in Renaissance seduction poetry. Just as the choir of birds echoes the words of the invisible singer in Acrasia's Bower, so Sidney's Astrophil (to take but one contemporary example) tells Stella: 'Smiling air allows my reason,/These birds sing, "Now use the season"' (Song No. 8, 55-6). To act in conformity with nature is to allow oneself to be controlled by the baser parts of one's being. Thus, Brooke is in one sense right when he argues that Spenser's enchantress has perverted the true function of art. Not, however, as he claims, because her artifice wars with nature, but because it *conspires with* nature to corrupt man instead of leading his mind to as high a perfection as his degenerate soul can be capable of.

As the setting for Guyon's supreme test of virtue the Bower of Bliss is rich in symbolic meaning. However, in some of its most important aspects this symbolism has escaped critical notice. Like Philotime's court, Acrasia's garden is a parody, not simply of an abstract ideal of virtue, but of a specific example of that virtue. The first thing that Spenser tells us about the garden is that 'Goodly it was enclosed round about' (II, xii, 43). Within its pale are pleasances whose beauty – the combined effects of art and nature – is such as to suggest (ironically) all the freshness of Flora appearing from her 'virgin bowre' (50). Among the delights of this garden of pleasure are a fountain 'Of richest substaunce' (60), aromatic breezes (51) and beguiling music (70 ff.).

Gardens are, of course, a familiar feature of medieval and Renaissance art and literature, and they can take many forms.[59] Spenser's principal literary sources for the Bower of Bliss are the garden of Armida in the sixteenth book of *Jerusalem Delivered* and, less directly, the walled gardens of the *Roman de la Rose* and Chaucer's *Knight's Tale* and *Merchant's Tale*. The medieval garden of love is a secular version of a religious symbol which originates in the Canticles. From the time of the early Church Fathers the Virgin Mary had been identified with the bride of the Canticles.[60] The phrases 'My sister my spouse is as a garden inclosed, as a spring shut vp, and a fountaine sealed vp' (Song of Solomon, IV, 12) were interpreted as a prefiguration of the Virgin's uncontaminated womb. In the Middle Ages, and indeed well into the seventeenth century, the *hortus conclusus* was one of the most familiar of all Marian images.[61] So firmly linked with the Virgin Mary was this composite image that each of its principal features became in turn a metonymic symbol of the Virgin. Thus not only do we find her universally referred to in medieval literature as a 'closid gardeyn',[62] a 'chast bowre'[63] or a 'Paradys of plesaunce';[64] but also as a 'cristall wall'[65] or a 'closed gate';[66] a 'swete smellynge lyllye',[67] a 'fragrant rose'[68] or a 'redolent cedyr';[69] and as a 'Cristallyn welle'[70] or 'welle of grace'.[71]

By a process of secularization the religious symbol of the enclosed garden became a familiar feature of medieval love poetry. In poets like Guillaume de Lorris and Chaucer the *hortus conclusus* no longer has the precise connotations it originally possessed and is used to symbolize the futility of man's efforts to create an earthly paradise through worship of the senses. Their gardens are not so much Marian parodies as humanistic adaptations of a religious image. However, in Spenser's Bower of Bliss each of the traditional features of the *hortus conclusus* has been inverted. Unlike the chaste bower of Marian tradition, Spenser's garden is 'enclosed round about', not with an impregnable wall, but with a fence 'but weake and thin' (43); its gate is not locked fast, but is 'wrought of substaunce light,/Rather for pleasure, then for battery or fight' (43); its well is not 'a spring shut vp, and a fountaine sealed vp', but an overflowing 'flood' which provides the scene for a display of the most blatant eroticism (60-8). In short, Spenser's Bower of Bliss is a parody of one of the most widely used of all Marian symbols. The contemporary reader, familiar as he was with the body of traditional iconography upon which this episode is based, could scarcely fail to compare the ironically titled 'Virgin Rose' (74) of canto xii with the 'heauenly pourtraict' of Belphoebe in canto iii, or the destructive effects of Acrasia's sensual charms with Belphoebe's 'ambrosiall odours' and miraculous healing powers (22). If Belphoebe represents Elizabeth in the character of 'a most vertuous and beautifull Lady', then Acrasia is just as clearly her antithesis.

The special significance of a corrupt garden in a poem addressed to Queen Elizabeth needs no emphasizing. Like the Virgin Queen of Heaven, England's maiden queen was regularly addressed in hortulan terms – terms which in her own case reflected the garden-like state with which she was, in a sense, synonymous.[72] Identification of a prince with an idealized landscape was a traditional device of epideictic poetry, and Elizabeth's poets made full use of the convention (see Chapter 4). But there was a particular reason why it was deemed appropriate to associate Elizabeth with nature's garden: as Astraea *rediviva* it was natural that she should be identified with a world transformed by art and restored to its golden-age purity. A song from the entertainments at Elvethem in 1591 is an example of the way Elizabeth was portrayed in the progresses not simply as the *genius loci* of an idealized landscape, but as identical with it:

Elisa is the fairest Quene
That ever trode upon this greene.
Elisaes eyes are blessed starres,
Inducing peace, subduing warres.
Elisaes hand is christal bright,
Her wordes are balme, her lookes are light,
Elisaes brest is that faire hill,
Where Vertue dwels, and sacred skill,
O blessed bee each day and houre,
Where sweet Elisa builds her bowre.[73]

By investing Acrasia's corrupt bower with Marian associations Spenser is hinting at the providential nature of Elizabeth's temperate reign – a reign foretold by prophecy and prefigured in the annals of history. However, in doing so he is also warning her that the artifice with which her court was virtually synonymous is a two-edged weapon. If history is the record, in part, of man's attempts to curb his 'natural' passions, then art – the antithesis of all that is natural – may be seen to be the very basis of civilization. But if that art is abused, it will destroy all that temperance has achieved.

## Notes

1. Fowler, *Spenser and the Numbers of Time*, pp. 63-79.
2. Fowler, pp. 66-79.
3. Smith and de Selincourt, p. 407.
4. Fowler, p. 83.
5. Though not all of these images are exclusive to the Virgin Mary, as a composite image they are. For a discussion of their significance in Marian literature and art see Warner, Chs. VI, XVI and XVII. Since she is a type of Elizabeth it was necessary for Spenser to avoid any suggestion of maternity on Belphoebe's own part. However, in associating her with the ideas of miraculous impregnation and

anaesthetic parturition Spenser may have been thinking of the imagery traditionally used in accounts of Christ's conception. Just as the impregnation of Mary was commonly compared to sunbeams piercing translucent material, so Belphoebe is conceived by 'sunne-beames' bright which 'pierst into her [mother's] womb' (III, vi, 7) (see Lydgate's *Life of Our Lady*, pp. 347 and 680).

6. The phrases 'flower of womanhood', 'flower of virtue', 'flower of chastity', and the phrases 'morning star' and 'star of the sea' occur countless times in late medieval Marian literature. See in particular Lydgate's 'Ballade at the Reverence of Our Lady', MacCracken, I, 254-60 and the carols addressed to the Virgin in *The Early English Carols*, edited by Richard Leighton Green (Oxford, 1935), pp. 129-62.

7. See, for example, *The Myroure of oure Ladye*: 'Heyle vyrgyn mother of god. thou arte the sonne of the day aboue. and the mone of the nighte of the worlde . . . As the sonne lyghtneth the day. and the mone the nyghte. so lyghtnest thow heuen and erthe' (p. 306).

8. *The Progresses and Public Processions of Queen Elizabeth*, I, 28.

9. *The Boke Named the Governour*, p. 257.

10. Pierre de la Primaudaye, *The French Academie*, translated by T. Bowes (London, 1586), p. 181.

11. See Howard Rollin Patch, *The Other World* (New York, 1950).

12. A notable exception is Lewis H. Miller, 'A Secular Reading of *The Faerie Queene*, Book II', *ELH*, 33 (1966), 154-69. For a general survey of criticism up to 1957 see Harry Berger, *The Allegorical Temper: Vision and Reality in Book II of Spenser's 'Faerie Queene'* (New Haven, Conn., 1957), pp. 3 ff.; a survey of more recent criticism will be found in Patrick Cullen, 'Guyon *Microchristus*: The Cave of Mammon Re-examined', *ELH*, 37 (1970), 153-4n.

13. 'The Cave of Mammon', in *Shakespeare, Spenser, Donne*, pp. 66-83.

14. See Berger, pp. 3-38.

15. Humphrey Tonkin, 'Discussing Spenser's Cave of Mammon', *SEL*, 13 (1973), 1.

16. Tonkin, p. 13.

17. See, for example, Hesiod, *Works and Days*, 109-20; Tibullus, *Elegies*, I, iii, 35-50: Seneca, *Phaedra*, II, 525-39; Ovid, *Metamorphoses*, I, 89-112; Boethius, *De Consolatione Philosophiae*, II, metre 5. See also Harry Levin, *The Myth of the Golden Age in the Renaissance* (London, 1969).

18. It may be worth noting that the first action performed by Milton's rebel angels after their expulsion from heaven is mining:

> Soon had his crew
> Opened into the hill a spacious wound
> And digged out ribs of gold.
> (*Paradise Lost*, I, 688-90)

19. John Erskine Hankins, *Source and Meaning in Spenser's Allegory: A Study of 'The Faerie Queene'* (Oxford, 1971), p. 130.

20. See Thomas Warton, *Observations on the Fairy Queen of Spenser* (1752) in *Variorum Spenser*, Book II, 264.

21. See John Upton (ed.), *The Faerie Queene of Edmund Spenser* (1758) in *Variorum Spenser*, Book II, 262.

22. See Rosemond Tuve, 'Spenser and the "Zodiake of Life"', *JEGP*, 34 (1935), 3-6.

23. *Shakespeare's Ovid, Being Arthur Golding's Translation of The Metamorphoses*, edited by W.H.D. Rouse (London, 1961), p. 23. All quotations from the *Metamorphoses* are from this edition.

24. *Spenser and the Numbers of Time*, p. 13.

25. On the origin of this idea see Arthur O. Lovejoy, *The Great Chain of Being: A Study of the History of an Idea* (1936; rpt. New York, 1960), pp. 58-66 and passim.

26. *Life of Our Lady*, p. 611. For other possible sources see Henry Gibbons Lotspeich, *Classical Mythology in the Poetry of Edmund Spenser*, Princeton Studies in English, IX (Princeton, 1932), p. 64.

27. See A.J. Magill, 'Spenser's Guyon and the Mediocrity of the Elizabethan Settlement', *SP*, 67 (1970), 167-77.

28. See Roberta D. Cornelius, *The Figurative Castle: A Study in the Medieval Allegory of the Edifice with Especial Reference to Religious Writings* (Bryn Mawr, Pa., 1930), Ch. IV, 'The Blessed Virgin as a Castle' (pp. 37-48). A late medieval example not mentioned by Cornelius is in Lydgate's *Life of Our Lady*, p. 349.

29. Peter Bayley, *Edmund Spenser: Prince of Poets* (London, 1971), p. 127.

30. Sir Walter Ralegh, *The Historie of the World* (London, 1614), p. 25.

31. Elyot, *The Governour*, p. 1.

32. See Ernst H. Kantorowicz, *The King's Two Bodies: A Study in Medieval Political Theology* (Princeton, 1957), p. 7.

33. Letter to Ralegh, p. 407.

34. The *locus classicus* for the analogy between the proportions of architecture and those of the human body is Vitruvius's *De Architectura* (see S.K. Heninger, Jr., *Touches of Sweet Harmony: Pythagorean Cosmology and Renaissance Poetics* (San Marino, 1974), p. 193). See also Cornelius, pp. 1-9; Leonard Barkan, *Nature's Work of Art: The Human Body as Image of the World* (New Haven, Conn., 1975), pp. 8-174.

35. See Olivier Marc, *Psychology of the House* (1972), translated by Jessie Wood (London, 1977), p. 67 and passim.

36. Guillaume de la Perriere, *The Mirrovr of Policie* (London, 1599), Sig.Riii$^{v}$.

37. See Vincent Foster Hopper, 'Spenser's "House of Temperance"', *PMLA*, 55 (1940), 958-67; Fowler, pp. 260-88; R.M. Cummings, 'A Note on the Arithmological Stanza: *The Faerie Queene*, II, ix, 22', *JWCI*, 30 (1967), 410-14; Jerry Leath Mills, 'Spenser's Castle of Alma and the Number 22: A Note on Symbolic Stanza Placement', *NQ*, 212 (1967), 456-7.

38. See Marc, p. 102; Heninger, p. 159.

39. John Case, *Sphaera Civitatis* (Oxford, 1588), Sig. ¶ 2.

40.

Omnibus impendet globus is, cui MOBILE PRIMVM
Nomen, & amplexu nexus qui continet omnes.
TU VIRGO, REGINA Potens, tu MOBILE PRIMVM
ELISABETHA, rapistecum molimina Gentis.
Inde reluctantes animos, mentesq; rebelles
Debilitas, Motvque trahis Suprema DIVRNO. (Case, Sig. ¶ 2)

41. See, for example, John Hayward: 'As one GOD ruleth the worlde, one maister the familie, as all the members of one bodye receiue both sence and motion from one heade, which is the seate and tower both of the vnderstanding and of the will: so it seemeth no lesse naturall, that one state should be gouerned by one commaunder' (*An Answer to the First Part of a Certaine Conference Concerning Svccession* (London, 1603), Sig. Bi$^{v}$).

42.

Hic ordo: sic conspirat status ORBIS, & VRBIS:
Haec tamen hoc tantum discrimine distat ab ILLO,
Quod non perpetua firmari possit vt ILLE. (Case, Sig. ¶ 2)

43. La Perriere, Sig. Ci$^{v}$.

44. On the moral significance of Alma's chronicles see Michael O'Connell, 'History and the Poet's Golden World: The Epic Catalogues in *The Faerie Queene*', *ELR*, 4 (1974), 241-67; Jerry Leath Mills, 'Spenser and the Numbers of History: A Note on the British and Elfin Chronicles in *The Faerie Queene*', *PQ*, 55 (1976), 281-6; Douglas Brooks-Davies, *Spenser's Faerie Queene: A Critical Commentary on Books I and II* (Manchester, 1977), p. 171.

45. Ralegh, p. 382.

46. William Baldwin, in the dedication to the 1559 edition of *The Mirror for Magistrates*, writes: 'here as in a loking glas, you shall see (if any vice be in you) howe the like hath bene punished in other heretofore, whereby admonished, I trust it will be a good occasion to move you to the soner amendment' (*Mirror for Magistrates*, edited by Lily B. Campbell (New York, 1960), pp. 65-6).

47. *A Defence of Poetry*, p. 79.

48. Many critics have noticed the allusion in the description of Belphoebe in stanza 31 to *Aeneid*, I, 502-3.

49. C.S. Lewis, *The Allegory of Love* (Oxford, 1936), p. 326.

50. R. Nevo, 'Spenser's "Bower of Bliss" and a Key Metaphor from Renaissance Poetic', *Studies in Western Literature*, X, edited by D.A. Fineman (Jerusalem, 1962), p. 26.

51. N.S. Brooke, 'C.S. Lewis and Spenser: Nature, Art and the Bower of Bliss', *The Cambridge Journal*, 2 (1949), 434.

52. For a discussion of the 'art' of this lyric see Robin Headlam Wells, 'Song from Spenser's *The Faerie Queene*', *CritS*, 6 (1973), 7-11.

53. A classic Elizabethan statement of this belief is the following stanza from a lyric in Francis Davison's *Poetical Rhapsody*:

> Praise-worthy Music is, for God it praiseth;
> And pleasant, for brute beasts therein delight;
> Great profit from it flows: for why? it raiseth
> The mind o'erwhelmed with rude passions' might;
> When against reason passions fond rebel,
> Music doth that confirm, and those expel.

(*Davison's Poetical Rhapsody* (1602), edited by A.H. Bullen, 2 vols (London, 1890), II, 98.) See also Gretchen Ludke Finney, *Musical Backgrounds for English Literature: 1580-1650* (New Brunswick, n.d.), pp. 47-68; John Hollander, *The Untuning of the Sky: Ideas of Music in English Poetry 1500-1700* (Princeton, 1961), pp. 36-43; 91-122; Heninger, pp. 103-4.

54. The parallel is noted by A.C. Hamilton, *The Structure of Allegory in 'The Faerie Queene'* (Oxford, 1961), pp. 104-5.

55. See, for example, Castiglione: 'it hath beene the opinion of most wise Philosophers, that the worlde is made of musike, and the heavens in their moving make a melodie, and our soule is framed after the verie same sort and therefore lifteth up it selfe, and (as it were) reviveth the vertues and force of it selfe with Musicke' (*The Book of the Courtier*, p. 75).

56. The clearest statement of the moral responsibility of the musician is probably in the *Timaeus*: 'Harmony', writes Plato, 'was given by the Muses to him who makes intelligent use of the Muses, not as an aid to irrational pleasure . . . but as an auxiliary to the inner revolution of the Soul, when it has lost its harmony, to assist in restoring it to order and concord with itself' (*Timaeus*, translated by R.G. Bury, Loeb Classical Library (London, 1929), p. 109). In claiming that the key to the problem of the role of music in the Bower of Bliss lies in the 'morally unwholesome blending of its musical categories', John Hollander seems to miss

the essential point that music is here being misused ('Spenser and the Mingled Measure', *ELR*, 1 (1971), 230).

57. See, for example, C.S. Lewis's essay on 'Nature' in *Studies in Words* (Cambridge, 1960), pp. 71-2. For general discussions of the subject of nature and art in Renaissance literature see Haydn, *The Counter-Renaissance*, pp. 468-524; Madeleine Doran, *Endeavours of Art: A Study of Form in Elizabethan Drama* (Madison, Wisc., 1954), pp. 54-70; Edward William Tayler, *Nature and Art in Renaissance Literature* (New York, 1964), pp. 11-37; Lawrence Manley, *Convention, 1500-1750* (Cambridge, Mass. and London, 1980), pp. 15 ff.

58. Seneca, *Ad Lucilium Epistulae Morales*, XC, 44-5, translated by Thomas Lodge, quoted by Tayler, *Nature and Art in Renaissance Literature*, p. 21.

59. See D.W. Robertson, Jr., *A Preface to Chaucer: Studies in Medieval Perspectives* (Princeton, 1963), pp. 386-8.

60. See Warner, pp. 61-2.

61. See Stanley Stewart, *The Enclosed Garden: The Tradition and the Image in Seventeenth-Century Poetry* (Madison, Wisc. and London, 1966), pp. 41-5. The music, though not derived from the Canticles, is a typical feature of the Marian garden. See Hans H. Hofstätter, *Art of the Late Middle Ages*, translated by Robert Erich Wolf (New York, 1968), pp. 162-3.

62. Lydgate, 'Ballade at the Reverence of Our Lady', MacCracken, I, 256.

63. *Early English Carols*, p. 151.

64. 'Ballade at the Reverence of Our Lady', MacCracken, I, 256.

65. Lydgate, *Life of Our Lady*, p. 349.

66. *Early English Carols*, pp. 143, 152.

67. *The Myroure of oure Ladye*, p. 216.

68. *Early English Carols*, p. 152.

69. 'Ballade at the Reverence of Our Lady', MacCracken, I, 256.

70. Ibid.

71. *Early English Carols*, pp. 143, 152.

72. See Bruce R. Smith, 'Landscape with Figures: The Three Realms of Queen Elizabeth's Country-House Revels', *RenD*, N.S. 8 (1977), 57-115.

73. *The Progresses and Public Processions of Queen Elizabeth*, III, 119.

# 3 A SECOND EVE

There are two assumptions which underlie much recent critical discussion of the 'Legend of Chastitie'. The first is that love, as it is depicted in the romance of Britomart and Artegall, 'ceases to be a metaphor and is treated in its own right';[1] the second is that Book III, in narrating the adventures of 'a heroine whose mission is to fit herself for the husband through whom she may fulfil her destiny . . .'[2] is the book of 'married love'.[3] While many readers may be reluctant to accept Lewis's claim that the subject of Book III is 'the final defeat of courtly love by the romantic conception of marriage',[4] there would appear to be little with which to quarrel in the view that Britomart's story shows the 'transformation of passionate love into matrimonial love'.[5]

Unexceptionable as such a reading may seem, it presents us with a problem when we find that the introductory stanzas of Book III, like those of Book II, are devoted entirely to explaining that the poem is a mirror in which Elizabeth may see her own 'glorious pourtraict' (3). Comparing his own poem with Ralegh's *Cynthia*, Spenser supplicates for permission similarly to 'sing his mistresse prayse' (5). Later, in canto iv, he claims that Elizabeth is the 'matter', or subject, of his song (3). If Spenser means what he says here and in his proem, this makes Book III not merely tactless, but illogical. For to address an epideictic poem celebrating the ideal of married love to a virgin queen who is on record as highly commending the single life[6] is nonsensical. There are, I believe, two answers to this problem, and they will form the substance of the present chapter: first, Book III is the book, not of marriage, but of courtship and all its attendant doubts, uncertainties and difficulties; and second, this courtship, in addition to its literal meaning, is a metaphor for the idea – familiar enough in Elizabethan royal panegyric – of Elizabeth's betrothal to her 'lover', England. Although this courtship does end finally in a marriage, the marriage – itself a metaphor – is not the subject of Book III.

A substantial part of the previous chapter was devoted to an analysis of the house of Alma. As one of the most important allegorical sequences of Book II this episode is crucial to our understanding of Spenser's technique as an epideictic poet. In this imaginative symbol of the temperate state are combined both a general moral statement concerning the need to regulate the passions which threaten to destroy body natural and body politic alike, and also a celebration of the Queen's 'two persons'. The Garden of Adonis serves an equally important function in Book III. As a symbol of prelapsarian sexuality the Garden provides a frame of reference against which the events of the book may be judged; but contained within this complex image of chaste fruitfulness is a subtle compliment to Elizabeth as the unique embodiment of the paradoxical virtue which it symbolizes.

The Garden of Adonis is one of the great set pieces of *The Faerie Queene*. But it differs from such comparable passages as the Bower of Bliss or Mount Acidale in so far as it contains a more or less coherent theory of creation. While this cosmogony is clearly Platonic in its general outlines it is sufficiently imprecise in its details to have left room for a wealth of speculation concerning the sources for Spenser's ideas.[7] Much of this scholarly investigation has proceeded on the assumption that the Garden of Adonis is a 'great philosophic poem . . .'[8] and that to trace its intellectual pedigree is to unlock its meaning. Judging by its results such an assumption would appear to be mistaken. That exhaustive studies of Spenser's supposed sources have a way of confusing rather than illuminating the important issues is scarcely surprising. Book III is not, after all, a philosophic, but a moral poem. Its purpose is to adapt 'antique praises vnto present persons' (III, proem, 3). This is not to deny that it contains a great deal of philosophic material. But Spenser uses this material as a poet in order to illustrate and embroider his theme, and not as a philosopher in order to promote a certain metaphysical theory. As Evans reminds us, it is allegory, not philosophy that we are reading in the Garden of Adonis.[9] While it would be unwise to minimize its difficulties, *The Faerie Queene* is to a remarkable degree self-elucidating. Since the significance of events in the poem, like those in life, is so often revealed retrospectively in the light of other incidents, it means that 'the most important single technique [of interpretation] is internal comparison or correlation'.[10] Nevertheless, because Spenser draws on certain literary and moral commonplaces which are no longer part of our general cultural experience, it may be necessary to provide such background information as would have been possessed by the Elizabethan reader.

As a symbol of prelapsarian sexuality the Garden of Adonis forms part of a long tradition of thought on the subject of the consequences of man's fall from his primitive state of grace. Classical accounts of the golden age speak of a time when man lived unrestrained by institutions and customs.[11] No judges existed for there were no laws to administer.[12] And since there were no rules of marriage, lovers came together freely in the woods, united by Venus.[13] In the Middle Ages these ideas receive their most explicit treatment in the witty and ironic Jean de Meun. In the golden age, says Ami to the Dreamer in Jean's encyclopaedic expansion of Guillaume de Lorris's allegory, lovers were able to indulge in their favourite pastime unhindered by rapacity or greed. In these moments of pleasure the greenwood trees would spread their branches over the embracing couples as they lay entwined together, creating canopies to protect them from the sun (*Roman de la Rose*, 8401-8).

Orthodox Christian opinion, too, regarded the prelapsarian world as a world of innocent pleasures. For all its asceticism, medieval theology was prepared to concede that unfallen man enjoyed a happy sexuality. Indeed Aquinas even goes so far as to argue that before the Fall 'the pleasure of sense would have been all the greater, given the greater purity of man's nature and sensibility of his body'.[14] Christian writers did not, of course, see unfallen man as innocently promiscuous (with only one representative of each sex this would not have been possible even had it been thought desirable). Aquinas explains that, if the pleasures of sensuality were superior before the Fall, 'the pleasure urge would not have squandered itself in so disorderly a fashion . . . when it was ruled by reason'.[15]

In the Renaissance we find a return to the idea of the golden age as a time when man's sexual needs were as freely supplied as his other appetites. In the chorus from the first act of *Aminta* beginning '*O bella età de l'oro* . . .' Tasso characterizes the golden age as pre-eminently an age of free love:

O happy golden Age,
Not for that Riuers ranne
With streames of milke, and hunny dropt from trees;
Not that the earth did gage
Vnto the husband-man
Her voluntary fruites, free without fees:
Not for no cold did freeze,
Nor any cloud beguile,
Th'eternall flowring Spring
Wherein liu'd euery thing,
And whereon th'heauens perpetually did smile;
Not for no ship had brought
From forraine shores, or warres or wares ill sought.
But onely for that name,
That Idle name of wind:

That Idoll of deceit, that empty sound
Call'd HONOR, which became
The tyran of the minde,
And so torments our Nature without ground;
Was not yet vainly found:
Nor yet sad griefes imparts
Amidst the sweet delights
Of ioyfull amorous wights.
Nor were his hard lawes knowne to free-borne hearts.
But golden lawes like these.
Which nature wrote. *That's lawfull which doth please.*
Then amongst flowres and springs
Making delightfull sport,
Sate Louers without conflict, without flame;
And Nymphs and shepheards sings,
Mixing in wanton sort
Whisp'rings with Songs, then kisses with the same
Which from affection came:
The naked virgin then
Her Roses fresh reueales,
Which now her vaile conceales:
The tender Apples in her bosome seene.
And oft in Riuers cleere
The Louers with their Loues consorting were.

(*Aminta*, I, 656-94)[16]

Tasso's defence of free love is a deliberate parody of traditional accounts of the golden age. The same idea can be found in Elizabethan erotic verse. 'How happy were our Syres in ancient time,/Who held plurality of loves no crime . . .' writes one poet,

Women were then no sooner ask'd then won,
And what they did was honest and well done.
But since this title honour hath been us'd,
Our weak credulity hath been abus'd;
The golden laws of nature are repeald,
Which our first Fathers in such reverence held . . .[17]

By the next century appeal to the golden age as a time of unrestricted sexual freedom had become a favourite device among rakish poets seeking fresh arguments for their cause.[18] It is this tradition of thought upon which Spenser is drawing when he describes the Garden as a place where

> all plentie, and all pleasure flowes,
> And sweet loue gentle fits emongst them throwes,
> Without fell rancor, or fond gealosie;
> Franckly each paramour his leman knowes,
> Each bird his mate, ne any does enuie
> Their goodly meriment, and gay felicitie.
> (III, vi, 41)

As Ovid had described the golden age as a time when

> The Springtime lasted all the yeare, and *Zephyr* with his milde
> And gentle blast did cherish things that grew of owne accorde.
> The ground untilde, all kinde of fruits did plenteously avorde.
> (*Metamorphoses*, I, 122-4)

so in Spenser's Garden

> There is continuall spring, and haruest there
> Continuall, both meeting at one time:
> For both the boughes doe laughing blossomes beare,
> And with fresh colours decke the wanton Prime,
> And eke attonce the heauy trees they clime,
> Which seeme to labour vnder their fruits lode:
> The whiles the ioyous birdes make their pastime
> Emongst the shadie leaues, their sweet abode,
> And their true loues without suspition tell abrode.
> (III, vi, 42)

The Garden of Adonis is the antithesis of Proserpina's Garden where the only fruits which grow are the apples of discord. In the middle of this paradise is Venus's secret cave where the goddess enjoys her lover 'when euer that she will' and 'Possesseth him, and of his sweetnesse takes her fill' (46). The function of this image of eternal copulation is to establish the Garden as a sexual paradise. The idea of sex as an elysium into which lovers are privileged to retreat is probably as old as love poetry itself. Since 'lovers' houres be full eternity'[19] it affords, as the poet himself knows 'by tryall' (29), a fleeting taste of the joys of a prelapsarian world.

With this image of prelapsarian sexuality Spenser interweaves his myth of transmigration. Though it may not impress us as philosophy, its poetic meaning is plain enough. Each time a soul leaves the Garden to be born into the world and is clothed 'with sinfull mire' (32), that birth is a repetition of man's fall from the golden age.[20] By reminding us of the fact that the springs of life are sexual, the Garden of Adonis expresses through symbolism what the rest of Book III teaches by narrative example: namely the paramount importance of preserving the purity of this sexual fountainhead.

The Garden of Adonis, then, is a complex symbol of uncorrupted sexuality. Since lovers experience no impediment to their happiness in the form of jealousy or envy, there is no seduction and no pursuit. By contrast the stories which go to make up the bulk of Book III are stories of 'louers sad calamities' (IV, i, 1): they illustrate in varying degrees the effects of man's fall on his sexual life. The dominant motif of the book is the chase. Peregrination, encounter and flight are, of course, distinctive characteristics of *The Faerie Queene* and an inevitable device in an allegory where the individual's struggle to harmonize the warring elements of his personality is expressed by means of the interaction of different characters. Nevertheless, although there is no book of *The Faerie Queene* in which we do not witness characters pursuing each other, this motif is so frequently employed in Book III as to become its outstanding feature. At one extreme we see Britomart pursuing her vision of Artegall; at the other we see Argante pursuing the objects of her depraved affections. Between these two extremes fall most of the rest of the cast in this heroic-tragi-comedy of love: Marinell, Florimell, Timias, Amoret, Paridell, Hellenore, Malbecco – all of them either pursuing or being pursued.

Noticeable also is the fact that in so few cases does Book III provide the conclusion to these stories. This is usually explained by pointing out that whereas Spenser's principal literary models for the first two books of *The Faerie Queene* were the Bible and classical epic respectively, his main literary source for Books III and IV was Ariosto. Whatever Spenser's reasons were for this choice it is clear that the effect of Ariosto's technique of narrative interlacement and suspended resolution is to emphasize the sense of tension and frustration which is the hallmark of the book as a whole. In a fallen world where jealousy and mistrust have made their appearance and where natural sympathy of choice seems rarely to be found, lovers can no longer meet freely as they do in the Garden of Adonis, but must undergo trial and hardship in the cause of love. Nor is it only the corrupt or depraved characters such as Malecasta or Malbecco who experience the pain of rejection or frustration:

Marinell, Timias and Proteus all suffer the pangs of unrequited passion. Epitomizing the suffering caused by discordant love is the tableau of Venus and Adonis depicted in the tapestries of Castle Joyeous (III, i, 34-8). Indeed the prophecy which Shakespeare's Venus makes on the death of her lover is a fitting comment on a world ruled by the caprice of Cupid:

> Since thou art dead, lo, here I prophesy
> Sorrow on love hereafter shall attend:
> It shall be waited on with jealousy,
> Find sweet beginning but unsavoury end,
> Ne'er settled equally, but high or low,
> That all love's pleasure shall not match his woe.
> (*Venus and Adonis* 1135-40)[21]

The privation of fallen humanity is summed up in the symbolic fate of Florimell, whose story, as Frye and other critics have suggested,[22] forms an allusion to the myth of Proserpine – itself an image of the Fall. As Proserpine is condemned perpetually to spend six months of every year in Hades while the upper world mourns her loss, so Florimell 'is imprisoned under the sea during a kind of symbolic winter in which a "snowy" Florimell takes her place'.[23]

Not even the heroine of Book III is exempt from the trials of love. Where the heroes of Books I and II embark on their missions in a mood of buoyant self-confidence (see in particular I, i, 28 and II, vii, 2), Britomart is tormented by doubt and uncertainty. Her complaint at love's cruelty is no less sincere for being couched in conventional terms:

> Huge sea of sorrow, and tempestuous griefe,
> Wherein my feeble barke is tossed long,
> Far from the hoped hauen of reliefe,
> Why do thy cruell billowes beat so strong,
> And thy moyst mountaines each on others throng,
> Threatning to swallow vp my fearefull life?
> O do thy cruell wrath and spightfull wrong
> At length allay, and stint thy stormy strife,
> Which in these troubled bowels raignes, and rageth rife.
>
> For else my feeble vessell crazd, and crackt
> Through thy strong buffets and outrageous blowes,
> Cannot endure, but needs it must be wrackt

On the rough rocks, or on the sandy shallowes,
The whiles that loue it steres, and fortune rowes;
Loue my lewd Pilot hath a restlesse mind
And fortune Boteswaine no assuraunce knowes,
But saile withouten starres gainst tide and wind:
How can they other do, sith both are bold and blind?
(III, iv, 8-9)

Suffering is an inescapable consequence of man's fall from his golden-age state of sexual innocence. The experience may, Spenser claims, degrade him still further, or it may inspire noble deeds:

Wonder it is to see, in diuerse minds,
How diuersly loue doth his pageants play,
And shewes his powre in variable kinds:
The baser wit, whose idle thoughts alway
Are wont to cleaue vnto the lowly clay,
It stirreth vp to sensuall desire,
And in lewd slouth to wast his carelesse day:
But in braue sprite it kindles goodly fire,
That to all high desert and honour doth aspire.
(III, v, 1)

Much of the narrative of Book III is devoted to illustrating the varieties of love and the perverted ends to which man is capable of turning it. With none of the more or less depraved characters is Britomart at all closely involved: some of them she never meets. She is, after all, a virtuous woman inspired by a noble vision and it is unlikely that she would be attracted to a professional seducer like Paridell, much less to such deviants as Ollyphant. If Britomart is to be tempted to forsake her mission, the temptation must clearly take a much subtler form than simple eroticism or blatant sexual perversion. The one incident in which she does become closely involved and which demands considerable courage on her part is the adventure with which the book concludes.

The rescue of Amoret from the House of Busirane is the culminating incident in a book which contrasts uncorrupted, prelapsarian sexuality with the various ways in which love may be abused or distorted in a fallen world. To Scudamour's rhetorical complaint concerning the injustice of fate (III, xi, 9), Britomart replies with a philosophic reminder that suffering is the unavoidable lot of fallen man: 'For who nill bide the burden of distresse,/Must not here thinke to liue: for life is wretchednesse' (14). On a literal level the story presents few difficulties. Roche aptly sums it up as 'the romance motif of the distressed maiden's rescue from the evil magician . . .'[24] On a tropological level, however, it seems to be more problematic. Interpretations of the story range from the view which sees the defeat of Busirane as representing 'the rejection of a now untimely passion'[25] to the exact opposite position which sees it as the defeat of 'Amoret's fear of sexual love in marriage'.[26] Although the incident is invested with a certain amount of deliberate mystery, its difficulty has probably been exaggerated, for, as is usually the case, Spenser provides the reader with sufficient clues to unravel the meaning.

A common device in Spenserian allegory is to employ different literary forms in presenting the same topic. Thus symbolic treatment of a theme may be either preceded or followed by presentation of the same moral idea in some other form such as an exemplary tale, a debate or an epigram. The episode of the House of Busirane is immediately preceded by the fabliau of Malbecco and Hellenore, a tale whose purpose is to illustrate in comic terms the absurdities to which jealousy can lead. The next canto begins with an apostrophe to the same vice:

O hatefull hellish Snake, what furie furst
Brought thee from balefull house of *Proserpine*,
Where in her bosome she thee long had nurst,
And fostred vp with bitter milke of tine,
Fowle Gealosie, that turnest loue diuine
To ioylesse dread, and mak'st the louing hart
With hatefull thoughts to languish and to pine,
And feed it selfe with self-consuming smart?
Of all the passions in the mind thou vilest art.
(III, xi, 1)

The elevated tone of stanza 1 suggests that, although the poet is still concerned with jealousy, he will now treat his subject in a manner befitting the 'vilest' of all the passions. Once we know that the story of Amoret's torture and Scudamour's helpless inability to assist her is a tale illustrating the power of jealousy to turn 'loue diuine/To ioylesse dread' the details fall into place. As we recall the events of the previous canto we realize that the narrator's comment on Malbecco applies equally to Scudamour: 'So doth he punish her and eke himselfe torment' (III, x, 3). Scudamour is unable to rescue Amoret because it is his own lack of faith in her ability to withstand temptation which is the real cause of her torture. This is why Amoret must warn Britomart not to kill Busirane, since 'none but hee/Which wrought it, could the same recure againe' (III, xii, 34). Though Britomart passes through the circumvallatory flames of desire with apparent ease we discover that even she is not immune to the anxieties and doubts (symbolized in the tapestries and the masque of Cupid) which may afflict the minds of the most virtuous of lovers. But, as Spenser has already told us in an earlier context, 'Despair breeds not . . . where faith is staid' (I, vii, 41). Once the evil spell has been broken by steadfast faith, these figments of the troubled imagination are seen to vanish, and she and Amoret are able to leave the castle in safety.

The incident may be interpreted as a warning of the way in which mutual love may be destroyed by the jealousy and suspicion which seem to be an inseparable part of courtship. To read the story in this way is to see the characters as personifications of the virtues and vices we name in our interpretation. In one sense, of course, Amoret, Scudamour and Busirane are indeed merely personifications of the conflicting parts of Britomart's psyche, so that the whole drama may be seen as an objectification of the struggle which is taking place in the mind of the heroine as she tries to conquer her own fears and doubts concerning the mission she has been appointed to undertake.

If love is a source of frustration and suffering, it can also, as Spenser repeatedly reminds us, inspire 'noble deeds and neuer dying fame' (III, iii, 1; see also III, i, 49 and III, v, 1). But the story of Britomart's quest is more than simply the story of a girl who triumphs over adversity by remaining true to an idealistic vision of love; for Spenser takes pains not only to insist on the historic significance of her destined union with Artegall, but also to identify this 'royall Mayd' (III, ii, 11) with the 'dred Soueraine' whom he addressed in the proem to Book III:

O dred Soueraine
Thus farre forth pardon, sith that choicest wit
Cannot your glorious pourtraict figure plaine
That I in colourd showes may shadow it,
And antique praises vnto present persons fit.

But if in liuing colours, and right hew,
Your selfe you couet to see pictured,
Who can it doe more liuely, or more trew,
Then that sweet verse, with *Nectar* sprinckeled,
In which a gracious seruant pictured

His *Cynthia*, his heauens fairest light?
That with his melting sweetnesse rauished,
And with the wonder of her beames bright,
My senses lulled are in slomber of delight.

But let that same delitious Poet lend
A little leaue vnto a rusticke Muse
To sing his mistresse prayse, and let him mend,
If ought amis her liking may abuse:
Ne let his fairest *Cynthia* refuse,
In mirrours more then one her selfe to see,
(III, proem, 3-5)

By invoking Ralegh's panegyric to Elizabeth, Spenser reminds us of the fact that Cynthia was the most popular of the Queen's mythological pseudonyms; in doing so he prepares us for the identification of Britomart herself with the chaste goddess:

As when faire *Cynthia*, in darkesome night,
Is in a noyous cloud enueloped,
Where she may find the substaunce thin and light,
Breakes forth her siluer beames, and her bright hed
Discouers to the world discomfited;
Of the poore traueller, that went astray,
With thousand blessings she is heried;
Such was the beautie and the shining ray,
With which faire *Britomart* gaue light vnto the day.
(III, i, 43)

The identification of Britomart with Elizabeth is completed by the prophetic revelations of canto iii. Spenser's approach to the portentous subject of Britomart's destiny is heralded by an appropriate elevation of tone as the poet invokes the muse of history:

Begin then, O my dearest sacred Dame,
Daughter of *Phoebus* and of *Memorie*,
That doest ennoble with immortall name
The warlike Worthies, from antiquitie,
In thy great volume of Eternitie:
Begin, O *Clio*, and recount from hence
My glorious Soueraines goodly auncestrie,

Till that by dew degrees and long protense,
Thou haue it lastly brought vnto her Excellence
(III, iii, 4)

In Merlin's cave Britomart learns that her passion is by no means the 'sad evill' her nurse assumes it to be, but the 'streight course of heauenly destiny':

Most noble Virgin, that by fatall lore
Hast learn'd to loue, let no whit thee dismay
The hard begin, that meets thee in the dore,
And with sharpe fits thy tender hart oppresseth sore.

For so must all things excellent begin,
And eke enrooted deepe must be that Tree,
Whose big embodied braunches shall not lin,
Till they to heuens hight forth stretched bee.
For from thy wombe a famous Progenie
Shall spring, out of the auncient *Troian* blood,
Which shall reuiue the sleeping memorie
Of those same antique Peres the heuens brood,
Which *Greeke* and *Asian* riuers stained with their blood.
(III, iii, 21-2)

Though Merlin alludes to Britomart's Trojan ancestry, he does not name the 'antique Peres' from whom she is descended, and it is only during the course of an after-dinner conversation in Malbecco's castle that she learns the details of the Troy story. As a prophet Merlin is more concerned with the future than the past. He explains that from Britomart's union with Artegall there will spring a line of 'Renowmed kings, and sacred Emperours' (23) culminating in a 'royall virgin' (49) who will usher in an age of 'vniuersall peace' (23):

Thenceforth eternall vnion shall be made
Betweene the nations different afore,
And sacred Peace shall louingly perswade
The warlike minds, to learne her goodly lore,
And ciuile armes to exercise no more:
(III, iii, 49)

What for Britomart is prophecy is, of course, 'history' for the reader.

But although Paridell's anecdotes and Merlin's prophecies form part of the same historical narrative, they serve quite different poetic functions. In cantos ix and x, history teaches a moral lesson. As Paridell and Hellenore elope, setting fire to Malbecco's castle, we witness a bathetic repetition of the events narrated in canto ix. Paridell and Hellenore are, as their names suggest, ignoble parodies of their prototypes, Paris and Helen: their story is an absurd echo of the past. Though the two events – the sack of Troy and the sack of Malbecco's castle – are quite independent of one another and have their own significance, they are mutually illuminating. History repeats itself because the same human types exist in all ages. The lesson to be drawn from Paridell's narrative with all its prospective irony is the importance of sexual temperance, or chastity. (The thematic overlapping of which this is an obvious example is a familiar feature of *The Faerie Queene* and one which is probably inevitable in a poem which undertakes to anatomize a number of closely related moral virtues.)

In canto iii history reveals not a moral, but a mystical, truth. Unlike Paris, who is merely the prototype of many Paridells, Britomart is unique. Her relation to Elizabeth is not analogical, but typological: that is to say, while she adumbrates Elizabeth, the true significance of her story is only revealed by its conclusion in the distant future. The most that can be said of Paridell is that he is *like* Paris; but Britomart's story *involves* Elizabeth in a way in which Paris's cannot in any sense be said to involve Paridell. The special significance of this typological relationship is suggested by the image of the Tree of Jesse at III, iv, 3.[27] As the Virgin Mary provided an iconographic link in Book I, completing the identification of Una with Elizabeth, and both with the idea of the one true church, so the Tree of Jesse, as a well-known figure of the Virgin, serves an equally important function in revealing the historic nature of Britomart's quest.

There are two aspects of the Virgin's character, as it has been traditionally represented, which are relevant to Britomart's story. These are her roles of mystical bride of Christ and of second Eve. As literal narrative Britomart's quest for her lover Artegall requires no explanation; on a tropological level it illustrates, as we have seen, the power of steadfast faith to overcome adversity. But if Britomart is a type of Elizabeth, then what is the significance of her courtship? The answer is not far to seek. In comparing their queen with the Virgin Mary, Elizabethan panegyrists drew upon the traditional idea of Christ's betrothal to his 'spouse' the church. Like her heavenly counterpart, England's royal virgin was also espoused to a sacred cause. The idea of her 'courtship' by her 'lover' England had been a popular one from the very earliest years of her reign. It is best characterized by the following well-known 'Songe betwene the Quene's Majestie and Englande' celebrating the accession:

E. Come over the born Bessy,
Come over the born Bessy,
Swete Bessey come over to me;
And I will the take,
And my dere Lady make
Before all other that ever I see.

B. My thinke I hear a voice,
At whom I do rejoyce,
And aunswer the now I shall: –
Tel me, I say,
What art thou that biddes me com away,
And so earnestly doost me call?

E. I am thy lover faire,
Hath chose the to mine heir,
And my name is mery Englande;
Therefore, come away,
And make no more delaye,
Swete Bessie! give me thy hande.

B. Here is my hand,
My dere lover Englande,
I am thine both with mind and hart,
For ever to endure,
Thou maiest be sure,
Untill death us two do part.

E. Lady, this long space
Have I loved thy grace,
More then I durste well saye;
Hoping, at the last,
When all stormes were past,
For to see this joyfull daye . . .[28]

Spenser himself had already used the conceit of the wooing of Elizabeth in the 'January' eclogue of *The Shepheardes Calender*, in the story of Colin's love for Rosalind.[29] Now, in the story of Britomart's quest for a 'half-human' lover,[30] the mere 'shade and semblant of a knight' (III, ii, 38), Spenser returns to the theme of Elizabeth's betrothal to her country.

As a celebration of the mystical love of Elizabeth for her 'spouse', the 'Legend of Chastitie' belongs to a long tradition of erotic allegory in which the language of love and the language of religion were interchangeable. On the one hand courtly love poetry, from its earliest manifestations, had parodied the language of religious experience,[31] while on the other, religious writers had used erotic allegory to describe sacred mysteries. The archetypal example of such erotic allegory is, of course, The Song of Solomon. 'You must bring chaste ears to listen to this Discourse of Love . . .' writes St Bernard in the twelfth century, 'and, when you think about the Lovers in it, you must not understand by them a man and a woman, but . . . Christ and the Church . . .'[32] By the sixteenth century such a reading of the Canticles could be regarded as standard.[33]

In the eroticism of the Canticles is the same paradox that we find in *The Faerie Queene*. Fundamental to the Christian doctrine of original sin is the evilness of concupiscence; yet it is in the most blatantly sensual language that the virgin bride of the Canticles declares that she is 'sicke of loue' for her spouse (V, 8). It is because Mary (the bride of the Canticles is a type of the Virgin) was untainted by concupiscence that she is transfigured and not debased by her passionate desire. In the Marian doctrine of immaculacy is enshrined the paradox which lies at the heart of Christianity's view of woman's nature. At one extreme is Eve, archetypal temptress and author of all man's sorrows; at the other is a second Eve who, in reversing the effects of the Fall, restores the prelapsarian ideal of chaste fruitfulness. It is fundamentally the same antinomy which forms the basis of Spenser's allegory in Book III.[34] Much of the narrative of Book III consists, as we have seen, of stories which show the effects of man's fallen nature on his sexual life. But at the centre of the book is a powerful image of uncorrupted sexuality: the *hortus conclusus*, type of the Virgin's uncontaminated womb. Unlike the sterile paradise of Acrasia's bower, this garden – the birthplace of all mankind – is enclosed by a wall which 'none might thorough breake' (III, vi, 31). Beyond this wall is a world where not even the virtuous can hope to escape the trials and frustrations of their fallen sexuality. Britomart is unique, however, in her triumph over the flesh. Like the bride of the Canticles, she is sick with passion for her visionary lover (see III, ii, 5, 28-9, 39; III, iii, 18; III, iv, 6 ff.). But for all her ardour she is without concupiscence. The passion which inspires her is 'no vsuall fire, no vsuall rage' (III, ii, 37), but the 'sacred fire' (III, iii, 1) of a mystical love. As the burning bush of Moses (Exodus, III, 2) signifies the mystery of Mary's combining of divine ardour with immunity from lust,[35] so Britomart, for all her lover's sickness, is untouched by the flames which surround Busirane's castle.

If Spenser was not the first to celebrate Elizabeth's mystical marriage to England, nor was he alone in portraying her in the character of a second Eve. To John Stubbs the prospect of Elizabeth's marriage to a Frenchman – albeit a Huguenot sympathizer – seemed like a recapitulation of the seduction of Eve: 'they have sent us hither', he wrote of the Duke of Alençon, 'not Satan in body of a serpent, but the old serpent in shape of a man, whose sting is in his mouth, and who doth his endeavor to seduce our Eve, that she and we may lose this English paradise.'[36] Like the Virgin Mary of the *hortus conclusus* and the *virga Iesse*, Elizabeth was popularly seen as a 'matchlesse flower' springing from royal stock.[37] Indeed, with her dynastic emblem the Tudor Rose and her personal motto *semper eadem*, she even attracted to herself the title *rosa sine spina*,[38] an image traditionally used to characterize the Virgin of immaculate conception, and which was supposed to have grown only in the Garden of Eden.[39] It is to this traditional Marian image of the flower of paradise that Spenser is alluding in his praise of Belphoebe in canto v:

> Eternall God in his almighty powre,
> To make ensample of his heauenly grace,
> In Paradize whilome did plant this flowre,
> Whence he it fetcht out of her natiue place,
> And did in stocke of earthly flesh enrace,
> That mortall men her glory should admire:
> In gentle Ladies brest, and bounteous race
> Of woman kind it fairest flowre doth spire,
> And beareth fruit of honour and all chast desire.
> (III, v, 52)[40]

As a type of England's 'Eternall Virgin',[41] Britomart, like Belphoebe, embodies an ideal of 'chast desire' which centuries of Marian doctrine had defined with great precision. In proclaiming unambiguously that virginity is the 'highest staire/Of th'honorable stage of womanhead' (III, v, 54), Spenser is not denying the meaning of his own allegory: for although Britomart does eventually marry, her marriage, like her courtship, is a mystical one; its purpose is to fulfil the 'streight course of heauenly destiny' (III, iii, 24).

## Notes

1. Mark Rose, *Heroic Love: Studies in Sidney and Spenser* (Cambridge, Mass., 1968), p. 77. Cf. Evans: in Book III Spenser 'moves from the world of myth to that of psychology' (*Spenser's Anatomy of Heroism*, p. 178).
2. Evans, p. 151.
3. Joanne Craig, 'The Image of Mortality: Myth and History in *The Faerie Queene*', *ELH*, 39 (1972), 535.
4. Lewis, *The Allegory of Love*, p. 298.
5. Rose, p. 112.
6. In 1560 Elizabeth wrote to the King of Sweden: 'we do not conceive in our heart to take a husband but highly commend this single life . . .', *The Letters of Queen Elizabeth*, edited by G.B. Harrison (London, 1935), p. 32.
7. The most important of such source studies are summarized in *Variorum Spenser*, Book III, 340-52. See also Nelson, *The Poetry of Edmund Spenser*, pp. 209-22 and Rose, pp. 118-19n.
8. Thomas P. Roche, Jr., *The Kindly Flame: A Study of the Third and Fourth Books of Spenser's 'Faerie Queene'* (Princeton, 1964), p. 116.
9. Evans, p. 153.
10. Alastair Fowler, 'Six Knights at Castle Joyous', *SP*, 56 (1959), 583.
11. See above, Chapter 2.
12. Ovid, *Metamorphoses*, I, 91-3.
13. Lucretius, *De Rerum Natura*, V, 958-64; Tibullus, II, iii, 71-4.
14. Aquinas, *Summa Theologiae* Ia, quae. 98, art. 2, edited by Thomas Gilbey, O.P. and others, 60 vols (London, 1963-76), vol. XIII translated by Edmund Hill, O.P., 157.
15. *Summa Theologiae* Ia, quae. 98, art. 2, vol. XIII, 157-9.
16. Translated by Samuel Daniel as 'A Pastorall', *The Complete Works in Verse and Prose of Samuel Daniel*, edited by Alexander B. Grosart, 5 vols (London, 1885), I, 260-1.
17. 'Variety', 37-47, *John Donne: The Elegies and The Songs and Sonnets*, edited by Helen Gardner (Oxford, 1965), p. 105. On the authorship of this poem see the editor's introduction, pp. xliii-xliv.
18. See Louis I. Bredvold, 'The Naturalism of Donne in Relation to Some Renaissance Traditions', *JEGP*, 22 (1923), 471-502; J.B. Leishman, *The Art of Marvell's Poetry* (London, 1966), p. 302.
19. Donne, 'The Legacy', 1.4.
20. As Eric Smith notes, Spenser sees the Fall as 'a recurring fact of life' (*Some Versions of the Fall: The Myth of the Fall of Man in English Literature* (London, 1973), p. 94).
21. Quotations from Shakespeare are from *The Complete Works*, edited by Peter Alexander (1951; rpt. London, 1971).
22. Northrop Frye, 'The Structure of Imagery in *The Faerie Queene*', *UTQ*, 30 (1961), 123. See also Kathleen Williams, 'Venus and Diana: Some Uses of Myth in *The Faerie Queene*', *ELH*, 28 (1961), 118; William Blissett, 'Florimell and Marinell', *SEL*, 5 (1965), 101.
23. Frye, p. 123.

24. *The Kindly Flame*, p. 72.
25. Rose, p. 112.
26. Roche, p. 77.
27. See Introduction. The root (*radix*) of Jesse (Isaiah, XI, 1) was taken to prophesy the royal line of David, in which the *virga* (stock or branch) was Mary and the *flos* was Jesus (see Watson, *The Early Iconography of the Tree of Jesse*, p. 3). However, proponents of the Immaculate Conception held that both stem and flower signified Mary (see D'Ancona, *The Iconography of the Immaculate Conception*, pp. 46-9; Mâle, *Religious Art in France*, p. 166n; Réau, *Iconographie De L'Art Chrétien*, II, 129-40).
28. Quoted by Wilson, *England's Eliza*, pp. 4-5.
29. See Paul E. McLane, *Spenser's Shepheardes Calender: A Study in Elizabethan Allegory* (Notre Dame, Ind., 1961). McLane argues that, like Skelton's Colyn Cloute, Spenser's character represents not only the poet himself, but also the *vox populi* (p. 38).
30. Judith H. Anderson, '"Nor Man it is": The Knight of Justice in Book V of Spenser's *Faerie Queene*', *PMLA*, 85 (1970), 73.
31. See Lewis, p. 20.
32. Saint Bernard, *On the Song of Songs:* Sermones in Cantica Canticorum, translated and edited by 'A Religious of C.S.M.V.' (London, 1951), p. 16. The traditional identification of the Bride of the Canticles with the church may be traced back as far as Hippolytus of Rome (d. 235) (see Herbert Musurillo, *Symbolism and the Christian Imagination* (Dublin, 1962), p. 130).
33. In the Geneva Bible the Song of Solomon is prefaced by the following 'argument': 'In this Song, Salomon by moste swete and comfortable allegories and parables describeth the perfite loue of Iesus Christ, the true Salomon and King of peace, and the faithful soule or his Church, which he hathe sanctified and appointed to be his spouse, holy, chast and without reprehension. So that here is declared the singular loue of the bridegroom toward the bride, and his great and excellent benefites wherewith he doth enriche her of his pure bountie and grace without anie of her deseruings. Also the earnest affection of the Church which is inflamed with the loue of Christ desiring to be more and more ioyned to him in loue, and not to be forsaken for anie spot or blemish that is in her' (Sig. & iv$^{v}$).
34. As Evans rightly says, 'The concept of the "fruitful virgin" is central to *The Faerie Queene* . . .' (*Spenser's Anatomy of Heroism*, p. 111).
35. See, for example, *The Myroure of oure Ladye*: 'By this busshe ys vnderstonde our lady that was fyred & brente not. for she was moder without losse of maydenhod' (p. 296).
36. *John Stubbs's 'Gaping Gulf' with Letters and Other Relevant Documents*, edited by Lloyd E. Berry, Folger Documents of Tudor and Stuart Civilization (Charlottesville, Va., 1968), pp. 3-4.
37. See, for example, the lines from the well-known prophecy in Greene's *Friar Bacon and Friar Bungay* quoted by Wilson, p. 104.
38. Stephen Batman wrote in 1582: 'There is one rose growing in *England*, is worth all [others], *Rosa sine spina*: which royall Rose growing in hir proper soyle, is borne vp of a well settled stalke . . .' (quoted by Wilson, p. 219n).
39. See Woolf, *The English Religious Lyric*, p. 288.
40. Though it is literally Belphoebe's chastity which Spenser is praising in this metonymic image, vehicle and tenor are, in effect, indistinguishable: Belphoebe *is* the flower of paradise 'enraced' in 'stock of earthly flesh'. Cf. the description of Una at I, i, 48 quoted in Chapter 1.
41. The phrase is from the first line of Hymn II in Sir John Davies's 'Hymnes of Astraea', *The Poems of Sir John Davies*, edited by Robert Krueger (Oxford, 1975), p. 71.

# 4 QUEEN OF LOVE

Friendship, like temperance, is not in itself a problematic virtue. Scholarship has shown that in his portrayal of friendship Spenser was drawing on certain proverbial commonplaces which were classical in origin. It was believed, for example, that true friendship is based on virtue and can only exist between equals; that friends possess one soul so that a true friend is a second self; that friends hold their goods in common; and that false friendship cannot last.[1] In addition to its literal meaning, friendship has for Spenser a metaphoric meaning and signifies that principle which underlies all social and cosmic concord.[2] This wider view of friendship was also an Elizabethan commonplace.[3] But although there is general agreement among Spenser's commentators concerning the essential nature of friendship, its relevance in an epideictic poem addressed to Queen Elizabeth is not immediately clear. Where holiness and temperance require no justification as attributes of Elizabeth, friendship does. For if, as Aristotle argues, one of the first conditions of true friendship is propinquity,[4] it is not easy to see how this virtue can be said to belong to a prince whose unique nature was expressed in the emblem of the phoenix, and whose poets spoke of her as a 'myracle of Nature, of tyme, of Fortune'.[5]

An explanation of this paradox is to be found in the proem to Book IV, where, once again, Spenser hails Elizabeth as a type of princely virtue. In this case, however, it is not as an exemplar of friendship that he addresses her, but as a goddess of love:

> To her I sing of loue, that loueth best,
> And best is lou'd of all aliue I weene:
> To her this song most fitly is addrest,
> The Queene of loue, and Prince of peace from heauen blest.
>
> (IV, proem, 4)

The role of the chaste mistress who inspires all men's affections is a familiar aspect of the cult of Elizabeth: Ralegh alludes to it when he claims, in his commendatory sonnet on *The Faerie Queene*, that he has seen the soul of Petrarch weep at the deposition, by Spenser's Gloriana, of Laura from her place in the temple of fame. But the quasi-sexual rivalry that was such an essential feature of Elizabeth's own court of love is something which is far more likely to generate discord than amity. Our first concern in this chapter must therefore be to consider what place this 'Queene of loue' has in the book of friendship.

Books III and IV are often treated by commentators as parts of a single whole. And with good reason, for not only are the four main stories of the former carried over into the latter, but both books deal with different aspects of love. Where Book III portrays the strife caused by passion and recounts tales 'Of louers sad calamities' (IV, i, 1), Book IV shows that love in its highest form is capable of reconciling the conflicts generated by sexual competition in a fallen world. As usual, Spenser's method is to portray good 'by paragone/Of euill'. If the dominant motif of Book III is the chase, that of Book IV is battle. In fact well over a hundred stanzas are devoted to quarrels, fights, tournaments and other forms of competition. Sometimes, as for example in the vivid account of Scudamour's restless night in the House of Care, the battle is internal; but for the most part the conflicts of Book IV take the form of ritualized physical encounters between armed knights. The excessive length and frequency of these battle descriptions may suggest that Spenser's subject was proving to be unpropitious, and that he was finding it necessary to pad out his narrative with descriptive material. However, careful scrutiny of Spenser's imagery would seem to indicate that this was not the case.

The similes used in the battle descriptions are of two main types. Spenser will either compare his combatants to ferocious animals, including tigers (IV, iii, 16), lions (IV, iii, 39; IV, iv, 32; IV, iv, 41), bulls (IV, iv, 18), boars (IV, iv, 29), mastiffs (IV, ix, 31) and vultures (IV, iii, 19); or he will compare them with the elements (IV, i, 42; IV, iii, 27; IV, v, 32; IV, ix, 23; IV, ix, 26; IV, ix, 33). The conventions of epic style allow for the elaboration of a simile beyond the immediate functional demands of illustration so that attention is directed away from the tenor of the image to its vehicle. The effect of Spenser's images of winds, tides, currents, waves, storms and wild animals is to suggest that the human discord we are witnessing is part of a universal state of strife. The description of the battle between the rivals for the love of the false Florimell, for example, is amplified with an image of the four winds:

> As when *Dan AEolus* in great displeasure,
> For losse of his deare loue by *Neptune* hent,
> Sends forth the winds out of his hidden threasure,
> Vpon the sea to wreake his fell intent;
> They breaking forth with rude vnruliment,

> From all foure parts of heauen doe rage full sore,
> And tosse the deepes, and teare the firmament,
> And all the world confound with wide vprore,
> As if in stead thereof they Chaos would restore.
> (IV, ix, 23)

Spenser's image of elemental strife recalls Ovid's account of the creation. Ovid explains how in order to prevent the four winds from tearing the world apart with their violence the creator assigned them each a separate territory. Where Spenser speaks of men in terms of the elements, Ovid does the opposite and describes the four winds as if they were contentious brothers ('tanta est discordia fratrum'):

> But yet the maker of the worlde permitteth not alway,
> The windes to use the ayre at will. For at this present day,
> Though ech from other placed be in sundry coasts aside:
> The violence of their boystrous blasts things scarsly can abide.
> They so turmoyle as though they would the world in pieces rend,
> So cruell is those brothers wrath when that they doe contend.
> (Golding, I, 63-8)

Though Spenser may very well have had Ovid in mind as he was writing Book IV, the parallel is not in itself remarkable. Similes such as these in which comparison is made between man and the elements are the natural expression of a mind which conceives of the universe as an integrated whole. In evoking the familiar truth that man is a mirror of the macrocosm, Spenser's elemental images suggest that human friendship cannot be considered independently of the universal principle of which it is a reflection. If the law which governs human conflict is the same as that which is observable in nature, so too is the law which underlies all social concord.

According to the traditional body of Pythagorean thought which the sixteenth century inherited from the Middle Ages, the natural antagonism of the four elements was stabilized by a system of mutual repulsion and attraction, so that although 'Water fights/With Fire, and Aire with Earth approaching neere:/Yet all are in one body, and as one appeare' (*FQ*, VII, vii, 25).[6] The inherent stability of the cosmos was explained by the fact that the four elements were bound together in a tetrad, that is to say, a configuration of two pairs of opposites linked together by their two mean terms. This arrangement was the principle upon which God created the universe. (It is because the tetrad was the very basis of the Pythagorean cosmos that the number four was considered to be of such paramount importance.[7]) The clearest account of the way the four elements are united in a tetradic relationship is in Macrobius's *Commentary on the Dream of Scipio*. Macrobius explains that the Creator gave to each of the elements two qualities, one of which it shared with the element closest to it in character. These shared qualities, or mean terms, form a series of bonds, linking element to element in an indissoluble union.[8]

Macrobius's account of the cosmic tetrad is based on the *Timaeus*. Like Plato, he insists that it is the natural antagonism of the four elements which is paradoxically the secret of their stability. The same idea is reflected in John Norden's *Vicissitudo Rerum* (1600). In answer to the question why discord is essential to the harmony of the cosmos, Norden explains that, if the mutually antagonistic elements were not kept in check by one another, the result would be an imbalance in nature:

For why? supremest have no fatall let,
But will preuaile, as they become too strong.
Therefore such *meane* must them be set among,
As though things bee compact of *contraryes*,
They must by *ballance*, have like quantities.[9]

*Vicissitudo Rerum* was not published until the year after Spenser's death. Of the many contemporary accounts of this cosmic principle with which Spenser would have been familiar[10] the most vivid is Du Bartas's story of the creation.[11] Though the elements are naturally in a state of discord, like 'Truce-hating Twins, where Brother eateth Brother', says Du Bartas, they are joined together in a 'holy Chain' which only God can break:

Water, as arm'd with moisture and with cold,
The cold-dry Earth with her one hand doth hold;
With th'other th'Aire: The Aire, as moist and warme,
Holds Fire with one; Water with th'other arme:
As Country Maydens in the Month of *May*
Merrily sporting on a Holy-day.
And lustic dauncing of a lively Round,
About the May-pole, by the Bag-pipes sound;
Hold hand in hand, so that the first is fast,
By meanes of those betweene, unto the last.
(*La Semaine*, I, ii, 323-33)[12]

Du Bartas's picturesque image of country maidens celebrating the rites of May will not seem incongruous if we recall that the dance was a familiar metaphor for the cosmos. 'Dancing', says Sir John Davies in the most celebrated Elizabethan defence of this favourite Renaissance art,

> then began to be,
> When the first seedes whereof the world did spring,
> The Fire, Ayre, Earth and Water did agree,
> By Loves perswasion, Natures mighty King,
> To leave their first disordred combating;
> And in a daunce such measure to observe,
> As all the world their motion should preserve.
> (*Orchestra*, 113-19)[13]

Although Spenser does not actually use the metaphor of dance in Book IV, the linking of hands (IV, x, 33) and the elaborate grouping and re-grouping of characters which are such a distinctive feature of the book are strongly suggestive of the formal patterns of a dance. In a brilliant analysis of Book IV Fowler has shown that the pattern of paired opposites linked together by their two mean terms which is the basis of the cosmos is also the principle which governs Spenser's character groupings. The quartet consisting of Cambell, Triamond, Canacee and Cambina interacts in a tetradic pattern which mirrors that of the cosmos. In just the same way as the mutually antagonistic elements are pacified and united by the quality which each pair holds in common, so the emotional conflict which exists between the characters is balanced by a corresponding affinity. The result is 'a system of interlocking relationships linking all four characters permanently together'.[14] In a similar fashion the various groupings of evil characters illustrate 'gross travesties of the tetrad'.[15]

In using the term friendship to connote the idea of cosmic concord, Spenser was following a widely accepted tradition.[16] According to conventional belief the essential nature of the cosmos was a *discordia concors*, an amicable reconciliation of fundamentally opposed qualities in a uniquely stable union. Traditional also was the belief expressed by Davies in the stanza from *Orchestra* quoted above that love is the architect of this union. It is love, Boethius tells us in the classic medieval account of the cosmos, 'that gouernythe both the land and the sea, and likewyse commaundethe the heuen, and kepyth the world in due order and good accorde, that is to saye: causythe ye due seasons of the yere to come successyuely accordying to their nature'. It is the same love which

> conserueth vertuous folke, and suche as be ioyned together in the bond of frendship. And this loue knytteth together the sacrament of wedlocke, with chast loue betwene man and wyfe. Thys loue also settith his lawes whych is trewe frendeshipe to faythful frendes and felowes. O howe happye were mankynd yf this loue of God that rulyth heuen, myght rule and gouerne theyr myndes, that is to say: that they myght so agre together in such perfyte frendeshyp, that one myght loue another, and agre as the elements do agre.[17]

For Spenser, too, love is the power by which

> the world was made of yore,
> And all that therein wondrous doth appeare.
> For how should else things so far from attone
> And so great enemies as of them bee,
> Be euer drawne together into one,
> And taught in such accordance to agree?
> (*Colin Clout*, 841-6)

It is because love is the author of universal concord that Spenser begins Book IV with an apostrophe, not as one might have expected, to a pair of archetypal representatives of friendship, such as Damon and Pythias, but to a 'Queene of loue'.

In praising Elizabeth as a queen of love, Spenser is suggesting comparison with the figure of Venus in canto x, who, like her, rules 'an Island . . . wall'd by nature gainst inuaders wrong' (IV, x, 6). If Ate, the 'mother of debate,/And all dissention' (IV, i, 19), is the antithesis of harmony, Venus is the personification of this principle. Through the agency of her handmaid Dame Concord she is the source of order in the cosmos:

> By her the heauen is in his course contained,
> And all the world in state vnmoued stands,
> As their Almightie maker first ordained,
> And bound them with inuiolable bands;
> Else would the waters ouerflow the lands,
> And fire deuoure the ayre, and hell them quight,
> But that she holds them with her blessed hands.
> (IV, x, 35)

It is Venus who, having first made the world (IV, x, 47), pacifies its warring elements:

> Great *Venus*, Queene of beautie and of grace,
> The ioy of Gods and men, that vnder skie
> Doest fayrest shine, and most adorne thy place,
> That with thy smyling looke doest pacifie
> The raging seas, and makst the stormes to flie;
> Thee goddesse, thee the winds, the clouds doe feare,
> And when thou spredst thy mantle forth on hie,
> The waters play and pleasant lands appeare,
> And heauens laugh, and al the world shews ioyous cheare.
> (IV, x, 44)

Control of the elements is a familiar device in the literature of praise. The idea is used by Virgil in the first book of the *Georgics* where Augustus is celebrated as a 'god of the boundless sea' ('deus immensi maris', I, 29), and again in the first book of the *Aeneid* in the extended simile of Neptune pacifying the stormy sea like a noble and pious man quelling the passions of an angry mob (I, 126-56).[18] The device also features prominently in Elizabethan panegyric. In a poem written in 1593 to celebrate the installation of the Earl of Northumberland as a Knight of the Garter, Peele incorporated the following visionary tribute to Elizabeth:

> I sawe a Virgin Queene, attyrde in white,
> Leading with her a sort of goodly Knights,
> With Garters and with Collers of S. George.
> Elizabeth on a compartiment
> Of gold, in Bysse was writ, and hunge a skue
> Upon her head, under an imperiall crowne:
> She was the Soveraigne of the Knights she led.
> Her face me thought I knewe: as if the same,
> The same great Empresse that we here enjoy,
> Had clymed the clowdes, and been in person there;
> To whom the earth, the sea, and elements
> Auspicious are.
> (*The Honour of the Garter*, 320-31)[19]

The same idea is used by Davison in a lyric from the *Poetical Rhapsody*:

Lands and seas she rules below,
Where things change, and ebb, and flow,
  Spring, wax old, and perish;
Only Time, which all doth mow,
  Her alone doth cherish.
      ('Of Cynthia', 11-15)[20]

When, in the first stanza of canto ii, Spenser evokes an image of universal discord which 'None but a God or godlike man can slake' he is probably preparing the reader for his tribute in canto x to Elizabeth in her familiar role as empress of the sea.[21] The metaphor may be read in two ways: the idea of control of the sea may either be taken to signify Elizabeth's position as head of the world's greatest maritime power, or, as in the case of Virgil's idealization of Augustus in the guise of Neptune, it may be taken to suggest the idea of the prince who pacifies the discordant elements within the state. In Elizabeth's case this latter role is linked with the idea of motherhood in the complex image of a maternal yet virgin goddess who, like Venus, bestows loving care on her children.

The island where Venus rules is a *hortus amoenus* in which lovers and friends enjoy 'spotlesse pleasures, and sweet loues content' (IV, x, 26) and where the joys of sex are uncontaminated by fear and jealousy (IV, x, 28). Unlike the frankly sensuous Venus of Book III, however, the queen of this paradisal garden remains aloof and detached from the lovers who throng her temple. Though worshipped as the author of love, she herself is chaste and inviolate. Yet paradoxically she is the goddess of generation:

Then doth the daedale earth throw forth to thee
  Out of her fruitfull lap aboundant flowres,
  And then all liuing wights, soone as they see
  The spring breake forth out of his lusty bowres,
  They all doe learne to play the Paramours;
  First doe the merry birds, thy prety pages
  Priuily pricked with thy lustfull powres,
  Chirpe loud to thee out of their leauy cages,
And thee their mother call to coole their kindly rages.

Then doe the saluage beasts begin to play
  Their pleasant friskes, and loath their wonted food;
  The Lyons rore, the Tygres loudly bray,

The raging Buls rebellow through the wood,
And breaking forth, dare tempt the deepest flood,
To come where thou doest draw them with desire:
So all things else, that nourish vitall blood,
Soone as with fury thou doest them inspire,
In generation seeke to quench their inward fire.
(IV, x, 45-6)

The explanation of this paradox lies in Venus's androgynous nature:

But for, they say, she hath both kinds in one,
Both male and female, both vnder one name:
She syre and mother is her selfe alone,
Begets and eke conceiues, ne needeth other none.
(IV, x, 41)

In medieval literature the hermaphrodite was a symbol of the creative union of opposites.[22] This is the meaning of the hermaphrodite image which Spenser uses in his description of the union of Scudamour and Amoret in the original 1590 conclusion to Book III:

Had ye them seene, ye would haue surely thought,
That they had beene that faire *Hermaphrodite*,

* * *

So seemd those two, as growne together quite.

The differences of temperament and sex which have been the cause of so much strife have been finally reconciled in a creative marriage of opposites. The androgynous Venus of Book IV has a similar significance. Combining, as she does, the antithetical qualities of chastity and fecundity she reconciles the two Venuses of popular tradition: the *Venus Vulgaris* who stood for animal beauty, sensual pleasure and generative power, and the *Venus Coelestis* who symbolized for the neo-Platonist ideal beauty.[23] Above the strife of sex by virtue of her unique nature, Spenser's dual Venus is a beneficent deity who superintends the Temple of Love and smiles on the union of her servants (IV, x, 56).

The principal source for Spenser's Venus is Lucretius.[24] But there are certain aspects of this goddess of love which suggest that, in addition to the fertility figure who is invoked in the opening lines of the *De Rerum Natura*, Spenser may have had another model in mind. It is, in particular, her garden that evokes biblical, rather than classical, associations. Its impenetrable wall (6); its aromatic flowers (22); its cedars (22); and its springs (24) mark this 'second paradise' (23) as another variation on the *hortus conclusus* theme. Although cedar trees are a familiar feature of the Marian aromatic garden,[25] their origin is not in the Canticles, but in Ecclesiasticus, whose 'wise sayings, and darke sentences, and similitudes'[26] became an important source of Marian imagery in the Middle Ages.[27] It is her identification with this 'mother of beautiful loue' (Ecclesiasticus, XXIV, 20) who 'possessed the waues of the sea, and all the earth, and all people, and nacion' (XXIV, 9) which must, in part, account for the Virgin Mary's traditional role as empress of the sea – a role which was naturally and easily assumed by Elizabeth as a post-figuration of the Virgin.

Thus, although her name and her literary ancestry are classical, Venus, like Belphoebe, also owes much to a tradition of Christian iconography. The fact that she is portrayed as a hermaphrodite is not the anomaly it may at first appear to be. For it should be recalled that one of the devices which the Virgin Mary shares with Queen Elizabeth – the phoenix – was regarded as androgynous because of its ability to regenerate itself unassisted by a mate.[28] As an emblem of chaste fruitfulness the phoenix is a fitting symbol for Mary's (and Elizabeth's) miraculous combination of fecundity and chastity.[29] The reason why Venus's Marian associations have gone unnoticed is probably the fact that, as a fertility figure, the Virgin Mary owes much to her mythological forbears.[30] The classical goddesses to whom she is most closely related in this capacity are Ceres and Astraea, both of whom were popularly identified with Elizabeth.[31] Indeed the Virgin is often undistinguishable iconographically from these two pagan types of chaste fruitfulness.[32]

In view of the close similarities between the cult of the Virgin and the cults of the classical fertility goddesses, it may be asked whether there is in fact any point in distinguishing between the pagan and Christian aspects of a character like Venus. The question is an important one; but it can only be answered within the context of the whole poem. For Venus is only one of the many figures in *The Faerie Queene* whom Spenser uses to 'shadow' Elizabeth. Although singly these characters may sometimes be interpreted quite satisfactorily in classical terms alone, together they form a composite image in which Pagan elements are subsumed by a Christian meaning. Only in the cult of the Virgin Mary do we find the full complex of powers, attributes and privileges that Spenser accords Elizabeth in *The Faerie Queene*. It is the special and unique nature of the relationship between Elizabeth and Mary which distinguishes it from the many classical parallels that Spenser draws in the poem. Whereas the analogies with pagan deities are simply metaphoric, those with the Virgin Mary are typological, having a prophetic and providential application concerning the destiny of the Queen and her nation. Thus when Spenser celebrates Elizabeth as a 'Queene of beautie and of grace' whose 'smyling looke doest pacifie/The raging seas, and makst the stormes to flie' his praise has a political and theological meaning beyond its merely metaphoric significance.

It has frequently been noted that there is a general movement in Book IV from the discord of the earlier cantos to the harmony of its conclusion. It remains to consider the significance of the river marriage of canto xi and to see how this concluding symbol of harmony relates to the celebratory themes we have been discussing.

As the culminating symbolic episode of Book IV, the river marriage would appear to correspond to those episodes in the first three books of *The Faerie Queene* which represent the climax of the allegory and which take the form of the completion of a mission or the ritualized defeat of a particular evil. It is clear that in general terms a marriage of natural forces is an appropriate way in which to conclude a book which has shown that human discord is part of the larger order of things. As Nelson rightly says: 'The marriage celebrated by so numerous and so distinguished a company in Proteus' hall becomes a symbol of cosmic harmony and plenitude . . .'[33] It is also a fitting way of resolving symbolically the stories of 'louers sad calamities' which Book III left uncompleted. However, the function of an epideictic poem is not merely to anatomize a virtue in general terms, but to show that this virtue is exemplified in some special way by the personage to whom the poem is addressed. If we are right in suggesting that Venus, as a personification of the principle of concord, is intended to evoke Queen Elizabeth, then it would seem reasonable to expect there to be a more specific meaning in the marriage of the Thames and the Medway than that proposed by Nelson.

Among those critics who have explored the literary as distinct from the local background of the pageant materials of canto xi,[34] there is general agreement that the catalogue of rivers was designed as a chorographical celebration of Britain. In one of the most thorough of such background studies, Roche argues that the marriage of the Thames and the Medway belongs to a Renaissance tradition of river marriage which is peculiar to England. The object of this literary sub-genre was to 'unite political praise with descriptions both historical and geographical'.[35] Although, as a description of canto xi, this clearly has much to recommend it, it leads Roche to the rather unexceptional conclusion that the whole episode 'is simply a universal expression of the love that moves the universe and lovers alike'.[36]

In Fowler's view the marriage of the Thames and the Medway may best be seen not as an example of a single sub-genre – the river marriage – but as an entirely original conflation of a number of quite different literary devices: 'After the manner of the pageant composer, Spenser has worked together several festival motifs, in themselves traditional, but original in their fresh combination and their unusual river-god setting.'[37]

Of the various literary devices and genres which form the background of canto xi the most relevant to this discussion is the topographical poem, for topographical poetry was traditionally employed as a form of indirect praise. In what has been claimed to be the 'first important local poem in English'[38] Dunbar identifies the virtues of London and the Thames with those of the Lord Mayor whom he compliments in the final stanza. As a topographical poem which employs local detail for epideictic purposes, Dunbar's *London*[39] marks the inception of a long and continuous tradition of English local poetry whose most celebrated exemplars are Jonson's *To Penshurst*, Denham's *Cooper's Hill* and Pope's *Windsor Forest*. In each case the topographical features of a landscape, a river or an estate are used as a means of complementing a sovereign or a patron. Less well known are the sixteenth-century antecedents of these seventeenth- and eighteenth-century topographical poems. The writers to whom Spenser probably owes most are Leland and Camden.

The monumental *Itinerary*, not published until the eighteenth century, bears witness to the fact that Leland's real genius was for topography; and when, in 1543 and 1545, he composed a pair of Latin panegyrics – the first celebrating the birth of Edward, Prince of Wales, the second complimenting the child's father – it was through the medium of topography that Leland addressed the King.[40] *Genethliacon Eaduerdi Principis Cambriae* is a political poem. Ostensibly a panegyric to the infant Prince of Wales, it is actually a celebration of the house of Tudor in terms of the familiar myth of Troy. The British people are portrayed as a chosen race (176-9) and their new-born prince as a descendant of Aeneas's who will usher in a new golden age ('Aurea jam sunt reditta nobis/Secula', 247-8). As befitting so auspicious an occasion, ceremony and ritual form an important part of the poem. Like Spenser, Leland devotes a considerable portion of his poem to an account of the procession of oceanitides, naiedes and other nymphs who come to pay their homage at the royal event. But the bulk of the poem is taken up with a recital of 'many names of venerable antiquity' ('multa vetustatis venerandae nomina', 777). An account of how news of the royal birth is spread through the kingdom provides Leland with an excuse for an extended topographical survey of Wales and the south-west of England.

Topography is similarly used as a form of indirect praise in Leland's *Cygnea Cantio*, or swan-song, as the poem is punningly titled. The passage of a company of swans from Oxfordshire up to London affords Leland another opportunity for local description, this time of London and the Thames Valley. Like the earlier poem, however, *Cygnea Cantio* is essentially a poem of praise in which local detail and historical anecdote are employed as a means of glorifying the House of Tudor.

The idea of a river journey as a device for giving structural unity to a topographical survey was borrowed by William Vallans in a poem entitled *A Tale of Two Swannes* (1590). Vallans's poem was included with Leland's two panegyrics in Hearne's edition of the *Itinerary*. But despite its superficial similarity with *Cygnea Cantio*, its purpose is quite different. For although several passing compliments to Queen Elizabeth are made in the course of the journey, these are only incidental, and royal praise does not constitute the real subject of the poem as it does in *Cygnea Cantio*. Nor is it true to describe the poem, as Roche does, as a river-marriage poem. The idea is mentioned only in the final lines of the poem and in no way constitutes its subject.

If *A Tale of Two Swannes* forms any part of the background of Book IV, it is a very minor one. Of far greater significance is Camden's *De Connubio Tamae et Isis*.[41] Here mythico-historical matter, local description and royal panegyric are united by the device of a marriage of rivers. Although *De Connubio Tamae et Isis* exists only as a series of fragments included in the *Britannia*, it is not difficult to form an idea of the poem as it must have existed in its entirety. Like *Cygnea Cantio*, its form is determined by the idea of a journey from Oxfordshire to London, where, in the climax of the poem, the nuptial pair, now united in the single figure of the Thames, 'endeavoureth to set forth, as well the dignitie of the place, as the majestie of Queene Elizabeth . . .'[42] In the final lines of the fragment Elizabeth is identified with the Thames in much the same way as Charles is half a century later in *Cooper's Hill*:

> Who can descrive in waving verse [her] noble vertues all?
> Praise-worthy parts shee hath alone, what all ye reckon shall.
> Then happinesse, long life and health, praise, love, may her betide.
> So long as waves of mine shall last, or streams and banks abide;

So long may shee most blessed Prince, all Englands scepter sway,
Let both my course, and her life end, in one and selfe-same day.[43]

The identification of a prince's virtues with those of a town or a river is a traditional device of epideictic poetry. It may be seen in its most explicit form in Elizabethan poetry in Drayton's *Idea, the Shepherd's Garland* and in Campion's Latin poem *Ad Thamesin*. In the third eclogue of *Idea* the singer praises 'fairest Beta' as queen of the river nymphs:

O thou fayre silver Thames: o cleerest chrystall flood,
*Beta* alone the Phenix is, of all thy watery brood,
The Queene of Virgins onely she:
And thou the Queene of floods shalt be:
Let all thy Nymphes be joyfull then to see this happy day,
Thy *Beta* now alone shalbe the subject of my laye.
(49-54)[44]

Campion likewise hails Elizabeth in the first line of his poem as 'Nympha potens Thamesis'.[45]

Our survey of sixteenth-century local poetry, brief as it is, may serve to show that the eleventh canto of Book IV belongs to a clearly defined tradition of epideictic topography. The procession of nymphs and dryads; the recitation of 'many names of venerable antiquity'; even the wedding of rivers are all devices which were familiar in later sixteenth-century poetry. What is unique to Spenser's poem is the adaptation of the river-marriage conceit for the purpose of symbolizing the popular idea of Elizabeth's 'marriage' to England.[46] Having dealt with the subject of Elizabeth's 'betrothal' to her country's cause in Book III, it remained for Spenser to show the completion of that mission in Book IV. A river marriage was an appropriate way of suggesting this event, for it was a symbolic device which allowed him to draw together the various strands of the two books, and at the same time to resolve their discords in a single conceit of great expressive power.

On the purely personal level the nuptial ceremony stands, like the multiple marriage of Elizabethan stage comedy, for the resolution of the discord generated by sexual strife; on the political level it signifies the amicable union between England and her prince – a political alliance which receives the approval of the assembled company of nations; finally, it signifies an elemental marriage of opposing forces where (in Hakewill's words) 'matter and forme like man and wife, are . . . married by . . . a sacred and inviolable knot'.[47] The sea, characterized until now as a place of turmoil and confusion, becomes the scene of a harmonious mingling of natural powers, and, as Proteus's harshness and cruelty are mollified, he becomes, like Prospero, the beneficent host of a wedding ceremony.

Although the critic may for his own convenience separate these various levels of meaning, in practice they are all interdependent. We have noticed that Spenser's imagery works in such a way that the personal, the political and the cosmic are shown to be aspects of one another. If we return briefly to consider one example from an earlier canto, the implications of this strategem will be clear.

In canto iii, stanza 27, Spenser uses the following epic simile in his description of the battle between Cambell and Triamond:

> Like as the tide that comes fro th'Ocean mayne,
> Flowes vp the Shenan with contrarie forse,
> And ouerruling him in his owne rayne,
> Driues backe the current of his kindly course,
> And makes it seeme to haue some other sourse:
> But when the floud is spent, then backe againe
> His borrowed waters forst to redisbourse,
> He sends the sea his owne with double gaine,
> And tribute eke withall, as to his Soueraine.

The effect of comparing the fluctuation of the battle to the movements of tide and current in a river estuary is to suggest, of course, that personal combat is part of a universal pattern. But contained within this formal simile is another image: the Shenan is itself compared to a colony, which for all its show of opposition, must inevitably submit to the superior might of an imperial power. In this complex image of elemental forces Spenser seems subtly to be implying that England's hegemony of the British Isles is a *natural* state of affairs. This suggests that the political alliance of canto xi is not merely a domestic one, but marks the inauguration of a state of international harmony sanctioned by nature and foretold by ancient prophecy. For if Elizabeth's 'marriage' is, in one sense, the culmination of Britomart's quest, then it must be seen as the fulfilment of Merlin's prophecy that Britomart, herself descended from 'the ancient Troian blood', would be the progenitor of a race of 'Renowmed kings, and sacred Emperours' (III, iii, 23). The cycle of history is complete: Troy has been reborn, and a sacred empire has been established.

The idea that the law of nations should reflect the *jus naturale* is not unique to Spenser; indeed it was fundamental to the theory of cosmos inherited by the Renaissance from the ancient world. *The Faerie Queene* owes its distinction not merely to the fact that it is one of the last statements of this belief, but also to the fact that it is one of the subtlest. If friendship is the principle which unites individuals and elements alike in peaceful harmony, it is also the principle which ensures stability both within the state and between nations. According to Starkey, a true commonwealth is one in which all the parts are united 'wyth perfayt loue and amyte one to a nother . . . as membrys and partys of one body . . .'[48] Just as the cosmos is regulated by a rational principle, so the amicable co-existence of disparate elements in human society depends upon the administration of justice by a wise and loving ruler. In portraying Elizabeth as a 'Queene of loue, and Prince of peace from heauen blest' Spenser is suggesting her unique qualification for this role. This is why he emphasizes her paradoxical character in the proem to Book IV. Like the lady of the *Amoretti* who displays a contradictory combination of 'Myld humblesse mixt with awfull maiesty', the character of this virgin 'mother' of her people is a unique fusion of antithetical qualities: though she is the embodiment of true affection, who 'loueth best,/And best is lou'd of all aliue', yet her imperious nature must be supplicated with prayers and petitions (5). Combining, like her heavenly counterpart Venus/Mary, contradictory qualities in harmonious equilibrium, she is shown to be the perfect living embodiment of the principle which it is her office to uphold.

## Notes

1. See Charles G. Smith, *Spenser's Theory of Friendship* (Baltimore, 1935), p. 27.

2. See Williams,'Venus and Diana: Some Uses of Myth in *The Faerie Queene*', p. 107; Nelson, *The Poetry of Edmund Spenser*, p. 255; Fowler, *Spenser and the Numbers of Time*, p. 26; Evans, *Spenser's Anatomy of Heroism*, p. 183; A.C. Hamilton (ed.), *The Faerie Queene* (London, 1977), p. 423.

3. Smith pp. 16-25. The most complete discussion of the theme of friendship in Renaissance English literature is by Laurens J. Mills, *One Soul in Bodies Twain: Friendship in Tudor Literature and Stuart Drama* (Bloomington, Ind., 1937).

4. *Nichomachean Ethics*, VIII, v, 5.

5. Lyly, *Endimion*, I, iv, 36-7.

6. The following paragraphs owe much to Heninger, *Touches of Sweet Harmony*. See also F.M. Cornford, 'Mysticism and Science in the Pythagorean Tradition', *CQ*, 16 (1922), 137-50; 17 (1923), 1-12; Leo Spitzer, 'Classical and Christian Ideas of World Harmony; Prolegomena to an Interpretation of the Word "Stimmung"', *Traditio*, 2 (1944), 409-64; 3 (1945), 307-64.

7. The number four provided a key to the cosmos because it embraced the

four elements, the four seasons, the four ages of man and the four humours. As La Primaudaye wrote: 'All the foundation of every deepe studie and invention must be settled upon the number fower, bicause it is the roote and beginning of all numbers' (*The French Academie*, quoted by Heninger, p. 170).

8. 'And so it happens that each one of the elements appears to embrace the two elements bordering on each side of it by single qualities: water binds earth to itself by coldness, and air by moisture; air is allied to water by its moisture, and to fire by warmth; fire mingles with air because of its heat, and with earth because of its dryness; earth is compatible with fire because of its dryness, and with water because of its coldness. These different bonds would have no tenacity, however, if there were only two elements; if there were three the union would be but a weak one; but as there are four elements the bonds are unbreakable, since the two extremes are held together by two means' (*Commentary on the Dream of Scipio*, translated by William Harris Stahl (New York, 1952), p. 105).

9. John Norden, Vicissitudo rerum, *An Elegiacall Poeme, of the interchangeable courses and variety of things in this world* (1600), with an introduction by D.C. Collins, Shakespeare Association Facsimiles, IV (London, 1931), stanza 85.

10. See Rosemond Tuve, 'A Medieval Commonplace in Spenser's Cosmology', *SP*, 30 (1933), 133-47; 'Spenser and the "Zodiake of Life"', pp. 1-19.

11. For Spenser's interest in Du Bartas see *Gabriel Harvey's Marginalia*, edited by G.C. Moore Smith (Stratford-upon-Avon, 1913), p. 161.

12. *The Divine Weeks and Works of Guillaume de Saluste Sieur Du Bartas*, translated by Joshuah Sylvester, edited by Susan Snyder, 2 vols (Oxford, 1979), I, 144.

13. *The Poems of Sir John Davies*, edited by Krueger, p. 94.

14. Fowler, p. 27.

15. Fowler, p. 30.

16. In Colville's translation of Boethius, for example, we find the 'contynuall peace and vnytye' of the four elements described as a state of 'mutuall amite' (*Consolation of Philosophy*, translated by George Colville (1556), edited by Ernest Belfort Bax, The Tudor Library Series, V (London, 1897), p. 52). Golding's translation of Ovid similarly describes the equilibrium of the elements as 'an endlesse freendship' (I, 25). Since neither Ovid nor Boethius actually uses the word *amicitia* in this context we may assume that those two sixteenth-century translators were simply reflecting a tradition which goes back to the *Timaeus*. For Plato the primary characteristic of the creation is amity ( φιλία ) (32C).

17. *Consolation of Philosophy*, p. 52.

18. Cf. Ovid's praise of Julius Caesar in *Metamorphoses*, XV, 830-1: 'quodcun que habitabile tellus/sustinet, huius erit: pontus quoque serviet illi!'.

19. *The Life and Works of George Peele*, edited by Charles Tyler Prouty, 3 vols (New Haven, Conn., 1952-70); *The Life and Minor Works*, edited by David H. Horne (1952; rpt. 1963), p. 256.

20. *Davison's Poetical Rhapsody*, edited by Bullen, II, 127.

21. It was as such that Elizabeth was celebrated in a sea masque which formed part of a City of London entertainment in 1594. See Nichols, *The Progresses and Public Processions of Queen Elizabeth*, III, 309-18.

22. See C.G. Jung, *The Archetypes and the Collective Unconscious*, translated by R.F.C. Hull (London, 1959), p. 174. See also Donald Cheney, 'Spenser's Hermaphrodite and the 1590 *Faerie Queene*', *PMLA*, 87 (1972), 195.

23. See Erwin Panofsky, *Studies in Iconology: Humanistic Themes in the Art of the Renaissance* (1939; rpt. New York, 1962), pp. 142-60; E.H. Gombrich, 'Botticelli's Mythologies: A Study in the Neoplatonic Symbolism of His Circle', *JWCI*, 8 (1945), 13; Edgar Wind, *Pagan Mysteries in the Renaissance* (London, 1958), pp. 73-5.

24. Stanzas 44-7 are an imitation of *De Rerum Natura*, I, 1-20. But Spenser was also familiar with Alain de Lille's hymn to nature in *The Complaint of Nature*, Metre IV (see *FQ*, VII, vii, 9).

25. See, for example, Lydgate's 'Ballade at the Reverence of our Lady':

O closid gardeyn al void of weedes wicke,
Cristallyn welle of clennesse cler consigned,
Fructifying olyve of foilys faire and thicke,
And redolent cedyr most derworthly ydyned
(36-9)

26. It is in these phrases that the Argument of the Geneva Bible describes the book of Ecclesiasticus (Sig. Nnnnii$^{v}$).

27. For a detailed Marian interpretation of Ecclesiasticus, XXIV, see *The Myroure of oure Ladye*, p. 282.

28. See Beryl Rowland, *Blind Beasts: Chaucer's Animal World* (Kent, Ohio, 1971), pp. 44-5. See also Ovid, *Metamorphoses*, XV, 391-2.

29. A similar symbolism may be intended by the description of Alma's castle, which combines the 'imperfect, mortall, foeminine' with the 'immortall, perfect, masculine' in one harmonious whole (II, ix, 22).

30. See E.O. James, *The Cult of the Mother-Goddess: An Archaeological Study* (London, 1959), pp. 61-2 and Warner, *Alone of All Her Sex*, pp. 269, 276-7.

31. The identification of Elizabeth with Astraea is well known. See Yates, 'Queen Elizabeth as Astraea'. Her identification with Ceres is less well documented. In Lyly's *Love's Metamorphosis*, Elizabeth is represented (rather less flatteringly than in the earlier *Sapho and Phao* and *Endimion*) by the 'somewhat stately' figure of Ceres. Ceres's dual nature as goddess of chastity and generation is best summed up in the following words of Cupid:

> Divine *Ceres*, *Cupid* accepteth any thing that cometh from *Ceres*; which feedeth my Sparrowes with ripe corne, my Pigeons with wholesome seedes; and honourest my Temple with chast virgines.
> (II, i, 83-6)

In representing Elizabeth by the figure of Ceres, Lyly was possibly thinking of a tradition among foreign travellers of evoking the idea of England's natural fertility in the phrase 'the very seat of Ladie *Ceres*'. See William Camden, *Britain, or a Chorographical Description of the Most flourishing Kingdomes . . .*, translated by Philemon Holland (London, 1610), p. 3.

32. See Warner, p. 276.

33. *The Poetry of Edmund Spenser*, p. 255.

34. Charles Grosvenor Osgood gives a survey of the latter in 'Spenser's English Rivers', *TCAS*, 23 (1920), 67-108. The most important discussions of the former are by A.M. Buchan, 'The Political Allegory of Book IV of *The Faerie Queene*', *ELH*, 11 (1944), 237-48; Roche, *The Kindly Flame*, pp. 167-84; Fowler, *Spenser and the Numbers of Time*, pp. 171-5; Jack B. Oruch, 'Spenser, Camden, and the Poetic Marriages of Rivers', *SP*, 64 (1967), 606-24; Michael O'Connell, 'History and the Poet's Golden World: The Epic Catalogues in *The Faerie Queene*', pp. 241-67; Gordon Braden, 'riverrun: An Epic Catalogue in *The Faerie Queene*', *ELR*, 5 (1975), 25-48.

35. *The Kindly Flame*, pp. 173-4.

36. *The Kindly Flame*, p. 184.

37. *Spenser and the Numbers of Time*, p. 173.

38. Ronald Arnold Aubin, *Topographical Poetry in XVIII-Century England*,

Modern Language Association of America Revolving Fund Series, VI (1936; rpt. New York, 1966), p. 14.

39. For the authorship of *London* see W. Mackay Mackenzie (ed.), *The Poems of William Dunbar* (1932; rpt. London, 1966), pp. 240-1.

40. Both *Genethliacon Eaduerdi Principis Cambriae* and *Cygnea Cantio* were published in the final volume of Thomas Hearne's edition of *The Itinerary*, 9 vols. Citations from both poems are from the third edition (Oxford, 1768-9).

41. For the authorship and complex publishing history of the poem see Oruch, p. 608.

42. *Britain*, p. 289.

43. *Britain*, p. 293.

44. *The Works of Michael Drayton*, edited by J. William Hebel, 5 vols (Oxford, 1931-41), I, 56.

45. *The Works of Thomas Campion*, edited by Walter R. Davis (1967; rpt. London, 1969), p. 362.

46. Fowler identifies the Thames with England and Elizabeth with the Medway (p. 172). While agreeing with his general conclusion I prefer to interpret the passage in a less specific way.

47. George Hakewill, *An Apologie or Declaration of The Power and Providence of God in the Gouernment of the World*, quoted by Victor Harris, *All Coherence Gone: A Study of the Seventeenth-Century Controversy Over Disorder and Decay in the Universe* (1949; rpt. London, 1966), p. 66.

48. *Dialogue between Pole and Lupset*, p. 55.

# 5 ASTRAEA REDUX

Justice was widely regarded in the Renaissance as the sovereign virtue. 'The moste excellent and incomparable vertue called iustice', writes Elyot, 'is so necessary and expedient for the gouernor of a publike weale, that without it none other vertue may be commendable, ne witte or any maner of doctrine profitable.'[1] As the most conspicuous attribute of a true prince, justice is of all the virtues the most obviously relevant to Queen Elizabeth. It is perhaps surprising, therefore, that Book V should be, by general critical consent, the least successful book of *The Faerie Queene*. What is wrong with the latter part of the book in particular is not simply the fact that the policy which Spenser undertook to defend is an abhorrent one to modern readers; it is the fact that he attempts to defend any policy at all in such a specific manner. For in doing so he has, in effect, abandoned his epideictic purpose. Fundamental to the theory of panegyric which the sixteenth century inherited from the ancient world is the distinction between praise and flattery, that is to say between the celebration of a moral ideal through the vehicle of a person, a city or an institution, and the defence of a particular individual's character, conduct or policies. Whereas praise, says Aristotle, 'sets forth greatness of virtue . . . encomium deals with achievements . . .'[2] The function of epideictic poetry is not to justify or to excuse, but to 'feign notable images of virtue or vice'. Its purpose is essentially moral.

This is not, of course, to suggest that a poet's artistic successes and failures may infallibly be judged in accordance with the prescriptions of a body of inherited criticism; rather that in abandoning a certain literary ideal Spenser has sacrificed the artistic integrity of his poem. Instead of inventing an imaginative fiction to embody an ideal of justice, he rather crudely allegorizes contemporary events. In his defence of the Elizabethan Church in Book I Spenser was fortunate in being able to draw upon a body of biblical imagery which combined so naturally and so successfully with the romance form of the poem that political quarrels were made to assume quasi-mythic proportions. In Book V there is no controlling myth of comparable authority to lift the narrative of the last four cantos above a merely historical level.

However, if Book V is notable for its preponderance of topical allegory,[3] it is also the most philosophic book of the poem. What gives it unique distinction as a document of sixteenth-century humanist culture is not the specific defence of Elizabethan foreign and domestic policy contained in the last four cantos, but the answers it provides to the larger philosophic and political questions which occupied the age. Spenser's theory of regal justice is based on the principle of natural law. Though the central importance of this controversial subject in the more profound literature of the period is familiar enough to students of Renaissance drama,[4] there has been little discussion of natural law as the underlying philosophic principle of Book V.[5]

As the concept of nature itself underwent a total transformation during the Renaissance and Enlightenment, so too the idea of natural law came, by the later eighteenth century, to mean the exact opposite of what it had meant for the orthodox Tudor humanist.[6] It is arguable that in Spenser's lifetime the question of the meaning of natural law presented itself in a more acute form than at any other period in European history. Indeed it was the stimulus afforded by the violent juxtaposition of the two world views, which, for the sake of convenience, we may call the medieval and the modern, that must in large measure account for the energy and vitality of Elizabethan literature. This crucial chapter in the history of ideas has been the subject of a number of scholarly studies.[7]

Reduced to its simplest terms the debate concerned itself with the question of whether human society was a divinely sanctioned institution or whether it was simply an aggregate of men united by no more lofty principle than fear and self-interest. According to the traditional conservative view all human societies approximated to a universal pattern. Although the pattern might be distorted by evil or ignorance, the principles upon which it was based could not be destroyed because they were precisely the same principles which governed the whole universe. As the cosmos was believed to be a rational creation in which every part was related to every other part in an orderly hierarchy, so, by analogy, social harmony depended upon the principle of degree. But the harmony which was the characteristic feature of the cosmos expressed itself in a pattern which did not merely exist spatially, but was extended in time. Just as the bodily humours mirrored the four classes of men and the four elements, so the seasons of the year mirrored the successive stages in man's life. Thus the natural processes of generation and decay could be seen as part of an orderly cycle of time. The most vivid contemporary illustration of this idea is Sir John Davies's *Orchestra*. Davies chooses the metaphor of a dance to expound a traditional view of the cosmos because in this image was combined in a unique fashion the idea of regularity, order and beauty expressed as a spatial pattern with that of duration in time. Freeze the dance and the rhythm is lost: only when the sequence of steps is completed does the spatial pattern reveal itself in all its 'comly order and proportion faire'.

The implications of this cyclical view of time were far-reaching. For it meant that not only could the apparently haphazard changes which were everywhere observable both in human affairs and in the natural world be seen as part of an eternal unchanging order, but also that a providential pattern could be discovered in the events of history. The political implications of such a providential view of history are obvious: if a prince could show that providence approved his reign, it added considerable weight to whatever other claims he might make to sovereignty.

Society, then, both in its structure and in its evolution, manifested the same principles which governed the natural world. However, since man and nature alike were contaminated by the Fall, it meant that no human society could ever be perfect. But fallen man was not without a guide in his attempts to approximate to the ideal pattern of social harmony established by the Creator. In the principle of natural law (*jus naturale*) he possessed an immutable system of ethical imperatives, and it was upon this principle that all human law (*jus gentium*) must be based. First formulated by the Stoics, the concept of natural law as the basis of social ethics became the central doctrine of European political thought from Cicero[8] to Hooker.[9] The classic Renaissance statement of its principles is contained in the *Laws of Ecclesiastical Polity*. 'Law rational', writes Hooker,

> which men commonly use to call the Law of Nature, meaning thereby the Law which human Nature knoweth itself in reason universally bound unto . . . comprehendeth all those things which men by the light of their natural understanding evidently know . . . to be beseeming or unbeseeming, virtuous or vicious, good or evil for them to do.[10]

In claiming that natural law is accessible to reason, Hooker is stating a principle which was fundamental to every humanist's credo, for, as Cicero had said, 'Truc law is right reason in agreement with nature . . .'[11] As an assertion of the power of human reason to participate in the divine law, natural law is an expression of the dignity and perfectibility of man.[12] To obey this law, Hooker explains, is to imitate 'the very manner of working which Nature herself doth necessarily observe in the course of the whole world'.[13] From this basic axiom could be deduced the whole system of practical dictates, which, even if they were widely challenged when Hooker wrote the *Laws*, were at least universally understood. If it is the love of God that 'gouerneth both the land and the sea, and likewyse commandethe the heuen, and kepyth the world in due order and good accorde', it followed that the same principle must govern all human relationships.[14] This is the law to which Macbeth refers in his ironic reply to Duncan's speech of welcome at Forres Castle, and it is the same law to which Cordelia appeals when she confesses that she loves her father according to her bond. Cordelia can say no more, because in saying this, she has said all. For the father who demands flattery from his daughter is also king, and as Jean Bodin says, 'A true king is one who observes the laws of nature as punctiliously as he wishes his subjects to observe his own laws . . .'[15] To deny these laws is to invite chaos. 'See we not plainly', says Hooker, 'that obedience of creatures unto the law of nature is the stay of the whole world?'[16] Thus nature herself commands us 'To worship God: to obey parents and gouernours, & thereby to conserue common society . . .'[17]

Such, in brief, was the theory of natural law which it is no exaggeration to say was held by practically every Elizabethan humanist. From the tone of contemporary political treatises such as Sir Thomas Smith's *De Republica Anglorum* (1583) the reader might be forgiven for supposing that this traditional body of theory was so secure as to be unassailable. Yet within a decade it was, if not actually dead, at least seriously ailing. When Donne complained that the world was 'crumbled out againe t'his Atomis' and that 'all Relation:/Prince, Subject, Father, Sonne are things forgot . . .'[18] it was not just the death of a fifteen-year-old girl he was lamenting, but the passing of a whole world order. Not that its demise was as unexpected or as unforeseen as these comparisons might suggest. For the best part of a century the whole edifice upon which the theory of natural law was based had been under attack by sceptical thinkers such as Machiavelli, Agrippa and Montaigne. Of these the most radical was Montaigne. Montaigne's well-known critique of the concept of natural law in the ironically titled 'Apology for Raimond Sebond' was the culmination of a current of ideas which had been gathering momentum since the early years of the century. Although the influence of the *Essays* – first published in 1580 and reissued in an expanded form in 1588 – was, of course, confined to the final years of the sixteenth century, the tradition of philosophic scepticism on which they drew was familiar enough in Tudor England.[19] In fact one of the most clear-headed contributions to the debate between ethical subjectivism and the theory of natural law is by an Englishman writing in the 1530s.

Starkey, like Elyot, is a traditionalist. What distinguishes his *Dialogue* from the treatises of Starkey's like-minded contemporaries is its serious attempt to defend Christian humanist principles against the attacks of thinkers such as Machiavelli and Agrippa.[20] Where Elyot simply ignores the existence of the materialist and sceptical political theories which were threatening the old order, Starkey confronts them with reasoned argument. He begins his analysis of human society with a debate on the meaning of nature. The primitivist argument is put into the mouth of Cardinal Pole, who claims that man's natural state is one of innocence and virtue and that it is city life which has corrupted him. This argument is countered by Thomas Lupset who says that if society is corrupt, this is not because of the influence of towns and cities, but because of 'the malyce of man, wych abusyth and turnyth that thyng wych myght be to hys welth and felycyte to hys owne dystructyon and mysery'.[21]

Pole then objects that Lupset's concept of 'the veray true polytyke and cyuyle life' is a meaningless one, since ideas about what constitutes the just society vary from one nation to another. Lupset sees Pole's subjectivist argument as an invitation to 'confusyon and tyranny' (p. 11). He admits that national customs do vary, but says that we must distinguish between civil law and natural law. Whereas civil law varies from one country to another, there are certain fundamental principles which are recognized by all nations and which are 'stablyschyd by nature' (p. 13):

> For [men] haue rotyd in theyr hartys a certayn rule . . . wych . . . is callyed of phylosopharys and wyse men, the vnyuersal and true law of nature, wych to al natyonys ys commyn . . . (p. 14)

Starkey is a lucid and forceful writer. But no amount of conservative eloquence could win an argument which would only be settled when the traditional theory of cosmos had been finally exploded. But that was not to come for well over a century, and when Spenser was writing *The Faerie Queene* the issue was still a live one.

In the proem to Book V Spenser explains that his subject is justice seen not simply as an abstract virtue, but as it is administered by Queen Elizabeth through her agent Artegall:

> Dread Souerayne Goddesse, that doest highest sit
> In seate of iudgement, in th'Almighties stead,
> And with magnificke might and wondrous wit
> Doest to thy people righteous doome aread,

That furthest Nations filles with awfull dread,
Pardon the boldnesse of thy basest thrall,
That dare discourse of so diuine a read,
As thy great iustice praysed ouer all:
The instrument whereof loe here thy *Artegall*.
(V, proem,11)

However, the bulk of the proem takes the form of an elegy on the progressive decline of the world since the golden age, when justice was revered by all and 'Peace vniuersall rayn'd mongst men and beasts' (V, proem, 9). A number of commentators have seen in this a contradiction. If, as stanza 11 claims, the object of Book V is to celebrate Elizabeth's justice, then why does the proem stress the absence of justice in a degenerate world, and not, as one might have expected, its glorious reaffirmation in Elizabeth and her government?[22]

In attempting to answer this objection we should first recall that the theme of the world's decay was a Renaissance commonplace which did not necessarily betoken a morbid sensibility.[23] It is a formula which may be found in even the most optimistic of writers. James Thomson is an example. In the opening section of 'Spring', Thomson concludes his introductory account of the golden age with a reflection on the state of the world in 'this late age' (372):

Such were those prime of days.
But now those white unblemished minutes, whence
The fabling poets took their golden age,
Are found no more amid these iron times,
These dregs of life! Now the distempered mind
Has lost that concord of harmonious powers
Which forms the soul of happiness; and all
Is off the poise within: the passions all
Have burst their bounds; and Reason, half extinct,
Or impotent, or else approving, sees
The foul disorder.
('Spring', 271-81)[24]

For all the apparent pessimism of these lines it would be difficult to find a more optimistic poem than *The Seasons*. By contrast it must be admitted that the fifth book of *The Faerie Queene* offers a gloomy view of its subject. Yet Spenser's purpose in introducing his poem with an account of the golden age myth is not altogether different from

Thomson's. *The Seasons* is not just a tribute to nature; like *The Faerie Queene*, it is a celebration of a national idea. But for Thomson, the neo-classicist, man is a degenerate creature inhabiting a fallen world (the four seasons only became distinguished from one another after the passing of the golden age and therefore serve as a permanent reminder of the fact that we inhabit a tarnished world). The promised return of the golden age may be imminent, but it will only be brought about by industry and by the civilizing influence of art.[25] As Thomson's contemporary, Dennis, wrote, 'The great Design of Arts is to restore the Decays that happen'd to human Nature by the Fall, by restoring Order.'[26]

In Spenser's poem, Astraea has already returned to the earth in the form of Queen Elizabeth. But the inauguration of her reign marks only the first step in the process of realizing the state of universal peace prophesied by Merlin. If, as many critics have complained, Artegall seems an unattractive hero,[27] this is because his task is an unpleasant one. It is precisely because Astraea/Elizabeth has come to rule a fallen world that she must employ the harsh and ruthless brand of justice which modern readers justly find objectionable. *The Faerie Queene*, as Evans reminds us, is not a utopian, but a heroic poem: to imagine an ideal commonwealth without laws or sanctions would be simply to indulge, like Shakespeare's Gonzalo, in an idle dream. The gloominess of the picture Spenser draws in the proem is a measure of the magnitude of the task to which Elizabeth has committed herself. Like Aeneas, she must exercise not only fortitude and piety, but also at times a ruthless justice in order to fulfil her political destiny.[28]

It may be seen that, in defining justice, Spenser is also defining a political ideal. But a coherent political theory presupposes a certain view not only of man, but of the kind of universe he inhabits. Having stated the former by implication in the proem, Spenser now establishes the latter in the first three incidents of the book. Artegall's role in these opening cantos is that of a Herculean hero 'Who now to perils great for iustice sake proceedes' (V, ii, 1).[29] In the first two episodes he acts the part of an impartial judge and executioner redressing wrong and restoring justice. While his first task is the adjudication of a private quarrel, his second concerns a case of social injustice. Pollente is a tyrannical landowner who, having acquired 'great Lordships' and 'goodly farmes' through 'strong oppression of his powre' (V, ii, 5), abuses that power by plundering rich and poor alike. From private tort and then social injustice, Spenser now extends his frame of reference to the whole universe.

The episode of the levelling giant is one of the most important in

Book V, for Artegall's reply to the giant's egalitarian arguments is classic statement of the principle of natural law. It is ironically the giant himself who, in his defence of his policy of reducing all men to a common level, appeals to nature's example. But because nature appears to have lost her ancient balance he must first undertake to restore the elements to their former equilibrium. When Artegall warns him of the folly of attempting to tamper with the natural order of things, the giant points to the manifest mutability of the natural world:

> Thou foolishe Elfe (said then the Gyant wroth)
> Seest not, how badly all things present bee,
> And each estate quite out of order goth?
> The sea it selfe doest thou not plainely see
> Encroch vppon the land there vnder thee;
> And th'earth it selfe how daily its increast,
> By all that dying to it turned be?
> Were it not good that wrong were then surceast,
> And from the most, that some were giuen to the least?
> (V, ii, 37)

Artegall explains that behind the apparent confusion of nature is an underlying principle of order. Moreover, the very inequality which the giant seeks to redress is a fundamental law of nature which all creatures are bound to obey:

> The hils doe not the lowly dales disdaine;
> The dales doe not the lofty hils enuy.
> He maketh Kings to sit in souerainty;
> He maketh subiects to their powre obay;
> He pulleth downe, he setteth vp on hy;
> He giues to this, from that he takes away.
> For all we haue is his: what he list doe, he may.
> (V, ii, 41)

Artegall's reply sums up the two most important principles of Spenser's universe: the principle of degree and the principle of analogy. Since man is a microcosm of the universe the same laws must govern the administration of social justice as govern the cosmos. The behaviour of the rabble which follows the giant in the hope of personal advantage illustrates the socially disruptive consequences of interfering with the law of degree. As Elyot warns, 'take away ordre from all thynges what shulde than remayne? Certes nothynge finally, except . . . *Chaos*'.

As an impartial agent of justice Artegall is not personally involved in any of these three incidents. But in canto v he discovers to his own cost another aspect of the law of degree. As men are separated by rank, so the sexes are distinguished by their innate qualities and abilities into superior and inferior; and

> vertuous women wisely vnderstand,
> That they were borne to base humilitie,
> Vnlesse the heauens them lift to lawfull soueraintie.
> (V, v, 25)[30]

The description in canto vii of Britomart's rescue of Artegall makes it clear that the hero's enslavement to Radigund is as blatant a form of injustice as the giant's experiments in social equality. When Britomart has subdued the Amazons she

> The liberty of women did repeale,
> Which they had long vsurpt; and them restoring
> To mens subiection, did true Iustice deale:
> (V, vii, 42)

Once again, Spenser shows that justice, whether personal or social, is dependent upon the law of nature.

Having introduced the subject of mutability as part of the natural order of the universe in canto ii, Spenser considers another aspect of nature's hidden wisdom in two further incidents. Both the sequel to Florimell's story and the story of the brothers Amidas and Bracidas serve to illustrate the truth that time, though it tries all, is ultimately beneficent.

After her long ordeal in Proteus's hall, Florimell had returned to the languishing Marinell at the end of Book IV like Proserpina bringing spring to the upper world:

> His cheared heart eftsoones away gan chace
> Sad death, reuiued with her sweet inspection,
> And feeble spirit inly felt refection;
> As withered weed through cruell winters tine,
> That feeles the warmth of sunny beames reflection,
> Liftes vp his head, that did before decline

And gins to spread his leafe before the faire sunshine.
(IV, xii, 34)

The significance of her suffering and joy is made clear in the first stanza of canto iii:

After long stormes and tempests ouerblowne,
The sunne at length his ioyous face doth cleare:
So when as fortune all her spight hath showne,
Some blisfull houres at last must needes appeare;
Else should afflicted wights oftimes despeire.
So comes it now to *Florimell* by tourne,
After long sorrowes suffered whyleare,
In which captiu'd she many moneths did mourne,
To tast of ioy, and to wont pleasures to retourne.
(V, iii, 1)

By linking the vicissitudes of human life with the seasonal cycle of time, the parallels between Florimell and Proserpina suggest, like the similar parallels in *The Winter's Tale*, that suffering and loss are merely part of a beneficent natural order.

The theme of the beneficence of fate is amplified in the next canto. When Artegall is asked to settle the dispute between the brothers Amidas and Bracidas he shows them that the sea which has robbed one brother of his inheritance has more than repaid him in the course of time. Though fate, symbolized in this episode by the 'mighty Sea', may appear cruel, it is, *sub specie aeternitatis*, just in its dealings with man:

For equal right in equall things doth stand,
For what the mighty Sea hath once possest,
And plucked quite from all possessors hand,
Whether by rage of waues, that neuer rest,
Or else by wracke, that wretches hath distrest,
He may dispose by his imperiall might,
As things at randon left, to whom he list.
So *Amidas*, the land was yours first hight,
And so the threasure yours is *Bracidas* by right.
(V, iv, 19)

The idea that fate is the unfolding of events in time in accordance with God's immutable law is, of course, a commonplace of medieval and Renaissance thought.[31] In illustrating this truth the emblematic Amidas/Bracidas episode presents its theme in a schematic form which takes little account of character or motive. In the drama of real life, the interplay between character and fate must be taken into account in any attempt to answer the question of whether there is justice in human suffering. If the divine order which lies behind the apparently random workings of fate is for the most part hidden from man, how is he to know when suffering, as part of a providential plan, is to be borne with patience, and when it must be resisted? It is this problem to which Spenser turns in the next episode – the story of Terpine and Artegall and their enslavement by the Amazons.

Having released Terpine from the gallows on which the Amazons had been about to hang him, Artegall demands, with an air of self-righteous indignation, an explanation for his shameful predicament. Terpine replies with an appeal to the inscrutability of fate:

> Most haplesse well ye may
> Me iustly terme, that to this shame am brought,
> And made the scorne of Knighthod this same day.
> But who can scape, what his owne fate hath wrought?
> The worke of heauens will surpasseth humaine thought.
> (V, iv, 27)

Artegall's answer to Terpine's passive fatalism anticipates Cassius's celebrated remark to Brutus:

> Right true: but faulty men vse oftentimes
> To attribute their folly vnto fate,
> And lay on heauen the guilt of their owne crimes.
> (V, iv, 28)

The irony of this interchange becomes apparent in canto v when Artegall discovers that it is one thing to prescribe a remedy for someone else's misfortune, but quite another to apply the same remedy to one's own sickness. Now that he has exchanged places with Terpine as captive of the Amazons, Artegall finds his own arguments less persuasive. It is (in Spenser's eyes) a mark of the depth to which he has sunk that it is a mere servant girl who exhorts him to awaken his 'dulled spirit' and escape his prison (V, v, 36). Artegall's reply is the more ironical for its seeming piety:

> Yet weet ye well, that to a courage great
> It is no lesse beseeming well, to beare
> The storme of fortunes frowne, or heauens threat,
> Then in the sunshine of her countenance cleare
> Timely to ioy, and carrie comely cheare.
> For though this cloud haue now me ouercast,
> Yet doe I not of better times despeyre;
> And, though (vnlike) they should for euer last,
> Yet in my truthes assurance I rest fixed fast.
>
> (V, v, 38)

In principle, of course, Artegall is right: indeed this is the very lesson he had taught Amidas and Bracidas. But so clouded is his judgement as a result of his infatuation with Radigund's beauty (V, v, 12-13), that he fails to see that, far from being the will of heaven, his imprisonment is a gross travesty of nature's law of degree.

The Radigund incident embodies two morals. The first, which is summed up in the first stanza of the next canto, concerns the dangers of perverting the natural hierarchy of the sexes and takes the form of a warning against the blandishments of women: 'For neuer yet was wight so well aware,/But he at first or last was trapt in womens snare' (V, vi, 1). The second is less simple. Having sworn to obey Radigund's law should she defeat him in battle (V, iv, 49), Artegall considers himself honour-bound to submit to the indignity of her patently unjust rule now that she is victor. His problem is the problem of accommodating human law to the law of nature, that is to say, of reconciling the demands of heavenly justice with a personal code of honour when the two are apparently in conflict. The problem is a familiar one because it is the question which most contemporary tragedies confront in one form or another. For tragedy is, above all, concerned with man's attempts to discover a just order in the universe. Nor is the problem simply a matter of choosing between conscience and desire. It is all very well to appeal, as Artegall does in the Amidas/Bracidas episode, to the principle of natural law. But before the virtuous man can resolve his conflict he must understand what heaven requires of him. The essential question which the incident poses is how we interpret natural law in morally ambiguous situations.

Now Artegall's problem is also Britomart's. Her predicament is almost a repetition of the situation at the end of Book III where Scudamour had despaired of rescuing Amoret from the House of Busirane. Her first reaction on learning of Artegall's imprisonment is to give way, as

Scudamour had done, to jealous passion (V, vi, 4-5). But her next is to do what Shakespeare's Isabella notably fails to do in an analogous situation. Confronted with a conflict between a private code of honour and the demands of natural law, she prays to heaven for guidance (V, vii, 7). As a neo-medieval temple of justice,[32] Isis Church is the allegorical 'core' of Book V. It provides not only an answer to the philosophic problem posed in canto v, but also Spenser's most complete statement concerning the function of the prince as an agent and deputy of divine justice.

For all its strangeness, Britomart's vision of the crocodile which impregnates her after consuming the 'outragious flames' which jeopardize the safety of the temple, does not present a serious exegetical problem, because, as is his usual custom, Spenser explains the allegory for the reader. The temple priest who interprets the vision begins his explanation by reminding Britomart of her royal lineage and claiming that it is the purpose of the dream to expound the nature and meaning of her royal office. He tells her that the crocodile, which has already been labelled as an emblem of 'forged guile,/And open force' (V, vii, 7), signifies her lover Artegall (V, vii, 22). Although the power he embodies is normally restrained by clemency, it must be unleashed if the 'troublous stormes' of rebellion threaten the crown (V, vii, 23). He concludes his interpretation by congratulating Britomart on the issue which will result from her union with the beast. The priest does not enlarge on the meaning of this liaison; but there is little need, for it is clear that what is signified is a marriage between justice and equity which will result in a strong nation. The typological significance of this marriage is hinted at in the strange metamorphosis which takes place in the heroine. As she sacrifices to the goddess of equity, Britomart is transformed from votary to queen: her priestess's clothing is replaced by royal robes 'adorn'd with gems and iewels manifold' and on her head appears a crown of gold (V, vii, 13). In her dream Britomart has become that which she prefigures.

The vision which Britomart receives in answer to her prayers provides a knife with which to cut the Gordian knot of canto v. Artegall had been unable to resolve the conflict between human and divine law himself, not so much (as Terpine had said) because the 'worke of heauens will surpasseth humaine thought', as because his reason had been impaired by passion. But a prince cannot afford to allow emotional considerations of this kind to influence his judgement – a point which Spenser amplifies in Book VI. Canto vii impresses on us that, as the agent of 'highest Iove', the prince has a unique function as an interpreter of natural law:

th'heuens themselues, whence mortal men implore
Right in their wrongs, are rul'd by righteous lore
Of highest Ioue, who doth true iustice deale
To his inferiour Gods, and euermore
Therewith containes his heauenly Common-weale:
The skill whereof to Princes hearts he doth reueale.
(V, vii, 1)

As a personification of the principle of equity,[33] the prince is a mediator between god and man. Armed with her new knowledge, Britomart sets out to liberate the sleeping crocodile, laying aside the law by which Artegall had been bound to Radigund, in order to re-establish natural law. The misgivings which had previously been such a distinctive mark of her character have now vanished. Incensed by the injustice of Radigund's behaviour, Britomart will not parley, but immediately resorts to open force (V, vii, 28). Having defeated the Amazon, she remorselessly decapitates her (V, vii, 34).

Once it is made clear that Spenser is arguing that 'forged guile/And open force' as a means of defending a prince's 'iust heritage' receives divine authorization, it clarifies much of the action of the book, even if it does not make it more acceptable to the modern reader. In an excellent study of Book V, Aptekar has shown that this policy is consistently reflected in the conduct of its hero: 'Throughout the Legend of Justice Artegall and his comrade, Arthur, repeatedly meet their twin foes, force and fraud, with the same twin means.'[34] That a conservative upholder of the theory of natural law should be advocating such tactics may at first seem surprising, since the use of calculated deception is something which we may more readily associate with Machiavelli[35] than an orthodox Elizabethan humanist. Indeed more than one critic has argued that there is evidence of extensive Machiavellian influence in Spenser.[36] This may seem surprising because Machiavelli represented all the sceptical iconoclastic tendencies which Spenser's conservative contemporaries most feared and deprecated.

As a servant of the crown who took a keen amateur interest in 'generall poyntes of government, and the great archpollycyes of all ould and newe common welthes',[37] Spenser was undoubtedly familiar with Machiavelli's ideas and even mentions the *Discourses on the First Ten Books of Titus Livius* in the *View of the Present State of Ireland*.[38] But advocacy of extreme measures to counter civil insurrection was by no means unique to Machiavelli. Jean Bodin, for example, argues that 'One must not . . . label as evidence of tyranny the executions, banishments, confiscations and other deeds of violence in a commonwealth . . . On the contrary it often happens that mildness in a prince would ruin a commonwealth, whereas severity saves it.'[39] Yet a more staunch upholder of the twin principles of natural law and absolute sovereignty than Bodin it would be difficult to find. Again, we find the pious and godly Lipsius devoting a complete chapter of his *Sixe Bookes of Politickes* to the principle of 'honest and laudable deceipt'.[40] If the Christian prince 'cannot prevaile by the Lions skinne', writes Lipsius, echoing Machiavelli, '[he] must put on the Foxes'.[41] It is because she rules in a fallen world, where, in Thomson's words, 'the passions all have burst their bounds' and men are deaf to reasoned argument, that Elizabeth is exhorted to employ ruthless measures against her enemies. As Bodin says, 'A prince . . . must not be judged a tyrant because he is harsh and severe, provided always he keeps the laws of God and of nature.'[42]

If canto vii gives the reader a prophetic glimpse of Britomart as the 'Magnificke Virgin' (V, vii, 21) she prefigures, the remaining cantos of Book V are concerned with the reality of administering justice in that 'future' kingdom. Mercilla, the 'mayden Queene of high renowne' (V, viii, 17) is Spenser's most explicit portrait of Elizabeth as Christian prince.[43] In Books I and II the characteristics of the godly ruler are defined in negative terms. From the portraits of Lucifera and Philotime we can deduce that the ideal ruler is one who displays 'Myld humblesse mixt with awfull maiesty'. In the character of Mercilla Spenser now presents us with a positive image of princely virtue. For all her 'dreaded soueraynti e' (V, ix, 34) this 'mightie Ladie' (35) is not without compassion. When Arthur and Artegall pay her homage she tempers 'that Maiestie and awe,/That whylome wont to doe so many quake' and listens to them with 'more myld aspect' (35). The significance of this particular combination of antithetical qualities would have been far more striking to the contemporary reader than it is to the modern student. For this portrait of mercy 'tempred with some maiestie imperiall' (34) is clearly intended to evoke an archetypal image of regal compassion. The possibility of the contemporary reader failing to recognize this allusion to the Virgin Mary is unlikely, since it is in her capacity as protecting intercessor who shelters mankind from God's just anger with her mantle of mercy[44] that the Virgin was (and still is) most widely venerated; not only that, but he would very likely have been familiar with the contemporary practice of attributing this role to Queen Elizabeth. In a ballad of 1584, for example, in which she is addressed in such standard Marian epithets as 'onely star of light', 'diamond of delight', 'peerles pearle' and 'phenix of most noble minde', Elizabeth is portrayed as the 'daughter of a noble king,/Descending of a royall race' who acts as a protectress of her people:

> The seruant of the mighty God,
> Which dooth preserue her day and night,
> For whome we feel not of his rod,
> Although the pope hath doon his spite.[45]

It is in precisely the same terms that Spenser celebrates Elizabeth in Book V. Clothed, as it were, with the sun in a mantle whose 'spreading wings did wyde vnfold' (28), Mercilla, like Mary, is an 'heyre of ancient kings' (29) who acts as protecting intercessor for mankind. It is Mercilla's handmaids who

> Vpon *Ioues* iudgement seat wayt day and night,
> And when in wrath he threats the worlds decay,
> They doe his anger calme, and cruell vengeance stay.
> (V, ix, 31)

If the final judgement at the trial in canto ix seems, for all Mercilla's show of tears (50), a ruthless one, it must be remembered that Duessa is not merely Mary Queen of Scots, but a personification of evil itself. The harsh measures which Mercilla must adopt in her fight against sedition prove her to be a true protectress of her people against Antichrist.

The Marian iconography of canto ix serves partly as a means of defining with great economy a well-known ideal of merciful justice. It also serves as a way of identifying Elizabeth with a traditional concept of the Christian prince. The idea of the godly ruler as a '*gemina persona*, human by nature and divine by grace'[46] has its origins in medieval political theory. Britomart's visionary initiation into sacred mysteries at the Temple of Isis recalls the medieval jurist's practice of personifying justice as a temple goddess whose function was to mediate between divine and human law.[47] The logical outcome of the idea that the prince is God's vicar on earth is the medieval belief in the principle of universal empire. Only under an absolute sovereign whose jurisdiction extended to the four corners of the world could the harmony of divine justice be realized on earth. It is to this traditional concept of the Christian prince that Spenser is appealing when he portrays Mercilla, in fulfilment of Merlin's prophecy, as a semi-divine being receiving, 'Angel-like', the homage of the 'kings and kesars' of the earth (V, ix, 29). That she has indeed been divinely appointed to this imperial office is confirmed by her providential kinship with the virgin empress of heaven and earth.

As a fountain of all earthly justice the prince is a mediator of the *jus naturale*, that is to say, the law of a harmonious, rational nature. But, as we have seen, the order which underlies the apparent chaos of events is only revealed in time. This is why Spenser begins Book V with an historical myth, and it is against the background of this myth that the apparent gloom of the proem must be seen. Though fate is ultimately beneficent, time must run its course, the nadir must be reached, before Astraea can return and the golden age can be renewed.

## Notes

1. *The Governour*, p. 195.

2. *The 'Art' of Rhetoric*, I, ix, 33, translated by John Henry Freese, Loeb Classical Library (London, 1926), p. 101.

3. For commentaries on the topical allegory of Book V see the *Variorium Spenser*, Book V, pp. 299-335. Notable recent commentaries are René Graziani, 'Elizabeth at Isis Church', *PMLA*, 79 (1964), 376-89; Douglas A. Northrop, 'Spenser's Defence of Elizabeth', *UTQ*, 38 (1969), 277-94; 'Mercilla's Court as Parliament', *HLQ*, 36 (1973), 153-8; O'Connell, *Mirror and Veil*, pp. 139 ff.

4. See in particular George C. Herndl, *The High Design: English Renaissance Tragedy and Natural Law* (Lexington, Ky., 1970).

5. The question is briefly discussed by Nelson, pp. 262 ff. See also B.E.C. Davis, *Edmund Spenser: A Critical Study* (Cambridge, 1933), p. 243.

6. See A.P. d'Entrèves, *Natural Law: An Introduction to Legal Philosophy* (1951; rpt. London, 1972), passim. On the general principles of natural law see also John Neville Figgis, *Studies of Political Thought: From Gerson to Grotius 1414-1625* (Cambridge, 1907), pp. 84-6; Otto Gierke, *Political Theories of the Middle Age*, translated and edited by Frederic William Maitland (Cambridge, 1922); *Natural Law and the Theory of Society 1500 to 1800*, translated and edited by Ernest Barker, 2 vols (1934; rpt. in one vol., Cambridge, 1958). For changing conceptions of natural law in the sixteenth century see Haydn, *The Counter-Renaissance*, pp. 131-66.

7. Several scholars have made excellent summaries of the body of ideas often referred to as the Elizabethan World Picture. See Hardin Craig, *The Enchanted Glass: The Elizabethan Mind in Literature* (1935; rpt. Oxford, 1960); E.M.W. Tillyard, *The Elizabethan World Picture* (London, 1943); Marjorie Hope Nicolson, *The Breaking of the Circle: Studies in the Effect of the 'New Science' upon Seventeenth-Century Poetry* (New York, 1960), pp. 11-46; Heninger, *Touches of Sweet Harmony*. Less numerous are accounts of what Haydn terms the Counter-Renaissance. See also Theodore Spencer, *Shakespeare and the Nature of Man* (1942; rpt. New York, 1961), pp. 1-50; John F. Danby, *Shakespeare's Doctrine of Nature: A Study of King Lear* (London, 1961), pp. 20-53; Herschel Baker, *The Wars of Truth: Studies in the Decay of Christian Humanism in the Earlier Seventeenth Century* (1952; rpt. Gloucester, Mass., 1969).

8. *De Legibus*, I, v, 17; I, vii, 23; *De Re Publica*, III, xxii.

9. Hooker, *Of the Laws of Ecclesiastical Polity*, I, 148-232.

10. Hooker, I, 182. For a popular contemporary exposition of the principle of natural law see John Bale, *A Comedy Concerning Three Laws*, II, 1 ff.

11. *De Re Publica*, III, xxii, translated by Clinton Walker Keyes, Loeb Classical Library edn (London, 1928), p. 211. Cf. Aquinas, *Summa Theologicae*, Ia 2ae, quae. 91, art. 2.

12. Such a view of human nature is incompatible with the Calvinist theology which many critics claim to find in Book I (see Chapter 1).

13. Hooker, I, 182.

14. See, for example, Sir John Cheke: 'Love is not the knot onely of the Commonwealth, whereby divers parts be perfectly joyned together in one politique bodie, but also the strength and might of the same, gathering together into a small room with order, which scattered would else breed confusion and debate' (*The True Subiect to the Rebell: Or the Hurt of Sedition, How Grievous it is to a Commonwealth* (1549; rpt. Oxford, 1641), pp. 52-3).

15. Jean Bodin, *Six Books of the Commonwealth*, abridged and translated by M.J. Tooley (Oxford, 1955), p. 59.

16. Hooker, I, 157.

17. Sir John Hayward, *An Answer to the First Part of a Certaine Conference Concerning Svccession* (London, 1603), Sig. Aiii$^{v}$.

18. *The Epithalamions, Anniversaries and Epicedes*, edited by W. Milgate (Oxford, 1978), p. 28.

19. See Felix Raab, *The English Face of Machiavelli: A Changing Interpretation 1500-1700* (London, 1964), pp. 30-76. See also Charles G. Nauert, *Agrippa and the Crisis of Renaissance Thought*, Illinois Studies in the Social Sciences, LV (Urbana, Ill., 1965), pp. 328-30.

20. Robert Ornstein has questioned the value of the notion of a body of sceptical, subjectivist thought running counter to the prevailing optimism of the sixteenth century (*The Moral Vision of Jacobean Tragedy* (Madison, Wisc., 1960), pp. 4-12). But while he is right to emphasize the bond that linked humanist with radical and which separated both from the 'mediocre talents' of the age (p. 12), there is, in doing so, a danger of 'defusing' the age, of removing the element of uneasiness and controversy which is so clearly evident in Starkey and which must be seen, in part at least, as the cause of the great Christian humanist works of the 1590s. It was precisely because they knew their world to be gravely threatened that Spenser, Sidney and Shakespeare produced their great defences of traditional values.

21. *Dialogue between Pole and Lupset*, p. 10.

22. Kathleen Williams, *Spenser's 'Faerie Queene': The World of Glass* (London, 1966), p. 155. See also O'Connell, *Mirror and Veil*, pp. 127 ff.

23. On the theme of the world's decay in sixteenth- and early seventeenth-century literature see Victor Harris, *All Coherence Gone: A Study of the Seventeenth Century Controversy over Disorder and Decay in the Universe* (1949; rpt. London, 1966), pp. 86 ff; Baker, *The Wars of Truth*, pp. 65-78.

24. James Thomson, *Poetical Works*, edited by J. Logie Robertson (1908; rpt. Oxford, 1965), p. 13. Cf. *Paradise Lost*, IX, 44.

25. See Robin Headlam Wells, 'Delight in Disorder: James Thomson and the Art of Landscape', *Comparison*, 8 (1978), 76-85.

26. 'The Grounds of Criticism in Poetry', *The Critical Works of John Dennis*, edited by E.N. Hooker, 2 vols (Baltimore, 1939), I, 336.

27. See in particular Anderson, '"Nor Man it is": The Knight of Justice in Book V of Spenser's Faerie Queene', p. 65. See also Hamilton, *The Structure of Allegory in 'The Faerie Queene'*, pp. 170-1; Williams, *Spenser's 'Faerie Queene': The World of Glass*, p. 152.

28. Spenser's belief in the restoration of a state of justice after man's progressive decline since the golden age is a form of chronological primitivism not to be confused with that cultural primitivism which attributes man's present ills

to the effects of civilization. See Arthur O. Lovejoy and George Boas, *Primitivism and Related Ideas in Antiquity* (1935; rpt. New York, 1973), pp. 1-22.

29. For discussions of Artegall as Hercules see Rosemond Tuve, 'Spenser's Reading: The "De Claribus Mulieribus"', *SP*, 33 (1936), 147-65; Nelson, *The Poetry of Edmund Spenser*, p. 257; Jean MacIntyre, 'Spenser's Herculean Heroes', *HACB*, 17 (1966), 5-12; T.K. Dunseath, *Spenser's Allegory of Justice in Book Five of 'The Faerie Queene'* (Princeton, 1968), pp. 46-85; Jane Aptekar, *Icons of Justice: Iconography and Thematic Imagery in Book V of 'The Faerie Queene'* (New York, 1968), pp. 153-200.

30. This stanza makes it clear that Elizabeth is to be regarded as an exception to the natural law governing the sexes. Douglas A. Northrop argues that Spenser saw this exception 'as an instance of equity, in which the law of men's rule is put aside so that the principle of the rule of the superior will be followed by conferring sovereignty on the divinely endowed woman' ('Spenser's Defence of Elizabeth', *UTQ*, 38 (1969), 277-8). For a discussion of the contemporary debate on this question see Kerby Neill, 'Spenser on the Regiment of Women: A Note on the *Faerie Queene*, V, v, 25', *SP*, 34 (1937), 134-7; James E. Phillips, Jr., 'The Background of Spenser's Attitude toward Women Rulers', *HLQ*, 5 (1942), 5-32; 'The Woman Ruler in Spenser's *Faerie Queene*', *HLQ*, 5 (1942), 211-34.

31. See Boethius, *The Consolation of Philosophy*, IV, prose 6 for a classic statement of this idea. For modern discussions of time in Renaissance literature see Baker, *The Wars of Truth*, pp. 65-78; Ricardo Quinones, *The Renaissance Discovery of Time*, Harvard Studies in Comparative Literature, XXXI (Cambridge, Mass., 1972); T. McAlindon, *Shakespeare and Decorum* (London and New York, 1973), pp. 10-11; G.F. Waller, *The Strong Necessity of Time: The Philosophy of Time in Shakespeare and Elizabethan Literature* (The Hague, 1976); S.K. Heninger, Jr., *The Cosmographical Glass: Renaissance Diagrams of the Universe* (San Marino, 1977), pp. 3-13. On Spenser's use of time imagery see Rawdon Wilson, 'Images and "Allegoremes" of Time in the Poetry of Spenser', *ELR*, 4 (1974), 56-82.

32. On the temple of justice in medieval literature see Kantorowicz, *The King's Two Bodies*, pp. 107-13.

33. Saint German defines equity as an exception to the 'general rules of the law of man, when they by reason of their generalty would in any particular case judge against the law of God, or the law of reason . . .' (quoted by James E. Phillips, 'Renaissance Concepts of Justice and the Structure of *The Faerie Queene*, Book V', *HLQ*, 33 (1970), 111). As this definition implies, the principle of equity could only be invoked if the application of any law resulted in the contravention of natural law (see Sir William Holdsworth, *A History of English Law*, 16 vols (1924, 3rd edn 1945; rpt. London, 1973), IV, 281). For the fullest discussion of equity in Book V see W. Nicholas Knight, 'The Narrative Unity of Book V of *The Faerie Queene*: "That Part of Justice which is Equity"', *RES*, N.S., 21 (1970), 267-94.

34. *Icons of Justice*, p. 116.

35. See, for example, *The Prince*, Ch. XVIII. In defence of his claim that a prince must be a 'great pretender and dissembler', Machiavelli explains that 'a prince, so long as he keeps his subjects united and loyal, ought not to mind the reproach of cruelty; because with a few examples he will be more merciful than those who, through too much mercy, allow disorders to arise . . .' (translated by W.K. Marriot, Everyman edn (1908; rpt. London, 1960), p. 91).

36. See Edwin A. Greenlaw, 'The Influence of Machiavelli on Spenser', *MP*, 7 (1909), 187-202; Davis, *Edmund Spenser: A Critical Study*, p. 72.

37. Gabriel Harvey, *The Works*, edited by Alexander B. Grosart, 3 vols (London, 1884-5), I, 139-40.

38. *Variorum Spenser*, *The Prose Works*, p. 229.

39. *Six Books of the Commonwealth*, pp. 63-4.

40. Justus Lipsius, *Sixe Bookes of Politickes or Civil Doctrine*, translated by William Jones (London, 1594), p. 114.

41. Lipsius, p. 114. Cf. Machiavelli, *The Prince*, Ch. XVIII.

42. *Six Books of the Commonwealth*, p. 64.

43. See Fowler, *Spenser and the Numbers of Time*, pp. 196-8; Northrop, 'Spenser's Defence of Elizabeth', pp. 277-94; 'Mercilla's Court as Parliament', pp. 153-8.

44. The most impressive graphic representation of this symbol is Piero della Francesca's *Madonna della Misericordia* (reproduced by Warner, *Alone of All Her Sex* in a plate facing p. 197). In his 'Ballade at the Reverence of Our Lady' Lydgate supplicates Mary, the 'Modyr of mercy' to spread her 'mantel of mysery-cord' upon the sins of mankind (MacCracken, I, 256). In the illustration from John Case's *Sphaera Civitatis* reproduced above (p. 60) Elizabeth is shown in the Marian role of protectress shrouding the body politic with the wings of her mantle.

45. *A famous dittie of the joyful receauing of the Queens most excellent maiestie* . . . quoted by Wilson, *England's Eliza*, p. 33.

46. Kantorowicz, *The King's Two Bodies*, p. 87.

47. See Kantorowicz, pp. 107-13.

# 6 PATTERN OF PRINCELY COURTESY

Book VI is by general consent the most attractive book of *The Faerie Queene*. After the barren landscapes of Book V it seems, says Lewis, almost as if Spenser is pausing to 'look down with relief at this delightful land, spacious and wide, and sprinkled with such sweet variety'.[1] The book owes much of its charm to the Greek romances upon which Spenser drew for his narrative material.[2] With their complex plots involving the capture, enslavement, separation and eventual reunion of lovers, these tales of suffering and joy have a universal appeal. But if there is general critical agreement concerning the success of Book VI as narrative poetry, there is none on the question of the precise meaning of the virtue for which its stories form a vehicle. Courtesy has been variously defined as 'acting towards others as a true friend would act', 'the fine art of living together nobly with all other human beings', 'the poetry of conduct'.[3] It has been argued that behind Spenser's portrayal of this virtue 'there exists a well-established and complex tradition' of courtesy books,[4] and that Spenser's courtesy has 'little . . . to do with the courtesy books';[5] that of all the virtues portrayed in *The Faerie Queene* this is 'the great *social* virtue',[6] and that it is 'a basically internal virtue'.[7] Furthermore, although Spenser says in the proem to Book VI that Elizabeth is the 'patterne . . . of Princely curtesie' (6), one of the most recent critical studies of *The Faerie Queene* claims that 'Book VI is remarkable for its failure to praise Elizabeth . . .'[8]

It is true that there is no equivalent in Book VI of Belphoebe or Venus or Mercilla; but it should be noted that the terms of Spenser's invocatory address to the Queen form part of a concatenation of Marian images linking Elizabeth with these her 'historical' types. In medieval Mariology courtesy is one of the most familiar attributes of the Virgin Mary. The author of the Middle English *Pearl*, for example, repeatedly describes her as 'Quen of cortaysye' (§ VIII). Although it is perhaps inevitable that in portraying Elizabeth as ideal Christian prince Spenser should describe her as a model of courtesy, his collocation of the phrases 'soueraine Lady Queene' and 'patterne of curtesie' recalls the emblematic portraits of the earlier books where he adapts images and epithets habitually associated with the Virgin to his own rhetorical purpose. Spenser's use of these phrases in the proem suggests that Book VI should be seen, not as a departure from the plan of the earlier books, but as an essential contribution to it. The fact that Elizabeth is not formally represented in this book does not mean that Spenser has lost sight of his original purpose: stanza seven of the proem makes it clear that, as the repository of 'all goodly vertues', she represents the ideal to which her courtiers must aspire. If each of the heroes is intended to evoke one aspect of Elizabeth's character as Christian prince, Calidore is no exception. In this chapter I shall argue that the virtue of which he is champion is just as essentially an attribute of the ideal ruler as justice is. For Spenser, the truly courteous man is one who not only observes the rule of decorum at all times, but who devotes his life to the good of the state, and who is prepared to sacrifice personal interests, even though these may be honourable and virtuous in themselves, to the higher good. He is, in short, a representative of civilization itself.

In the opening stanzas of Book VI we learn that at Gloriana's court Calidore is regarded as a model of civility, a man who 'loathd leasing, and base flattery,/And loued simple truth and stedfast honesty' (VI, i, 3). But, as Spenser has shown us so many times in the course of the poem, the world of *The Faerie Queene* is a world in which truth is seldom simple and steadfast honesty rarely sufficient as a protection against evil. Just as the Redcrosse Knight had to undergo the severest physical and mental trials before the meaning of Una's advice concerning the need for moral vigilance became clear to him, so Calidore must suffer in order to be wise. In his case, however, the advice whose true meaning he learns only by experience, is, ironically, advice which he himself gives to another character in the first canto of the book.

Sir Crudor, like Sir Terpine, is a gross and blatant example of discourteous conduct. In dealing with offenders against the laws of civility and hospitality Calidore acts with dignity and restraint. But the moral which he impresses on Crudor at the end of canto i is the very lesson which he himself must learn in the final cantos of the book. 'Nothing', he tells Crudor,

> is more blamefull to a knight,
> That court'sie doth as well as armes professe,
> How euer strong and fortunate in fight,
> Then the reproch of pride and cruelnesse.
> In vaine he seeketh others to suppresse,
> Who hath not learnd him selfe first to subdew:
> All flesh is frayle, and full of ficklenesse,
> Subiect to fortunes chance, still chaunging new;

> What haps to day to me, to morrow may to you.
> (VI, i, 41)

The burden of Calidore's advice can be summed up simply as the necessity for self-control. But for the Renaissance humanist it is axiomatic that self-control can only be achieved through self-knowledge; and while Calidore may be well equipped with good intentions, he does not, as yet, know himself and his own weaknesses. And so Book VI, like the earlier books, is, among other things, an adventure in self-awareness.

In the first three cantos Calidore acts as an agent of order and decorum, redressing wrong and correcting uncouth behaviour. But he is not subjected to temptation himself. The testing of Calidore's own virtue is the subject of the last four cantos of the book, and takes the form of a temptation to abandon his quest in favour of the pastoral life. In previous books the pitfalls which had threatened the heroes were, in most cases, clear to the reader even if they were not to the characters themselves. But Calidore's choice is complicated by the fact that the way of life he is tempted to embrace seems morally preferable to the world he rejects. Indeed the pastoral world seems, paradoxically, to epitomise the very virtue which it is his mission to uphold. Spenser emphasizes the ambiguity of Calidore's predicament in the introductory stanzas of canto x. After telling the reader that Calidore has decided to stay and woo Pastorella instead of hunting 'after shadowes vaine/Of courtly fauour' (VI, x, 2), the narrator remarks:

> Ne certes mote he greatly blamed be,
> From so high step to stoupe vnto so low.
> For who had tasted once (as oft did he)
> The happy peace, which there doth ouerflow,
> And prou'd the perfect pleasures, which doe grow
> Amongst poore hyndes, in hils, in woods, in dales,
> Would neuer more delight in painted show
> Of such false blisse, as there is set for stales,
> T'entrap vnwary fooles in their eternall bales.
> (VI, x, 3)

That Calidore's sojourn among the shepherds represents a neglect of his mission is a point on which few modern critics would disagree. But although the view that Spenser was recommending the virtues of country life in opposition to the life of the court is no longer widely accepted,[9] at the same time it is commonly felt that the pastoral episode is not entirely relevant to the central issues of the book. In an essay entitled 'The Truancy of Calidore', Maxwell suggests that the fact that 'certain aspects of Calidore's courtesy are displayed in this episode more clearly than elsewhere . . . makes it all the odder that the framework within which all this occurs is . . . Calidore's truancy from his central quest',[10] and concludes that 'Calidore's neglect of the quest cannot be presented as an offence ***against*** courtesy, comparable to the backslidings of the heroes of Books I and II . . .'[11] Maxwell's sense of a certain confusion in the episode is shared by Nelson who argues that 'If the attractions of Pastorella have led Sir Calidore astray, so too has the pastoral episode diverted the poet from his principal purpose',[12] and by Evans, who writes: 'The truancy of Calidore is one of the most puzzling episodes in *The Faerie Queene*, for Spenser appears to be censuring the knight for behaviour which in itself seems praiseworthy.'[13]

Before we can give a complete answer to the question of whether Calidore is to be considered at fault for wishing to embrace the pastoral life we have to know precisely what is signified by the quest he is abandoning. Involving as it does the subduing of a monster, Calidore's quest may perhaps best be compared with that of the Redcrosse Knight. The defeat of the dragon which has been tyrannizing Una's parents is a symbolic event rich in biblical association and draws together the historical, the tropological and the anagogical meanings of the narrative. As the only explicitly Christian book of *The Faerie Queene*, Book I is exceptional in responding to this kind of traditional threefold analysis. But while it would be wrong to expect each book to yield a similar set of meanings, it is reasonable to assume that the hero's mission will in each case have a specific bearing on the virtue which it is his task to uphold.

Although the Blatant Beast lacks the religious associations which the Old Dragon of Book I inherits from its prototype in St John, it is just as precise in its significance. The chief characteristic of the Beast is its thousand evil tongues with which it

> spake licentious words, and hatefull things
> Of good and bad alike, of low and hie;
> Ne Kesars spared he a whit, nor Kings,
> But either blotted them with infamie,
> Or bit them with his banefull teeth of iniury.
> (VI, xii, 28)

With its poisonous words and 'venemous intent' (VI, i, 8) the Blatant Beast is a personification of verbal falsehood. Because it destroys by verbal means, the wounds it inflicts will not respond to normal treatment and can only be cured by 'the art of words' (VI, vi, 6). The hermit from whom Timias and Serena seek medical help after being attacked by the Beast knows that the only remedy for their sickness is 'fit speaches' (VI, vi, 6).

For the Renaissance humanist the corruption of language is a matter of grave concern. Since barbarism signifies, literally, a state of inarticulacy,[14] it is easy to see how civilization came to be identified with speech, 'the only benefit man hath to expresse his excellencie of mind above other creatures'.[15] Language was held in profound veneration because this was the means which first enabled man to form civil communities. Starkey, echoing Cicero, explains that it was 'by perfayt eloquence and hye phylosophy [that] men were brought, by lytyl and lytyl, from the rude lyfe in feldys and wodys, to thys cyuylyte, wych you now se stablyschyd and set in al wel rulyd cytes and townys'.[16] Thus we find that the most distinctive feature of Spenser's feral man is his lack of speech:

> For other language had he none nor speach,
> But a soft murmure, and confused sound
> Of senselesse words, which nature did him teach,
> T'expresse his passions, which his reason did empeach.
> (VI, iv, 11)

By contrast, one of the chief characteristics of the courteous man is his eloquence (VI, ii, 3). If speech is, in Jonson's words, 'the Instrument of *Society*',[17] ignorance of language is closely identified by Spenser with uncivilized conduct. Despite the fact that he is 'borne of noble blood' (VI, v, 2), the inarticulate Salvage man acts in a dangerously impulsive manner and must twice be restrained by Prince Arthur from committing the acts of savage violence which earn him his name (VI, vi, 38-40). To suggest that this character is 'very nearly an ideal' of humanity[18] is to attribute to Spenser precisely that sentimental form of cultural primitivism which he is deprecating in Book VI.[19] While the Salvage man serves as a reminder that even the best of natures stand in need of the restraining influence of civilization, it is the 'salvage nation' which offers a true picture of what primitive uncivilized man is like. This band of cannibals who neither

> giue
> Them selues to any trade, as for to driue

> The painefull plough, or cattell for to breed,
> Or by aduentrous marchandize to thriue;

and who 'eate the flesh of men, whom they mote fynde' (VI, viii, 35-6) is both a grim parody of prelapsarian man as described by such writers as Ovid, and also, perhaps, an answer to Montaigne.[20]

Since speech is the basis of ordered social life, it follows that to distort or corrupt the true function of language is to strike at the very foundation of civilization. (We may note that in lasciviously praising Serena's body (VI, viii, 39) the salvage nation is, in effect, corrupting the highest office which poets can assume, namely, that of 'trumpetters of all praise'.[21]) As Starkey says, '*there can rayne no gud pollycy wher the jugement of the pepul ys corrupt by false opynyon* . . .'[22] Essentially the same point is made by Jonson when he says that corrupt language 'imitates the publicke riot'.[23] It is true that the Blatant Beast is perfunctorily characterized. But to have given further physical details would have been unnecessary. When Hamilton argues that the Beast 'cannot be defined further than to say that he is Antichrist' he unwittingly denies his own claim as he goes on to note that 'with his thousand defaming, blaspheming tongues he is that total perversion of the Word against the Word'.[24] In portraying the Blatant Beast as a perverter of the true function of language, Spenser has created a figure which would have been instantly recognizable to the Elizabethan humanist as a symbolic enemy of civilized life. The hero whose mission it is to destroy this beast must therefore be seen not merely as an exponent of the arts and graces of civilization, but as a defender of its most fundamental principle. This means that Calidore's choice cannot be discussed as if it involved no more than a simple decision between virtue and pleasure. Upon his choice depends the very existence of the court – the focus and centre of civilized life.

Behind the nominal debate in canto ix concerning the relative merits of court and country life is the subject, fundamental to Elizabethan pastoral, of the rivalry between art and nature. In its most serious form this debate is concerned, as we saw in the previous chapter, with the nature of civilization itself. As Starkey's interlocutors debate the question of natural law it becomes clear that their conflicting views of society are based on mutually antagonistic theories of nature. Where Lupset sees man as a corrupt and fallen creature whose natural passions must be restrained by the discipline of 'polytyke ordur', Pole believes that man's natural state is one of innocent simplicity. Since civil life is the source of so much evil, says Pole, the wise man will forsake the city and seek a life of virtue in harmony with the natural world:

> yf thys be cyuyle lyfe and ordur, to lyue in cytes and townys wyth so much vyce and mysordur, me seme man schold not be borne therto, but rather to lyfe in the wylde forest, ther more folowyng the study of vertue, as hyt ys sayd men dyd in the golden age, where in man lyuyd accordyng to hys natural dygnyte.[25]

However, Lupset argues that since the evil they both deplore lies not in the institution of society, but in man's own nature, a retreat to the 'woodys . . . and wyld forestys' will solve nothing. Instead of seeking to escape the problems of society the responsible man will devote his knowledge and experience to the cause of civilization:

> Therefor, Master Pole . . . me semyth, hyt schold be best for you to apply your mynd to be of the nombur of them wych study to restor thys cyuyle ordur, and maynteyn thys vertuose lyfe, in cytes and townys to the commyn vtylyte.[26]

In placing paramount value on enlightened public service Starkey is expressing a moral commonplace which may be found everywhere in the courtesy literature of the period.[27] In the early part of the sixteenth century, English humanism ceased to be the purely academic movement it had been in the previous century and assumed a distinctively social tone. In evolving a system of education based on a study of the classical writers of Greece and Rome, men like More, Starkey and Elyot were inspired by the Platonic ideal of a good and just state ruled by an elite of enlightened public servants.[28] Thus when Spenser tells his readers that it is his intention 'to fashion a gentleman or noble person in vertuous and gentle discipline' it is to a long tradition of humanist thought that he is appealing in the casual phrase 'Aristotle and the rest',[29] a tradition which regarded public service as the highest ideal to which a virtuous man could aspire.

From his colloquy with Meliboe it is clear that behind Calidore's sentimental view of pastoral life is a primitivistic conception of nature not unlike Cardinal Pole's. Although his motives are never less than honourable, Calidore's temptation differs little in its implications from that of Tasso's Rinaldo. When Rinaldo's rescuers arrive at Armida's magic island in the fifteenth book of *Jerusalem Delivered* they are welcomed with these words:

> This is the Place, wherein you may asswage
> Your Sorrows past; here is that Joy and Bliss,
> Which flourish'd in the antique *Golden Age*;
> Here needs no Law, here none doth ought amiss:
> Put off those Arms, and fear not *Mars* his Rage;
> Your Sword, your Shield, your Helmet needless is;
>   Then consecrate them here to endless Rest;
>   You shall Love's Champions be, and Soldiers blest:
> (Fairfax's translation, XV, lxiii)[30]

Calidore's particular weakness does not happen to be sensuality. Nevertheless, Armida's invitation sums up perfectly everything that the pastoral world stands for in Calidore's mind. In Arcadia he believes, like Cardinal Pole, that he will be able to live in innocent tranquillity 'as hyt ys sayd men dyd in the golden age'.

But Calidore's hope is based on an illusion, for he has apparently forgotten the advice which he had given to Sir Crudor in the first canto of the book. In warning Crudor that all men are 'Subiect to fortunes chance, still chaunging new' Calidore had summed up one of the central motifs of Book VI. Although there is no book of *The Faerie Queene* in which Spenser does not impress on his reader that it is a fallen world in which Gloriana rules, the devices he employs to remind us of this fact vary from book to book. In Book VI it is the repeated motif of interrupted tranquillity which serves to emphasize the fact we live in a world governed by chance, a world where, as Calidore had remarked, 'What haps to day to me, to morrow may to you'. In an article entitled 'Courtesy and the Fall of Man', Evans notes that 'it is a feature of the world of Book VI that lovers are always being interrupted, however legitimate their embraces'.[31] Examples he cites include those of Aladine and Priscilla who are 'Ioying together in vnblam'd delight' (VI, ii, 43) when they are attacked without provocation, and Serena, who is 'without suspect of ill or daungers hidden dred' (VI, iii, 23) when the Blatant Beast carries her off. By repeating the motif of shattered repose Spenser creates, in the words of another critic, 'an image of a world in which unexpected misfortune seemingly cannot be avoided, even in moments of apparent peace'.[32]

The truths which have been stated by implication in the events of cantos i-viii are now recapitulated in verbal form in Meliboe's discourse on resignation. In reply to Calidore's eulogy of the pastoral life he tells the knight that since fortune is unpredictable, it is folly to place our hopes of happiness in the external circumstances of our lives. The lesson which nature has taught him is that 'fittest is, that all contented rest/ With that they hold: each hath his fortune in his brest' (VI, ix, 29). But Meliboe's Boethian counsel is lost on Calidore. It is one of the nicest ironies of Book VI that, as the heroic opponent of falsehood begins to forget his mission, *he becomes deaf to verbal truth*. So much so that, as Cheney perceptively remarks, 'The different viewpoints of the two men are emphasized by a counterpoint of motive which suggests not so much a debate as a conversation carried on at cross purposes.'[33]

Since Calidore has failed to profit from Meliboe's 'sensefull words' (VI, ix, 26), he must be shown their wisdom by non-verbal means. In canto x he receives a vision which presents in emblematic form the same truths that Meliboe had hoped to impress on him. When Calidore approaches the visionary dancers on Mount Acidale they vanish, leaving only the piper Colin Clout. Calidore questions him concerning the meaning of this vision, and the shepherd tells him that the three figures within the outer circle of dancers are the Graces and that it is they who bestow on man the gifts of courtesy and

> teach vs, how to each degree and kynde
> We should our selues demeane, to low, to hie;
> To friends, to foes, which skill men call Ciuility.
> (VI, x, 23)

It has often been noted that Book VI marks a return to the structural pattern of the first two books. Mount Acidale, as the allegorical heart of the book, would appear to correspond roughly to the House of Holiness and the Castle of Alma where the Redcrosse Knight and Guyon receive the religious and moral instruction which enables them to complete their missions. But if the function of the Graces is to teach men the art of civility, Calidore cannot reasonably be said to be in need of their instruction, for he has already proved his ability to behave with grace and decorum to friends and enemies alike. Because Colin Clout's account of the Graces appears to do little more than sum up what we have already witnessed in Calidore's actions, it is often assumed that 'There is nothing to explicate in the legend of Courtesy . . .'[34] However the real significance of the episode lies not in the summary definition of stanza 23, but in the iconography of the Graces, which Colin Clout analyses in the next stanza:

> Therefore they alwaies smoothly seeme to smile,
> That we likewise should mylde and gentle be,

> And also naked are, that without guile
> Or false dissemblaunce all them plaine may see,
> Simple and true from couert malice free:
> And eeke them selues so in their daunce they bore,
> That two of them still froward seem'd to bee,
> But one still towards shew'd her selfe afore;
> That good should from vs goe, then come in greater store.
> (VI, x, 24)

The Graces are, of course, one of the most familiar of all classical images used in the Renaissance. Their conventional pose – two facing the viewer and one with her back towards us, linked together by interlacing arms – traditionally signifies that grace consists of a triple movement: giving, accepting and returning.[35] This traditional reading of the mythological group is summed up as well as anywhere in the gloss to the 'April' eclogue of *The Shepheardes Calender*:

> The Graces be three sisters, the daughters of Iupiter . . . otherwise called Charites, that is thanks. Whom the Poetes feyned to be the Goddesses of al bountie and comelines, which therefore (as sayth Theodontius) they make three, to wete, that men first ought to be gracious and bountiful to other freely, then to receiue benefits at other mens hands curteously, and thirdly to requite them thankfully: which are three sundry Actions in liberalitye. And Boccace saith, that they be painted naked . . . the one hauing her backe towards vs, and her face fromwarde, as proceeding from vs: the other two toward vs, noting double thanke to be due to vs for the benefit, we haue done.[36]

But if we compare E.K.'s reading of the classical triad with Colin Clout's explanation, we find that Spenser has reversed the traditional configuration of the group, so that now only one of the figures is facing us, while two have their backs towards us. This, Colin Clout tells Calidore, is to signify that while no man can hope to escape adversity, misfortune is often followed by good in greater measure.

The corollary of Colin Clout's account of the Graces, which ought to be clear to Calidore after hearing Meliboe's discourse on resignation, is that, since fortune is by nature mutable, bestowing and withholding her gifts regardless of men's wishes, we should not expect to find perfect happiness in this world. Although Colin Clout takes this as being understood, the narrator makes it clear for the reader in the first stanza of the next canto:

The ioyes of loue, if they should euer last,
Without affliction or disquietnesse,
That worldly chaunces doe amongst them cast,
Would be on earth too great a blessednesse,
Liker to heauen, then mortall wretchednesse.
Therefore the winged God, to let men weet,
That here on earth is no sure happinesse,
A thousand sowres hath tempred with one sweet,
To make it seeme more deare and dainty, as is meet.
(VI, xi, 1)

In bringing home to us by vivid pictorial means the lesson of fortune's mutability the allegory of the Graces serves to underline a truth which has both been implied in previous events of the narrative and also directly stated by Meliboe. Only incidentally is it the function of this speaking picture to provide us with a summary of the particular social graces for which Calidore is renowned.

Calidore's vision on Mount Acidale is a vision of perfect harmony, order and grace symbolized by a dance. But it is a poetic vision summoned by the piper Colin Clout and not a reality to be found on earth; and on Calidore's intrusion it vanishes. When he returns to the shepherds two events occur which serve to destroy his illusions about the pastoral life. The first is an attack by a tiger which very nearly results in Pastorella's death; the second is the abduction by a band of outlaws of the whole company of shepherds while Calidore is away hunting in the woods. He returns to find that the shepherds have gone, their cottages have been demolished and their flocks driven away:

He sought the woods; but no man could see there:
He sought the plaines; but could no tydings heare.
The woods did nought but ecchoes vaine rebound;
The playnes all waste and emptie did appeare:
Where wont the shepheardes oft their pypes resound,
And feed an hundred flocks, there now not one he found.
(VI, xi, 26)

The disappearance of the shepherds is like the vanishing of the visionary dancers on Mount Acidale: it is as if an idyllic pastoral dream has suddenly evaporated. Indeed this is exactly what has happened. Despite Meliboe's repeated warnings that happiness does not depend upon fortunate circumstances; despite the truth symbolized in the masque of the Graces that fortune is by nature mutable, Calidore had persisted in his belief that the shepherds' life was one of perfect happiness. Now this illusion has been destroyed. Spenser's pastoral world does not represent nature in its 'pristine, prelapsarian state', as Tayler argues it does;[37] it has been shown to be subject, like any other world, to the rule of fortune. In place of the dangers of political life there are wild beasts and bands of outlaws to threaten man's security. Just as Shakespeare is careful to show that the native inhabitants of his countryside are mostly knaves or fools who must eat garlic in order to disguise their bad breath (*The Winter's Tale*, IV, iv, 162), so Spenser makes it clear that boorish shepherds are no match for a courteous knight. And it is ironical that Pastorella, who seems to Calidore to symbolize everything that is best in the pastoral life, owes her graces not to her rustic upbringing, but, like Perdita, to her noble birth. Calidore has learned by bitter experience the wisdom of the precepts whose real meaning he had failed to grasp. He has learned that, since no man can escape fortune's tyranny, it is vain to deceive oneself with false hopes of finding perfect happiness in a fallen world.

But if the ways of fortune are inscrutable, they are not capricious. As the Graces complete the sequence of their dance, like the revolving cycle of the seasons, so the good which is withheld from us will, in due time, return 'in greater store'. The prophetic truth of Colin Clout's interpretation of the dance of the Graces is revealed in the sequel to Pastorella's story. In comparing the shepherdess imprisoned in the 'hellish dens' (VI, xi, 3) of the brigands to a fading flower 'that feeles no heate of sunne' (VI, x, 44), Spenser is again alluding to the myth of Proserpina. Just as the restoration of Florimell to her lover was compared to the return of spring to the earth (IV, xii, 34), so Pastorella's release from an underworld of 'darkenesse dred and daily night' (VI, x, 42) is like a resurrection from the dead:

> So her vneath at last he did reuiue
> That long had lyen dead, and made againe aliue.
> (VI, xi, 50)

In rehearsing the most powerful of all primitive myths Spenser shows once more that, although suffering, privation and loss are an inescapable part of human existence, the eternal self-renewal of life betokens a beneficent natural order. This is the meaning of the visionary dance which Calidore witnesses on Mount Acidale. To break the sequence of its steps, as he had done, is to destroy a pattern which can only reveal itself in its 'comely order and proportion faire' in the fullness of time.

Calidore's decision to embrace the pastoral life may be seen, then, to be based on a partial view of nature. In itself his sentimental primitivism is not a particularly dangerous form of self-deception, and in a private individual might result in nothing more serious than personal disillusionment. However, its implications are far-reaching. We saw from Starkey's *Dialogue* that the corollary of a primitivistic conception of nature was a denial of the very principle of which Calidore, the servant of the court, is champion. To say, as Lewis does, that courtesy 'has very little connexion with court'[38] may be sadly true as a matter of fact; as a matter of principle, however, courtesy has everything to do with the court. Spenser himself reminds us that Calidore's virtue is etymologically connected with the court (VI, i, 1), the 'great schoolmistresse of all curtesy' (III, vi, 1). Similarly we cannot ignore the fact that its synonym, civility, is rooted in the concept of civilization. Though all the important sixteenth-century courtesy writers tacitly identify courtesy with service of the court as the focus of civilized life, it is Starkey who is most explicit in linking it with the cause of civilization:

> You know ryght wel, Master Pole, that to thys al men are borne and of nature brought forth, to commyn such gyftys as be to them gyuen, ych one to the profyt of other, *in perfayt cyuylyte*; and not to lyue to theyr owne plesure and profyt, wyth[out] regard of the wele of theyr cuntrey, forgettyng al justyce and equyte.[39]

It is because man is an imperfect creature inhabiting a fallen world that he needs the restraining discipline of 'polytyke ordur'. The task of the courteous man is to protect the court, the centre and focus of civilized life, from those forces which threaten its existence.

There is, of course, no absolute reason why devotion to the cause of *humanitas* should be incompatible with personal fulfilment. Spenser was, after all, no rigid Puritan, but a Christian humanist who believed in an ideal of human conduct based on regulation of the natural affectations rather than on their complete suppression. Similarly we are given no good reason for Calidore's refusal of Tristram's offer to assist him in his mission (VI, ii, 33-7). It may be asked, then, why the quest of the courteous man is shown to be an essentially solitary affair? The answer is that Calidore, like Lyly's Alexander, is in part an evocation of Elizabeth. In portraying a hero who is temporarily diverted from his task Spenser is no more criticizing Elizabeth for neglect of her royal office than Lyly is reproving her for sexual indiscretion. Both are simply defining courtesy in a way which has a special relevance for a celibate queen who, for nearly five decades, had devoted herself exclusively to her country's needs. As Elizabeth is inseparable from the court she rules, so she is a symbolic embodiment of the virtues for which it stands. It is in the sense of a representative of *humanitas* that Elizabeth is to be seen as a 'patterne . . . of Princely curtesie'.

## Notes

1. *The Allegory of Love*, p. 350.
2. See Dorothy Woodward Culp, 'Courtesy and Fortune's Chance in Book 6 of *The Faerie Queene*', *MP*, 68 (1971), 255-6 and Charles Clay Doyle, 'As Old Stories Tell: *Daphnis and Chloe* and the Pastoral Episode of *The Faerie Queene*, Book VI', *Neohelicon*, 5 (1977), 51-70.
3. These phrases have been taken, almost at random, from the selection of essays printed in the *Variorum Spenser*, Book VI, 317-48.
4. Humphrey Tonkin, *Spenser's Courteous Pastoral: Book Six of the 'Faerie Queene'* (Oxford, 1972), p. 172.
5. Kathleen Williams, 'Courtesy and Pastoral in *The Faerie Queene*, Book VI', *RES*, N.S., 13 (1962), 337.
6. Kate M. Warren, Introduction to an edition of *The Faerie Queene*, in *Variorum Spenser*, Book VI, 324.
7. Daniel Javitch, *Poetry and Courtliness in Renaissance England* (Princeton, 1978), p. 139.
8. Cain, *Praise in 'The Faerie Queene'*, p. 155. Cf. Nelson, who writes, 'The Legend of Courtesie, alone of the books of *The Faerie Queene*, contains no celebration of the Queen . . .' (*The Poetry of Edmund Spenser*, p. 293).
9. This is the view taken by Warren in the introduction to her edition, in *Variorum Spenser*, Book VI, 318.
10. J.C. Maxwell, 'The Truancy of Calidore', *ELH*, 19 (1952), 146.
11. Pp. 147-8.
12. *The Poetry of Edmund Spenser*, p. 293.
13. Maurice Evans, 'Courtesy and the Fall of Man', *ES*, 46 (1965), 215.
14. From Gr. βαρβαρισμός , 'unintelligible speech' (Ernest Klein, *A Comprehensive Etymological Dictionary of the English Language* (Amsterdam, 1966)).
15. Ben Jonson, *Timber or Discoveries*, *Ben Jonson*, edited by C.H. Herford and Percy and Evelyn Simpson, 11 vols (Oxford, 1925-52), VIII (1947), 620-1.
16. *Dialogue between Pole and Lupset*, p. 53. Cf. Cicero, *De Inventione*, I, ii, 2-3.
17. *Discoveries*, p. 621.
18. Richard Neuse, 'Book VI as Conclusion to *The Faerie Queene*', *ELH*, 35 (1968), 338.
19. On the distinction between the chronological primitivism of which Spenser, like Starkey's Lupset, is an advocate, and the cultural primitivism to which this view of man is so radically opposed, see Chapter 5, note 28. On the history of the feral man in classical, medieval and Renaissance literature see Hoxie Neale Fairchild, *The Noble Savage: A Study in Romantic Naturalism* (New York, 1928), pp. 1-22; Lovejoy and Boas, *Primitivism and Related Ideas in Antiquity*, pp. 287-367; Hayden White, 'The Forms of Wildness: Archaeology of an Idea' in *The Wild Man Within: An Image in Western Thought from the Renaissance to*

*Romanticism*, edited by Edward Dudley and Maximillian E. Novak (Pittsburg, 1972), pp. 3-38. Richard Bernheimer, *Wild Men in the Middle Ages: A Study in Art, Sentiment, and Demonology* (1952; rpt. New York, 1970) contains much valuable material but fails to distinguish with sufficient precision between the mythological monster who is biologically half human and half animal and the feral man, who, though fully human, is innocent of civilization's influence.

20. See Montaigne's essay 'Of Cannibals'.

21. Puttenham, *The Arte of English Poesie*, p. 35.

22. *Dialogue between Pole and Lupset*, p. 66 (my italics).

23. *Discoveries*, p. 593.

24. *The Structure of Allegory in 'The Faerie Queene'*, p. 195.

25. *Dialogue between Pole and Lupset*, p. 9.

26. P. 10.

27. See, for example, Castiglione, *The Book of the Courtier*, pp. 260-1; Sir Thomas More, *Utopia*, translated by Raphe Robinson, Everyman edn, edited by John O'Hagan (1910; rpt. London, 1918), pp. 18-19; Elyot, *The Governour*, pp. 227-9. In emphasizing the public responsibilities of the courtier these writers owe much to Cicero, *De Officiis*, I, xx, 67-73.

28. See Caspari, *Humanism and the Social Order in Tudor England*, pp. 1-27.

29. Smith and de Selincourt, p. 407.

30. *Tasso's Jerusalem Delivered: or Godfrey of Bulloign*, translated by Edward Fairfax, 4th edn (London, 1749), p. 350.

31. 'Courtesy and the Fall of Man', p. 212.

32. Culp, 'Courtesy and Fortune's Chance', p. 258.

33. Donald Cheney, *Spenser's Image of Nature: Wild Man and Shepherd in 'The Faerie Queene'* (New Haven, Conn., 1966), p. 220.

34. Kathleen Williams, *Spenser's Faerie Queene: The World of Glass*, p. 191.

35. See Wind, *Pagan Mysteries in the Renaissance*, pp. 31 ff.

36. Smith and de Selincourt, p. 434.

37. *Nature and Art in Renaissance Literature*, p. 113.

38. *The Allegory of Love*, p. 350. Cf. H.C. Chang, *Allegory and Courtesy in Spenser: A Chinese View*, Edinburgh University Studies in Language and Literature, VIII (Edinburgh, 1955), p. 175.

39. *Dialogue between Pole and Lupset*, p. 2 (my italics).

# 7 *SEMPER EADEM*: A LEGEND OF CONSTANCY

The 'Legend of Constancie' is no more than a fragment; but it forms an important part of our discussion for two reasons: first, because it summarizes in an explicit fashion ideas which have been expressed through image and symbol in earlier books of the poem; and second, because as a fragment the 'Mutabilitie' cantos provide, as Lewis suggests,[1] a clue to Spenser's method of composition, and consequently a valuable indication of Queen Elizabeth's role in the whole poem. The fragment suggests that, in defining the title virtue of each book, Spenser was at the same time characterizing Elizabeth and her political destiny. Though the critic may, for the convenience of himself and his reader, treat the moral and political aspects of the poem independently of each other, the 'Mutabilitie' cantos show, quite indisputably, that the two are ultimately inseparable.

Our analyses of Books IV, V and VI in particular have shown that, in the face of the growing tide of sceptical thought in the later sixteenth century, Spenser adopts the standpoint of an orthodox Christian humanist, professing a traditional cosmos whose order, grace and harmony reflect the wisdom of a beneficent Creator. For all the apparent pessimism of the proem to Book V, his view of the world is essentially an optimistic one. In their different ways both the Amidas/Bracidas incident in Book V and the dance of the Graces in Book VI serve to show that, though fate may appear to be harsh, there is, nevertheless, a beneficent, unchanging order which underlies the seemingly random flux of events in the world. It is, however, a pattern which can only be revealed in the fullness of time. This truth is expressed in mythic terms in the parallel experiences of Florimell and Pastorella, both of whom undergo, like Proserpina, a period of privation before they are restored once more to the upper world. Their stories show that the same law which governs the cycle of the seasons also governs the operation of fate, ensuring that, although 'good should from vs goe', it will in due time 'come in greater store' (VI, x, 24) in the same way that spring follows winter. This cyclical view of time is fundamental to the conception of the whole poem. Though it is time which brings about change, suffering and loss, it is time also which reveals the divine pattern of which the portentous events celebrated in the poem form a part – a pattern which is observable in the span of a man's life, in the four seasons of the year and in the course of history itself. These ideas are now recapitulated at the trial of Mutabilitie. Concerning the essential nature of the philosophy expressed in canto vii, most modern Spenserians are in agreement. What no critic has attempted, however, is to show how these ideas form part of Spenser's epideictic purpose.

The speech in which the titaness defends her claim to universal sovereignty is one of the most eloquent passages in *The Faerie Queene*. The mutability of the natural world is, of course, a commonplace in Elizabethan literature; but nowhere is this familiar theme given more impressive statement than in the titaness's great address to the assembled company of gods on Arlo hill. The world she evokes is one ruled in all its aspects by change. Not only men and beasts, but even the earth itself, 'great mother of vs all' (VII, vii, 17), is subject to mutability:

> For, all that from her springs, and is ybredde,
> How-euer fayre it flourish for a time,
> Yet see we soone decay; and, being dead,
> To turne again vnto their earthly slime:
> Yet, out of their decay and mortall crime,
> We daily see new creatures to arize;
> And of their Winter spring another Prime,
> Vnlike in forme, and chang'd by strange disguise:
> So turne they still about, and change in restlesse wise.
> (VII, vii, 18)

In support of her claim that all things are ruled by change, Mutabilitie summons a procession of seasons, months, hours, day, night, and finally, life and death. In a poem celebrated for its pageantry this solemn spectacle of time's ineluctable passage is without comparison. 'Who sees not', demands the titaness when this majestic procession has passed by, 'that *Time* on all doth pray?' (VII, vii, 47). In reply to her challenge Jove points out that though 'all things . . . that vnder heauen dwell/Are chaung'd of *Time*', it is the gods who are responsible for directing the course of time (VII, vii, 48). But Mutabilitie will not accept his argument, claiming that not even the gods themselves are free from time's jurisdiction. Even Cynthia, first among goddesses, bears nightly testimony to the universal rule of mutability:

> Euen you faire *Cynthia*, whom so much ye make
> *Ioues* dearest darling, she was bred and nurst
> On *Cynthus* hill, whence she her name did take:

> Then is she mortall borne, how-so ye crake;
> Besides, her face and countenance euery day
> We changed see, and sundry forms partake,
> Now hornd, now round, now bright, now brown and gray:
> So that *as changefull as the Moone* men vse to say.
> (VII, vii, 50)

After demonstrating that the other heavenly bodies are equally changeable, Mutabilitie then sums up her argument:

> Then since within this wide great *Vniuerse*
> Nothing doth firme and permanent appeare,
> But all things tost and turned by transuerse:
> What then should let, but I aloft should reare
> My Trophee, and from all, the triumph beare?
> Now iudge then (O thou greatest goddesse trew!)
> According as thy selfe doest see and heare,
> And vnto me addoom that is my dew;
> That is the rule of all, all being rul'd by you.
> (VII, vii, 56)

Considering the length and the eloquence of the case for the defence, the judge's reply is a brief one:

> I well consider all that ye haue sayd,
> And find that all things stedfastnes doe hate
> And changed be: yet being rightly wayd
> They are not changed from their first estate;
> But by their change their being doe dilate:
> And turning to themselues at length againe,
> Doe worke their owne perfection so by fate:
> Then ouer them Change doth not rule and raigne;
> But they raigne ouer change, and doe their states maintaine.
> (VII, vii, 58)

Despite its brevity, however, nature's verdict must come as no surprise, for it is a view which has been implied many times during the course of the poem.[2]

A number of classical, medieval and Renaissance writers including Empedocles,[3] Aristotle,[4] Lucretius,[5] Ovid,[6] Boethius,[7] Alain,[8] Lipsius[9] and Bruno[10] have been adduced as sources for the view of nature expressed in canto vii. As an artist Spenser clearly drew extensively on the long speech of Pythagoras in the fifteenth book of the *Metamorphoses*. But the philosophy of the 'Mutabilitie' cantos cannot be traced to any one classical or medieval source. It is true also that similar ideas or even phrases may be found in such writers as Boethius, Alain or Lipsius. But books like *De Consolatione Philosophiae*, *De Planctu Naturae* and *De Constantia* are themselves popularizations of classical and medieval humanist commonplaces and cannot be regarded as, in any real sense of the term, philosophic source material. More important than attempting to establish a specific precedent for Spenser's ideas is to see what part this body of conventional wisdom plays in the definition of constancy.

Our understanding of what Spenser means by constancy is naturally limited by the fragmentary nature of Book VII, for we have none of the illustrative narrative material which he normally uses as a vehicle for displaying the various facets of his hero's virtue. What is clear from canto vii, however, is that, as a personal and social virtue constancy, like friendship and justice, is to be seen as the operation in the world of man of a cosmic principle.

Now constancy is one of the fundamental characteristics of the Pythagorean cosmos: though the four elements of which all things are framed are in a state of endless flux, continually dissolving one into another, the end result is a state of perfect equilibrium. Ovid's Pythagoras explains how

> The earth resolving leysurely dooth melt too water sheere,
> The water fyned turnes too aire. The aire eeke purged cleere
> From grossenesse, spyreth up aloft, and there becommeth fyre.
> (Golding, XV, 270-2)

But this series of transmutations is only a part of the complete pattern. As in a country dance (to borrow Du Bartas's simile) where a complex series of steps brings each dancer back to his original position, so the four elements continue their metamorphoses until they are restored once more to their original state, when the whole cycle can begin again: 'From thence in order contrary they back ageine retyre' (XV, 273). Thus, says Pythagoras, while it is true that all things are subject to mutability, this change takes place within a stable system so that the sum total of things remains constant:

> And though that varyably

Things passe perchaunce from place to place: yit all from whence they came
Returning, doo unperrisshed continew still the same.
(XV, 282-4)

It is, ironically, Mutabilitie herself who sums up this familiar idea in an argument which effectively undermines her own case:

Thus, all these fower (the which the ground-work bee
Of all the world, and of all liuing wights)
To thousand sorts of *Change* we subiect see:
Yet are they chang'd (by other wondrous slights)
Into themselues, and lose their natiue mights;
The Fire to Aire, the th'Ayre to Water sheere,
And Water into Earth: yet Water fights
With Fire, and Aire with Earth approaching neere:
Yet all are in one body, and as one appeare.
(VII, vii, 25)

In his interpretation of nature the apologist of a Pythagorean cosmos must explain a paradox: he must explain how discord is essential to harmony, how multeity is comprised in unity, how change is subsumed by constancy. Alain, for example, tells his reader that

> after the universal Maker had clothed all things with the forms for their natures, and had wedded them in marriage with proportions suitable to them individually, [He wished] that by the round of mutual relation of birth and death there should to perishable things be given *stability through instability, infinity through impermanence, eternity through transientness*, and that a series of things should be continually woven together in unbroken reciprocation of birth . . .[11]

These paradoxes are best explained by reference to the dual nature of time. Although, as Mutabilitie so vividly demonstrates, hours, days, months and seasons all follow one another in relentless succession, their sequence forms an eternally self-renewing cycle.[12] This cyclical nature of time is commonly represented by Renaissance cosmographers and poets either diagrammatically in the form of a pictorial calendar or by imagery and structural symbolism. The most brilliant example of the latter is Spenser's own *Epithalamion.*[13] While the course of a single day is symbolized by the chiming of the hourly bell in the concluding lines of each of the twenty-four stanzas, we are reminded, by the total number of long lines in the poem (365), that this one day is part of a larger unit of time. However, through imagery of flowers and garlands and by means of the circular form of the poem where 'opposite' stanzas are matched against each other, Spenser also symbolizes the eternal revolution of the heavens. In this way he shows that days and years are part of an unending cycle of time. What makes *Epithalamion* unique is not the idea of symbolizing the nature of time by structural means, but the subtlety and complexity of the poem's organization. Indeed so familiar is the calendar in medieval and Renaissance art and literature as a symbol of time's dual nature that the contemporary reader could scarcely be unaware of the irony of Mutabilitie's pageant. Far from clinching her argument, the procession she summons in support of her claim to universal sovereignty is the most eloquent proof she could have chosen had she been attempting to demonstrate nature's constancy. The phrase which sums up most succinctly the paradox which is implied by the term constancy is the phrase which Spenser uses in his account of the Garden of Adonis. Although Adonis is himself 'subject to mortalitie', as a symbol of life's eternal self-renewal he is 'eterne in mutabilitie' (III, vi, 47).

If constancy is analagous to friendship in the sense that it embodies one of the fundamental paradoxes of the Pythagorean cosmos, it is also like friendship in being one of the chief characteristics of another great enigma – that of England's virgin 'wife' and 'mother'. The fact that the canto which was clearly intended as the philosophic 'core' of Book VII is preceded by an allegory of the Queen,[14] depicted first as Cynthia, then as Diana, lends support to our claim that the character of Elizabeth forms an integral part of the poem's moral scheme.

The function of the allegory of Cynthia is twofold: it serves both as a vehicle for praising Elizabeth as universal empress, and also as a device for anatomizing the nature of constancy as it is embodied in her person. At the Ditchley entertainments of 1592, a debate between Constancy and Inconstancy is resolved by the silent presence of the Queen. In the final speech of the tableau, Inconstancy confesses that

> I am not, I cannot be as I was, the leaue that I did take of my selfe, is to leaue my selfe, and to change, or rather to be changed to that estate which admitteth no change: by the secret power of hir, who though she were content to let me be caried almost out of breath with the winde of inconstancie, doth now in hir silence put me to silence, and by the glorie of hir countenance, which disperseth the

flying cloudes of vaine conceites, commands me to wishe others, and to be my selfe as she is, *Semper eadem*.[15]

In a study of iconic representations of Elizabeth in *The Faerie Queene*, Cain argues that the story of Mutabilitie's attack on Cynthia represents a subversion of this cult.[16] It is true that in naming her page Vesper Spenser is hinting at the fact that the Queen is now in the evening of her life; true also that Mutabilitie does succeed in halting Cynthia's chariot, so that the world is momentarily plunged in darkness (VII, vi, 14). But lunar eclipses are only temporary phenomena, and in the next canto it is revealed that the titaness's claim to sovereignty of the heavens has been rejected. We do not need to be reminded, by such examples as *Paradise Lost*, that rebellions which fail have the effect, not of undermining authority, but of confirming it. To emphasize the point Spenser follows the story of Mutabilitie's attempted usurpation of Cynthia's throne with another allegory of rebellion, this time in the form of an anti-masque.[17] If there is any doubt concerning the integrity of Cynthia's reputation after Mutabilitie's futile attack, it is dispelled by the farcical tale of Faunus and his oafish attempt to spy on Diana as she bathes. But even this fabliau contains a serious meaning. By showing Faunus, Satan-like, corrupting the nymph Molanna with 'Queen-apples, and red Cherries from the tree' (VII, vi, 43), Spenser reminds us of a fact which has been brought to our attention many times in *The Faerie Queene*, namely that Elizabeth rules in a fallen world where authority is continually subject to threat from the baser elements of humanity.

Although, as Mutabilitie points out in her trial speech, Cynthia is renowned for her changeableness, it should be recalled that she is also nature's most accurate time-piece.[18] Combining as she does the antithetical qualities of mutability and regularity, she is the perfect symbol of the constancy which characterizes the cosmos as a whole. It was these paradoxes which Elizabeth's poets and artists[19] seized upon in their idealization of the Queen as Cynthia. In a lyric from Dowland's *Third Book of Airs* the neophyte who ponders the mystery of 'A woman with a constant mind' is invited to compare this unique 'Queen of love and beauty' with the moon 'That ever in one change doth grow/ Yet still the same':

Say, Love, if ever thou didst find
A woman with a constant mind?
None but one.
And what should that rare mirror be?

Some goddess or some queen is she?
  She, she, she, and only she,
She only Queen of love and beauty.

But could thy fiery poisoned dart
At no time touch her spotless heart,
      Nor come near?
She is not subject to Love's bow;
Her eye commands, her heart saith No,
  No, no, no, and only no!
One No another still doth follow.

How might I that fair wonder know
That mocks desire with endless No?
      See the moon
That ever in one change doth grow
Yet still the same; and she is so,
  So, so, so, and only so.
From heaven her virtues she doth borrow.

To her then yield thy shafts and bow
That can command affections so.
      Love is free;
So are her thoughts that vanquish thee.
There is no Queen of love but she,
  She, she, she, and only she,
She only Queen of love and beauty.[20]

With the possible exception of Ralegh's lost poem, the most complete expressions of the cult of Cynthia are Lyly's *Endimion* and Chapman's *The Shadow of Night*. In a long speech from the opening scene of the play Endimion begins his encomium of Cynthia by appealing to her absolute constancy:

> O fayre *Cynthia*, why doe others terme thee vnconstant, whom I haue euer founde vnmoueable? Iniurious tyme, corrupt manners, vnkind men, who finding a constancy not to be matched in my sweete Mistris, haue christned her with the name of wauering, waxing, and waning. Is shee inconstant that keepeth a setled course, which since her first creation altereth not one minute in her mouing? (I, i, 30-6)

But there is another reason why the moon was regarded as a peculiarly apt symbol for Elizabeth. As Endimion elaborates his conceit he observes: 'There is nothing thought more admirable or commendable in the sea, then the ebbing and flowing; and shall the Moone, from whom the Sea taketh this vertue, be accounted fickle for encreasing, & decreasing?' (I, i, 36-9). It is probably the fact of its world-wide influence over the tides which led to the moon's being seen as a symbol of empire.[21] In a pageant at Elvethem in 1591 Cynthia is described as 'the wide Oceans Empresse';[22] three years later in the enigmatic *Shadow of Night*, Chapman hails his goddess as empress of 'Earth, seas, and hell';[23] and when in the 'Mutabilitie' cantos an attempt is made to usurp Cynthia's throne, it is her twin dominions of the night and the sea over which the titaness seeks to gain control (VII, vi, 10). It is this tradition of lunar symbolism upon which Spenser is drawing when he praises Elizabeth as a 'glorious virgin Queene' who 'In widest Ocean . . . her throne does reare/That ouer all the earth it may be seene' (II, ii, 40). For him, as for Lyly, Cynthia symbolized the mystery of the Queen's paradoxical nature: her notoriously fickle temperament on the one hand, and her steadfast devotion (summed up in her personal motto *semper eadem*) to her imperial mission on the other.

These two quite separate aspects of lunar symbolism – the paradoxical constancy of the moon and its association with the idea of universal empire – are brought together in Book VII in a single image rich in emotive power. The figure of the 'mortall borne' (VII, vii, 50) virgin queen who can never be permanently eclipsed, but who reigns in heaven 'in euerlasting glory' (VII, vi, 8); who is identified with the moon and is environed with stars (VII, vi, 9); who exercises dominion over the seas; who miraculously defies change so that 'Time stands still with gazing on her face';[24] and who is a type of constancy and a 'ioy to weary wandring trauailers' (VII, vi, 9) is an unmistakable allusion to the Virgin Mary. All these ideas – the paradoxes of mortal divinity and inconstant constancy; sovereignty of the heavens; identification with the moon and the pole star; dominion over the seas; and miraculous defiance of time – are familiar aspects of the cult of the Virgin;[25] but it is now Elizabeth, as Cynthia, to whom these special powers and privileges are being applied. In much the same way that the providential nature of Britomart's mystical union with Artegall is implied by the Marian imagery of Book III, so the idea of Elizabeth's imperial destiny is reinforced by allusion to the Queen of Heaven. As Mary had, for centuries, been seen as a type of the Church and a symbol of its temporal aspirations, so Spenser is claiming that Elizabeth, as a post-figuration of the Virgin, is a predestined 'Prince of peace from heaven blest'. Only by ignoring these iconographic details is it possible to claim, with Cain, that the allegory of canto vi is a subversion of the cult of Elizabeth. Far from undermining her authority, the 'Legend of Constancie' is one of Spenser's most explicit apologies for Elizabeth's imperial claims.

Although we can only speculate about the kind of adventures which would have formed the bulk of the narrative of Book VII, we can be quite certain about the essential nature of the virtue this book was intended to portray. Constancy, like friendship and justice, is both a moral ideal to which the individual must attempt to approximate in his personal conduct, and also a cosmic principle. Elizabeth, as Cynthia, is at the centre of the book because she combines, in a unique fashion, both aspects of this virtue: she is not only a pattern and example of the former, but she is also, by virtue of her regal position as God's deputy on earth, a living embodiment of the latter. If the poet's epideictic purpose seems alien to the modern reader, it was a very familiar one to Spenser's contemporaries. The delicate balance it wished to achieve between gracious compliment and reverence for a divine principle is perhaps best caught by Lyly in a dialogue from the second act of *Endimion*:

*End.* . . . of *Cynthia* we are allowed not to talke but to wonder, because her vertues are not within the reach of our capacities.
*Tellus.* Why, she is but a woman.
*End.* No more was *Venus*.
*Tellus.* Shee is but a virgin.
*End.* No more was *Vesta*.
*Tellus.* Shee shall haue an ende.
*End.* So shall the world.
*Tellus.* Is not her beautie subiect to time?
*End.* No more then time is to standing still.
*Tellus.* Wilt thou make her immortall?
*End.* No, but incomparable.

(II, i, 77-88)

The particular importance of the 'Mutabilitie' fragment lies in the fact that it provides, as Lewis argues, an important clue to Spenser's method of composition. It suggests that he was in the habit of working from an allegorical 'core' containing the essence of his moral, and then filling out this definition with accretive narrative material. Of especial significance is what the fragment tells us about Elizabeth's role in the poem. It shows that she is not simply a gracious *dea ex machina* wheeled out at appropriately dramatic moments in order to provide the poet with an excuse for some discreet flattery, but that she is at the conceptual centre of the poem. *The Faerie Queene* was conceived, like the *Aeneid*, as a great national poem. As Virgil had praised Augustus through the noble deeds of his 'ancestor' Aeneas, so Spenser used the myth of Britain's Trojan origins as a means of suggesting the idea of providence working through history. But the myth of Troy was not capable of expressing the idea of Britain's specifically Protestant destiny. Drawing on the medieval interpretation of Virgil's fourth Eclogue as a prophecy of the return of the Virgin, Spenser employed a religious typology to portray Elizabeth – the one figure in whom are united the various virtues portrayed in *The Faerie Queene* – as a Christian prince restoring peace and justice to a fallen world.

## Notes

1. *The Allegory of Love*, p. 353.

2. In a subtly argued article Lewis J. Owen challenges nature's verdict, claiming that its failure to refute Mutabilitie's evidence may explain the pessimism of the two stanzas of the unfinished eighth canto ('Mutable in Eternity: Spenser's Despair and the Multiple Forms of Mutabilitie', *JMRS*, 2 (1972), 49-68). Persuasive as it is, Owen's discussion is open to the objection that it fails adequately to consider the argument of the 'Mutabilitie' cantos in the context (i) of the theory of nature developed in the completed books of the poem, and (ii) of the title virtue of Book VII.

3. Evelyn May Albright, 'Spenser's Cosmic Philosophy and His Religion', *PMLA*, 44 (1929), 715-59.

4. William Fenn De Moss, *The Influence of Aristotle's 'Politics' and 'Ethics' on Spenser* (Chicago, 1920), pp. 57-64.

5. Edwin Greenlaw, 'Spenser and Lucretius', *SP*, 17 (1920), 455-63.

6. William P. Cumming, 'The Influence of Ovid's *Metamorphoses* on Spenser's "Mutabilitie" Cantos', *SP*, 28 (1931), 241-56.

7. Brents Stirling, 'The Concluding Stanzas of *Mutabilitie*', *SP*, 30 (1933), 193-204.

8. Edwin Greenlaw, 'Some Old Religious Cults in Spenser', *SP*, 20 (1923), 219-31.

9. Albright, 'Spenser's Cosmic Philosophy and His Religion', p. 722.

10. Ronald B. Levinson, 'Spenser and Bruno', *PMLA*, 43 (1928), 675-81.

11. Alain de Lille, *The Complaint of Nature*, translated by Douglas M. Moffat, Yale Studies in English, XXXVI (New York, 1908), pp. 43-4 (my italics).

12. For a valuable discussion of this point see Sherman Hawkins, 'Mutabilitie and the Cycle of the Months' in *Form and Convention in the Poetry of Edmund Spenser, Selected Papers from the English Institute*, edited by William Nelson (New York and London, 1961), pp. 88 ff. See also Joanne Field Holland, 'The Cantos of Mutabilitie and the Form of *The Faerie Queene*', *ELH*, 35 (1968), 21-4; Michael Holahan, '*Iamque opus exegi*: Ovid's Changes and Spenser's Brief

Epic of Mutability', *ELR*, 6 (1976), 264.

13. See A. Kent Hieatt, *Short Time's Endless Monument: the Symbolism of the Numbers in Spenser's 'Epithalamion'* (New York, 1960).

14. For discussions of Cynthia as Elizabeth in canto vi see Judah K. Stampfer, '*The Cantos of Mutability*: Spenser's Last Testament of Faith', *UTQ*, 21 (1952), 152-3; William Blissett, 'Spenser's Mutabilitie' in *Essays in English Literature from the Renaissance to the Victorian Age, presented to A.S.P. Woodhouse 1964*, edited by Millar MacLure and F.W. Watt (Toronto, 1964), pp. 26-42; Richard N. Ringler, 'The Faunus Episode', *MP*, 63 (1965), 12-13; Robin Headlam Wells, '*Semper Eadem*: Spenser's "Legend of Constancie"', *MLR*, 73 (1978), 250-5; Holahan, '*Iamque opus exegi*: Ovid's Changes and Spenser's Brief Epic of Mutability', pp. 257-8.

15. 'The Ditchley Entertainment' printed by E.K. Chambers in *Sir Henry Lee: An Elizabethan Portrait* (Oxford, 1936), Appendix E, p. 289.

16. Cain, *Praise in 'The Faerie Queene'*, p. 182. See also Blissett, 'Spenser's Mutabilitie', pp. 31-4.

17. For discussions of the Faunus episode as parody of the allegory of Cynthia see Hawkins, p. 84 and Ringler, pp. 15-19.

18. These apparently contradictory aspects of lunar symbolism are fully documented by Warner, *Alone of All Her Sex*, pp. 261-2.

19. For a discussion of representations of Elizabeth as Cynthia in contemporary portraiture see Strong, *The Cult of Elizabeth*, pp. 48, 52.

20. John Dowland, *Third Book of Airs*, edited by Edmund Horace Fellowes, *The English School of Lutenist Song Writers* (London, 1923), p. 24.

21. See Yates, 'Elizabeth as Astraea', pp. 35, 72.

22. Quoted by Wilson, *England's Eliza*, p. 299.

23. 'Hymnvs in Cynthiam', *The Poems of George Chapman*, edited by Phyllis Brooks Bartlett (New York, 1962), p. 31.

24. The phrase is the first line of a lyric from Dowland's *Third Book of Airs*, p. 7.

25. The Virgin Mary's quasi-divine sovereignty of heaven and earth and her identification with the moon have been documented in earlier chapters. For the idea of the Virgin as a celestial luminary which can never be eclipsed see Lydgate's *Life of Our Lady*, p. 554. The image of the Virgin as a seafarer's guide is a commonplace of Marian literature; it is repeatedly used by Lydgate in his lyrics to the Virgin. See also Petrarch's *Hymn to the Virgin*.

# APPENDIX: POLYDORE VERGIL AND ENGLISH HISTORIOGRAPHY

Since it is clear that the Elizabethans were by no means naive in their attitude to history, it may be enquired how the notion arose of the 'incredibly uncritical . . . appetite shown by the Elizabethans for literature dealing with the myths or history of their country'.[1] The idea is based, to a large extent, on Greenlaw's claim that most sixteenth-century British historiographers sought for patriotic reasons to promote the Trojan myth which Polydore Vergil had discredited in his *Historia Anglica* (1534-55).[2]

Polydore wrote his history at the invitation of Henry VIII; but although he claims diplomatically neither to 'affirm as trew, nether reproove as false, the judgement of one or other as concerning the originall of soe auncient a people, referring all things . . . to the consideration of the reader . . .' he makes it abundantly plain that he has nothing but contempt for the 'easye credit' of those British chroniclers who treat the Trojan myth as historical fact.[3] 'In olde time', writes Polydore,

> mani nations weare so bowlde as to derive the beginninge of their stocke from the Goddes (as especiallie the Romaines did), to thentent the originall of there people and citties mighte bee the more princelie and prosperus, which things, albeit thei sownded more like fabels then the sincere witnesses of noble acts, yet weare thei receaved for trewthe; for the which cause even those things which last of all were committed to writinge of the antiquities of Britaines, were with soe easye credit receaved of the common sorte that thei have ascribid the fownteine of theire genialogie to Brutus . . .[4]

Greenlaw suggests that, in demolishing a national myth, Polydore 'precipitated a conflict of far-reaching importance'.[5] While popular opinion denounced him as a traitor, iconoclast and papist, historiographers (we are told) strenuously countered Polydore's history by reaffirming the truth of Geoffrey of Monmouth's early British chronicles.

Polydore may have been an unpopular figure, but he was also an influential one. While British historiographers might affect to despise him, they respected his scholarship and paid him the compliment of imitating his methods. Indeed it was Polydore's humanist principles which were, in a large part, responsible for the character of historiography in sixteenth-century England.[6] Before the sixteenth century the task of the chronicler was frankly moral. History was valuable because it revealed an eternal pattern of sin and divine punishment. If records of the past were valued for their moral utility, the criterion by which events were judged to be important was their illustrative power, not their historical veracity.

In the sixteenth century, historiographers did not cease to believe that the chief function of history was to teach; but they had learnt a new respect for historical accuracy. Polydore tells us that

> The fyrst office of an historiographer is to write no lye, the seconde that he shall conzel no trueth, for favoure, displeasure, or feare. The perfection of an historie resteth in matter and wordes. The order of the matter requyreth, observaunce of tymes, descripcions of places, the maners, lyves of men, theyr behavoures, purposes, occacions, dedes, saiynges, casaultes, achevynges, & finishyng of thynges. The tenour of the wordes asketh a brefe perspicuite and syncere trueth, with moderate and peaceable ornamentes.[7]

Polydore's credo could not be ignored, even if its consequences were sometimes unwelcome for patriotic Englishmen. Of particular delicacy was the matter of Britain's early history and the Galfridian claim that a British prince would return to rule the kingdom. Where did sixteenth-century English historiographers stand on this question? Greenlaw maintains that they upheld the old story in their glorification of the House of Tudor. He cites the following passage from Hall's *Chronicle* dealing with the accession of Henry VII:

> It was by a heavenly voyce reveled to Cadwalader last kyng of Brytons that his stocke and progeny should reigne in this land and bear domynion agayn: Whereupon most men were persuaded in their awne opinion by this heavenly voice he was provided and ordeined long before to enjoye and obteine this kyngdome, whiche thing kyng Henry the vi did also shewe before.[8]

Greenlaw's citation is misleading, however, because he omits the words with which Hall prefaces his account: 'Men commonly report that . . .' The omission is, admittedly, a small one; but its effect is to transform the record of hearsay into a statement of historical fact. It is difficult, furthermore, to take seriously the claim that Hall opposed himself to Polydore on this question when it is pointed out that his cautious observation concerning Cadwallader's revelation is a verbatim translation from the twenty-sixth book of the *Historia Anglica*.[9]

The great theme of Hall's *Chronicle* was the achievement of the House of Tudor in bringing peace to a divided nation: 'The olde deuided controuersie betwene the . . . families of Lancastre and Yorke', writes Hall in his introduction,

> by the vnion of Matrimony celebrate and consummate betwene the high and mighty Prince Kyng Henry the seuenth and the Lady Elizabeth his moste worthy Quene, the one beeyng indubitate heire of the hous of Lancastre, and the other of Yorke was suspended and appalled in the person of their most noble, puissant and mighty heire kyng Henry the eight, and by hym clerely buried and perpetually extinct.[10]

The moral to be drawn from the events related is a simple one: it is to enable men to perceive 'that by discord greate thynges decaie and fall to ruine, so the same by concord be reuiued and erected'.[11]

However, it is one thing to suggest that a marriage which brought peace to the country by uniting the houses of Lancaster and York received the blessing of heaven, and quite another to justify a claim to the throne on the basis of a legendary genealogy. Hall may well have been personally attracted to the Trojan myth, indeed it would have suited his purposes admirably; but we do him an injustice as a historiographer if we claim that he believed in its literal truth. Although he mentions Geoffrey in his dedicatory epistle, and refers briefly to the story of Brutus's division of the kingdom between his three sons in his defence of England's right to political hegemony of the British Isles,[12] Hall makes no attempt to verify or discredit the Trojan myth. In short, he treats the legends concerning Britain's ancient past as myth, and not as historical fact. Holinshed likewise reproduces Hall's translation of the *Historia Anglica* on the subject of Cadwallader's prophetic revelation;[13] while later writers, such as Camden and Speed, follow Polydore in treating the whole myth with politely damning scepticism.[14]

The importance of Greenlaw's work on national myth in Elizabethan literature must not be underestimated. But the suggestion that sixteenth-century British historiographers accepted the Trojan myth as a substantially veracious account of the past is misleading. For it not only devalues historiography, but also disguises the fact that the Elizabethans, far from being naïve in their espousal of the Troy story, had a highly sophisticated conception of myth and its relation to history.

## Notes

1. E.M.W. Tillyard, *The English Epic and its Background* (London, 1954), p. 321.
2. *Studies in Spenser's Historical Allegory*, pp. 4-15.
3. *Polydore Vergil's English History, from an Early Translation* (a contemporary translation of Books 1-VIII), edited by Sir Henry Ellis, Camden Society Reprints (London, 1846), p. 31.
4. Polydore Vergil, p. 31.
5. Greenlaw, p. 4.
6. See Denys Hay (ed.), *The* Anglica Historia *of Polydore Vergil A.D. 1485-1537* (a text, with English translation by the editor, of Books XXIV-XXVII), Camden Society Reprints, 3rd series, LXXIV (London, 1950), pp. xxvi ff.
7. *An Abridgement of the Notable Worke of Polydore Vergil*, translated by Thomas Langley (1546), quoted by Levy, *Tudor Historical Thought*, pp. 62-3.
8. *Hall's Chronicle*, quoted by Greenlaw, p. 9.
9. Fuit ille annus salutis MCCCCLXXXVI. Henricus sic regnum adeptus est, quod Dei nutu atque consilio gestum, & prouisum esse, uisum est, quanto abhinc, id est, ex hoc anno salutis 1486, annos DCCXCVII memoriae proditum ferunt, uocem divinitus Cadoualladro ultimo Britannorum regi, ut supra memoraui, redditam, eius progenium rursus regnaturam (*Historia Anglica* (Basel, 1555), p. 566).
10. *Hall's Chronicle*, p. 1.
11. *Hall's Chronicle*, p. 2.
12. *Hall's Chronicle*, p. 851.
13. Raphael Holinshed, *Chronicles of England, Scotland and Ireland*, 6 vols (1577-86; rpt. London, 1807-8), III, 481.
14. Camden, *Britain*, pp. 5-6; John Speed, Proem to *The Historie of Great Britaine* (London, 1611).

# LIST OF WORKS CITED

## Primary Sources

Note: this part of the bibliography does not list authors who have been quoted from secondary sources such as Wilson's *England's Eliza*.


Alain de Lille, *The Complaint of Nature*, translated by Douglas M. Moffat, Yale Studies in English, XXXVI (New York, 1908)

Aquinas, St Thomas, *Summa Theologiae*, translated and edited by Thomas Gilbey, OP and others, 60 vols (London, 1963-76)

Aristotle, *The 'Art' of Rhetoric*, translated by John Henry Freese, Loeb Classical Library (London, 1926)

— *The Nichomachean Ethics*, translated by H. Rackham, Loeb Classical Library (London, 1926)

Baldwin, William, *The Mirror for Magistrates* (1559), edited by Lily B. Campbell (New York, 1960)

Bale, John, *The Dramatic Writings of John Bale*, edited by John S. Farmer, Early English Dramatists Series (London, 1907)

— *The Image of Both Churches, Select Works of John Bale*, edited by Henry Christmas, Parker Society Reprints (Cambridge, 1849)

Bernard, St, *Saint Bernard on the Song of Songs:* Sermones in Cantica Canticorum, translated and edited by 'A Religious of C.S.M.V.' (London, 1952)

Bible, The Geneva, facsimile of the 1560 edition with an introduction by Lloyd E. Berry (Madison, Wisc., 1969)

Boccaccio, Giovanni, *Genealogie Deorum Gentilium Libri*, edited by Vincenzo Romano, 2 vols (Bari, 1951), *Opere*, edited by several hands, 7 vols (Bari, 1928-51)

Bodin, Jean, *Six Books of the Commonwealth*, abridged and translated by M.J. Tooley (Oxford, 1955)

Boethius, *Boethius' Consolation of Philosophy*, translated by George Colville (1556), edited by Ernest Belfort Bax, The Tudor Library Series, V (London, 1897)

Bryskett, Lodowick, *A Discourse of Civill Life: Containing the Ethike part of Morall Philosophie* (London, 1606)

Calvin, John, *Institutes of the Christian Religion*, translated by Henry Beveridge, 2 vols (London, 1949)

Camden, William, *Britain, or a Chorographicall Description of the Most Flourishing Kingdomes, England, Scotland, and Ireland . . .*, translated by Philemon Holland (London, 1610)

Campion, Thomas, *The Works of Thomas Campion*, edited by Walter R. Davis (1967; rpt. London, 1969)

Case, John, *Sphaera Civitatis* (Oxford, 1588)

Castiglione, Baldassare, *The Book of the Courtier*, translated by Sir Thomas Hoby, Everyman edn (1928; rpt. London, 1966)

Chapman, George, *The Poems of George Chapman*, edited by Phyllis Brooks Bartlett (New York, 1962)

Cheke, Sir John, *The True Subiect to the Rebell: Or the Hurt of Sedition, How Grievous it is to a Common-wealth* (1549; rpt. Oxford, 1641)

[Cicero], *Rhetorica ad Herennium*, translated by Harry Caplan, Loeb Classical Library (London, 1954)
Cicero, *De Inventione*, translated by H.M. Hubbell, Loeb Classical Library (London, 1949)
— *De Legibus*, translated by Clinton Walker Keyes, Loeb Classical Library (London, 1928)
— *De Officiis*, translated by Walter Miller, Loeb Classical Library (London, 1947)
— *De Oratore*, translated by E.W. Sutton, Loeb Classical Library, 2 vols (London, 1948)
— *De Re Publica*, translated by Clinton Walker Keyes, Loeb Classical Library (London, 1928)
Daniel, Samuel, *The Complete Works in Verse and Prose of Samuel Daniel*, edited by Alexander B. Grosart, 5 vols (London, 1885)
Davies, Sir John, *The Poems of Sir John Davies*, edited by Robert Krueger (Oxford, 1975)
Davison, Francis, *Davison's Poetical Rhapsody* (1602), edited by A.H. Bullen, 2 vols (London, 1890)
De Malynes, Gerrard, *Saint George for England, Allegorically Described* (London, 1601)
Dennis, John, *The Critical Works of John Dennis*, edited by Edward Niles Hooker, 2 vols (Baltimore, 1939)
Donne, John, *The Elegies and The Songs and Sonnets*, edited by Helen Gardner (Oxford, 1965)
— *The Epithalamions, Anniversaries and Epicedes*, edited by W. Milgate (Oxford, 1978)
Dowland, John, *Third Book of Airs*, edited by Edmund Horace Fellowes, The English School of Lutenist Song Writers (London, 1923)
Drayton, Michael, *The Works of Michael Drayton* edited by J. William Hebel, 5 vols (Oxford, 1931-41)
Dryden, John, *Essays of John Dryden*, edited by W.P. Ker, 2 vols (New York, 1961)
Du Bartas, Guillaume de Saluste, *The Divine Weeks and Works of Guillaume de Saluste Sieur du Bartas*, translated by Joshuah Sylvester, edited by Susan Snyder, 2 vols (Oxford, 1979)
Dunbar, William, *The Poems of William Dunbar*, edited by W. Mackay Mackenzie (1932; rpt. London, 1966)
*Early English Carols, The*, edited by Richard Leighton Greene (London, 1935)
Elizabeth I, *The Letters of Queen Elizabeth*, edited by G.B. Harrison (London, 1935)
Elyot, Sir Thomas, *The Boke Named the Governour* (1531), Everyman edn (London, 1907)
Erasmus, Desiderius, *A booke called in Latyn* Enchiridion militis christiani *and in englyssche the manuell of the christen knyght*, translated by William Tyndale (1533; rpt. London, 1576)
— *The Correspondence of Erasmus*, translated by R.A.B. Mynors and D.F.S. Thomson, 2 vols (Toronto, 1975)
— *De Libero Arbitrio*, translated and edited by E. Gordon Rupp in collaboration with A.N. Marlow in *Luther and Erasmus: Free Will and Salvation*, The Library of Christian Classics, XVII (London, 1969)
— *The Education of a Christian Prince*, translated by Lester K. Born, Columbia Records of Civilization, XXVII (New York, 1936)
— *Paraphrase of Erasmus upon the Newe Testamente*, translated by N. Udall (London, 1548)
Foxe, John, *The Acts and Monuments of John Foxe*, edited by George Townsend, 8 vols (London, 1843-9)

Geoffrey of Monmouth, The Historia Regum Britanniae *of Geoffrey of Monmouth*, edited by Acton Griscom with a translation by Robert Ellis Jones (London, 1929)

Gough, John, *Prologue to an Abridged Edition of Erasmus' 'Enchiridion'* (1561) in *Elizabethan Puritanism*, edited by Leonard J. Trinterud (New York, 1971)

Hall, Edward, *The Vnion of the Two Noble and Illustre Famelies of Lancastre & Yorke*. . . (Hall's Chronicle) (1548; rpt. London, 1809)

Harvey, Gabriel, *Gabriel Harvey's Marginalia*, edited by G.C. Moore Smith (Stratford-upon-Avon, 1913)

— *The Works of Gabriel Harvey*, edited by Alexander B. Grosart, 3 vols (London, 1884-5)

Hayward, Sir John, *An Answer to the First Part of a Certaine Conference Concerning Svccession* (London, 1603)

Hesiod, *The Poems and Fragments*, translated by A.W. Mair (Oxford, 1908)

Higgins, John and Thomas Blenerhasset, *Parts added to 'The Mirror for Magistrates'*, edited by Lily B. Campbell (Cambridge, 1946)

Holinshed, Raphael, *Chronicles of England, Scotland, and Ireland*, 6 vols (1577-87; rpt. London, 1807-8)

Hooker, Richard, *Of The Laws of Ecclesiastical Polity*, Everyman edn, 2 vols (1907; rpt. London, 1925)

Jewel, John, *An Apology of the Church of England*, edited by J.E. Booty, Folger Documents of Tudor and Stuart Civilization (New York, 1963)

Jonson, Ben, *Ben Jonson*, edited by C.H. Herford and Percy and Evelyn Simpson, 11 vols (Oxford, 1925-52)

La Perrière, Guillaume de, *The Mirrour of Policie* (London, 1599)

La Primaudaye, Pierre de, *The French Academie*, translated by T. Bowes (London, 1586)

Leland, John, *Cygnea Cantio* (1545), *Genethliacon Eduerdi Principis* (1543) both printed in *The Itinerary of John Leland*, edited by Thomas Hearne, 3rd edn, 9 vols (Oxford, 1768-9)

Lipsius, Justus, *Sixe Bookes of Politickes or Civil Doctrine*, translated by William Jones (London, 1594)

Lucretius, *De Rerum Natura*, translated by W.H.D. Rouse, Loeb Classical Library (London, 1937)

Luther, Martin, *De Servo Arbitrio*, translated and edited by Philip S. Watson in collaboration with B. Drewery in *Luther and Erasmus: Free Will and Salvation*, The Library of Christian Classics, XVII (London, 1969)

Lydgate, John, *A Critical Edition of John Lydgate's Life of Our Lady*, edited by Joseph A. Lauritis, Ralph A. Klinefelter and Vernon F. Gallagher, Duquesne Studies in Philology, II (Pittsburgh, 1961)

— *The Minor Poems of John Lydgate*, edited by Henry Noble MacCracken, Early English Text Society, 2 vols (London, 1911 and 1934)

Lyly, John, *The Complete Works of John Lyly*, edited by R. Warwick Bond, 3 vols (Oxford, 1902)

Machiavelli, Niccolo, *The Prince*, translated by W.K. Marriot, Everyman edn (1908; rpt. London, 1960)

Macrobius, *Commentary on the Dream of Scipio*, translated by William Harris Stahl (New York, 1952)

Menander, *Menander Rhetor*, edited and translated by D.A. Russell and N.G. Wilson (Oxford, 1981)

Milton, John, *The Poems of John Milton*, edited by John Carey and Alastair Fowler (London, 1968)

Montaigne, Michel de, *The Essays of Montaigne*, translated by E.J. Trechmann,

2 vols (Oxford, 1927)
More, Sir Thomas, *Utopia*, translated by Raphe Robinson, edited by John O'Hagan, Everyman edn (1910; rpt. London, 1918)
*Myroure of oure Ladye, The,* edited by John Henry Blunt, Early English Text Society (London, 1873)
Nichols, John (ed.), *The Progresses and Public Processions of Queen Elizabeth*, 3 vols (1788-1805; rpt. London, 1823)
Nicols, Richard, *Englands Eliza: or the Victorious and Triumphant Reigne of that Virgin Empresse of Sacred Memorie, ELIZABETH, Queene of England*, printed in *A Mirovr for Magistrates*, edited by John Higgins (London, 1610)
Norden, John, Vicissitudo rerum: *An Elegiacall Poeme* (1600), with an introduction by D.C. Collins, Shakespeare Association Facsimiles, IV (London, 1931)
Ovid, *Shakespeare's Ovid: Being Arthur Golding's Translation of the Metamorphoses*, edited by W.H.D. Rouse (London, 1961)
Peele, George, *The Life and Works of George Peele*, edited by Charles Tyler Prouty, 3 vols (New Haven, Conn., 1952-70)
Petrarch, *One Hundred Sonnets of Petrarch Together with His Hymn to the Virgin*, translated and edited by Albert Crompton (London, 1898)
Plato, *Timaeus*, translated by R.G. Bury, Loeb Classical Library (London, 1929)
Puttenham, George, *The Arte of English Poesie*, edited by Gladys Doidge Willcock and Alice Walker (1936; rpt. Cambridge, 1970)
Quintilian, *Institutio Oratore*, translated by H.E. Butler, Loeb Classical Library, 4 vols (London, 1933)
Ralegh, Sir Walter, *The Historie of the World* (London, 1614)
Seneca, *Seneca's Tragedies*, translated by Frank Justus Miller, Loeb Classical Library, 2 vols (London, 1927)
Shakespeare, William, *The Complete Works*, edited by Peter Alexander (1951; rpt. London, 1971)
Sidney, Sir Philip, *Miscellaneous Prose of Sir Philip Sidney*, edited by Katherine Duncan-Jones and Jan Van Dorsten (Oxford, 1973)
Skelton, John, *Magnyfycence*, edited by Robert Lee Ramsay, Early English Text Society (1908; rpt. London, 1925)
Speed, John, *The Historie of Great Britaine* . . ., 3rd edn (London, 1632)
Spenser, Edmund, *The Poetical Works of Edmund Spenser*, edited by J.C. Smith and E. de Selincourt, one vol. edn (Oxford, 1924)
— *The Works of Edmund Spenser*, variorum edn, edited by Edwin Greenlaw, Charles Grosvenor Osgood, Frederick Morgan Padelford and Ray Heffner, 10 vols (Baltimore, 1932-49)
Starkey, Thomas, *A Dialogue between Cardinal Pole and Thomas Lupset* in *England in the reign of King Henry the Eighth*, Early English Text Society, Extra Series, XXXII (1878; rpt. London, 1927)
Stubbs, John, *John Stubbs's 'Gaping Gulf' with Letters and Other Relevant Documents*, edited by Lloyd E. Berry, Folger Documents of Tudor and Stuart Civilization (Charlottesville, Va., 1968)
Tasso, Torquato, *Tasso's Jerusalem Delivered: or Godfrey of Bulloign*, translated by Edward Fairfax, fourth edn (London, 1749)
Thomson, James, *Poetical Works*, edited by J. Logie Robertson (1908; rpt. Oxford, 1965)
Tibullus, *Poems*, translated by J.P. Postgate in *Catullus, Tibullus and Pervigilium Veneris*, Loeb Classical Library (London, 1925)
Vallans, William, *A Tale of Two Swannes* (1590), printed in Hearne's edition of Leland's *Itinerary*
Vergil, Polydore, *The* Anglica Historia *of Polydore Vergil A.D. 1485-1537*, edited and translated by Denys Hay, Camden Society Reprints, 3rd series, LXXIV

(London, 1950)
— *Historia Anglica* (Basel, 1555)
— *Polydore Vergil's English History, from an Early Translation*, edited by Sir Henry Ellis, Camden Society Reprints (London, 1846)
Virgil, *The Aeneid, The Eclogues and the Georgics*, translated by H. Rushton Fairclough, Loeb Classical Library, 2 vols (London, 1935)

## Secondary Sources

Albright, Evelyn May, 'Spenser's Cosmic Philosophy and His Religion', *PMLA*, 44 (1929), 715-59
Anderson, Judith H., '"Nor Man it is": The Knight of Justice in Book V of Spenser's *Faerie Queene*', *PMLA*, 85 (1970), 65-77
Aptekar, Jane, *Icons of Justice: Iconography and Thematic Imagery in Book V of 'The Faerie Queene'* (New York, 1969)
Aubin, Ronald Arnold, *Topographical Poetry in XVIII-Century England*, MLA Revolving Fund Series, VI (1936; rpt. New York, 1966)
Auerbach, Erich, 'Figura' in *Scenes from the Drama of European Literature* (New York, 1959), pp. 11-76
— *Mimesis: The Representations of Reality in Western Literature* (1946; rpt. New York, 1953)
Baker, Herschel, *The Image of Man: A Study of the Idea of Human Dignity in Classical Antiquity, The Middle Ages, and the Renaissance* (1947; rpt. New York, 1961)
— *The Wars of Truth: Studies in the Decay of Christian Humanism in the Earlier Seventeenth Century* (1952; rpt. Gloucester, Mass., 1969)
Barkan, Leonard, *Nature's Work of Art: The Human Body as Image of the World* (New Haven, Conn., 1975)
Bayley, Peter, *Edmund Spenser: Prince of Poets* (London, 1971)
Bennett, Josephine Waters, *The Evolution of 'The Faerie Queene'* (1942; rpt. New York, 1960)
Bercovitch, Sacvan (ed.), *Typology and Early American Literature* (Amherst, Mass., 1972)
Berger, Harry, *The Allegorical Temper: Vision and Reality in Book II of Spenser's 'Faerie Queene'* (New Haven, Conn., 1957)
Bernheimer, Richard, *Wild Men in the Middle Ages: A Study in Art, Sentiment, and Demonology* (1952; rpt. New York, 1970)
Blissett, William, 'Florimell and Marimell', *SEL*, 5 (1965), 87-104
— 'Spenser's Mutabilitie' in *Essays in English Literature from the Renaissance to the Victorian Age, presented to A.S.P. Woodhouse 1964*, edited by Millar MacLure and F.W. Watt (Toronto, 1964), pp. 26-42
Braden, Gordon, 'riverrun: An Epic Catalogue in *The Faerie Queene*', *ELR*, 5 (1975), 25-48
Bredvold, Louis I, 'The Naturalism of Donne in Relation to Some Renaissance Traditions', *JEGP*, 22 (1923), 471-502
Brooke, N.S., 'C.S. Lewis and Spenser: Nature, Art and the Bower of Bliss', *Cambridge Journal*, 2 (1949), 420-34
Books-Davies, Douglas, *Spenser's 'Faerie Queene': A Critical Commentary on Books I and II* (Manchester, 1977)
Buchan, A.M., 'The Political Allegory of Book IV of *The Faerie Queene*', *ELH*, 11 (1944), 237-48

Burgess, Theodore, *Epideictic Literature* (Chicago, 1902)
Bush, Douglas, *The Renaissance and English Humanism* (1939; rpt. Toronto, 1958)
Buxton, John, *Elizabethan Taste* (London, 1963)
Cain, Thomas H., *Praise in 'The Faerie Queene'* (Lincoln, Nebr., 1978)
Caspari, Fritz, *Humanism and the Social Order in Tudor England* (Chicago, 1954)
Cassirer, Ernst, *The Platonic Renaissance in England*, translated by James P. Pettegrove (London, 1953)
Chalmers, George, *A Supplemental Apology for the Believers in the Shakespeare-Papers* (London, 1799)
Chambers, E.K., *Sir Henry Lee: An Elizabethan Portrait* (Oxford, 1936)
Chang, H.C., *Allegory and Courtesy in Spenser: A Chinese View*, Edinburgh University Studies in Language and Literature, VIII (Edinburgh, 1955)
Charity, A.C., *Events and their Afterlife: The Dialectics of Christian Typology in the Bible and Dante* (Cambridge, 1966)
Cheney, Donald, 'Spenser's Hermaphrodite and the 1590 *Faerie Queene*', *PMLA*, 87 (1972), 192-200
— *Spenser's Image of Nature: Wild Man and Shepherd in 'The Faerie Queene'* (New Haven, Conn., 1966)
Comparetti, Domenico, *Vergil in the Middle Ages*, translated by E.F.M. Benecke (London, 1895)
Cornelius, Roberta D., *The Figurative Castle: A Study in the Mediaeval Allegory of the Edifice with Especial Reference to Religious Writings* (Bryn Mawr, Pa., 1930)
Cornford, F.M., 'Mysticism and Science in the Pythagorean Tradition', *CQ*, 16 (1922), 137-50; 17 (1923), 1-12
Craig, Hardin, *The Enchanted Glass: The Elizabethan Mind in Literature* (1935; rpt. Oxford, 1960)
Craig, Joanne, 'The Image of Mortality: Myth and History in *The Faerie Queene*', *ELH*, 39 (1972), 520-44
Cullen, Patrick, 'Guyon *Microchristus*: The Cave of Mammon Re-Examined', *ELH*, 37 (1970), 153-74
Culp, Dorothy Woodward, 'Courtesy and Fortune's Chance in Book 6 of *The Faerie Queene*', *MP*, 68 (1971), 254-9
Cumming, William P., 'The Influence of Ovid's *Metamorphoses* on Spenser's "Mutabilitie" Cantos', *SP*, 28 (1931), 241-56
Cummings, R.M., 'A Note on the Arithmological Stanza: *The Faerie Queene*, II ix, 22', *JWCI*, 30 (1967), 410-14
Danby, John F., *Shakespeare's Doctrine of Nature: A Study of 'King Lear'* (London, 1961)
D'Ancona, Mirella Levi, *The Iconography of the Immaculate Conception in the Middle Ages and Early Renaissance*, Monographs on Archaeology and Fine Arts sponsored by The Archaeological Institute of America, VII (New York, 1957)
Danielou, Jean, S.J., *From Shadows to Reality: Studies in the Biblical Typology of the Fathers*, translated by Dom Wulstan Hibberd (London, 1960)
Davis, B.E.C., *Edmund Spenser: A Critical Study* (Cambridge, 1933)
Davis, Thomas M., 'The Traditions of Puritan Typology' in Bercovitch, pp. 11-45
De Moss, William Fenn, *The Influence of Aristotle's 'Politics' and 'Ethics' on Spenser* (Chicago, 1920)
De Neef, A. Leigh, 'Epideictic Rhetoric and the Renaissance Lyric', *JMRS*, 3 (1973), 203-31
d'Entrèves, A.P., *Natural Law: An Introduction to Legal Philosophy* (1951; rpt. London, 1972)

Dickens, A.G., *The English Reformation* (London, 1964)

Doran, Madeleine, *Endeavours of Art: A Study of Form in Elizabethan Drama* (Madison, Wisc., 1954)

Doyle, Charles Clay, 'As Old Stories Tell: *Daphnis and Chloe* and the Pastoral Episode of *The Faerie Queene*, Book VI', *Neohelicon*, 5 (1977), 51-70

Drew, D.L., *The Allegory of the 'Aeneid'* (Oxford, 1927)

Dudley, Edward and Maximillian E. Novak (eds), *The Wild Man Within: An Image in Western Thought from the Renaissance to Romanticism* (Pittsburgh, 1972)

Dunseath, T.K., *Spenser's Allegory of Justice in Book Five of 'The Faerie Queene'* (Princeton, 1968)

Evans, Maurice, 'Courtesy and the Fall of Man', *ES*, 46 (1965), 209-20

— *Spenser's Anatomy of Heroism: A Commentary on 'The Faerie Queene'* (Cambridge, 1970)

Fairchild, Hoxie Neale, *The Noble Savage: A Study in Romantic Naturalism* (New York, 1928)

Farrer, Austin, 'Typology', *The Expository Times*, 67 (1956), 228-31

Figgis, John Neville, *Studies of Political Thought: From Gerson to Grotius 1414-1625* (Cambridge, 1907)

Finney, Gretchen Ludke, *Musical Backgrounds for English Literature: 1580-1650* (New Brunswick, n.d.)

Fletcher, Angus, *The Prophetic Moment: An Essay on Spenser* (Chicago, 1971)

Fowler, Alastair, 'Six Knights at Castle Joyeous', *SP*, 56 (1959), 583-99

— *Spenser and the Numbers of Time* (London, 1964)

Froehlich, Karlfried, '"Always to Keep the Literal Sense in Holy Scripture Means to Kill One's Soul": The State of Biblical Hermeneutics at the Beginning of the Fifteenth Century' in Miner, pp. 20-48

Frye, Northrop, 'The Structure of Imagery in *The Faerie Queene*', *UTQ*, 30 (1961), 109-27

Garrison, James D., *Dryden and the Tradition of Panegyric* (Berkeley, Los Angeles and London, 1975)

George, Charles H. and Katherine, *The Protestant Mind of the English Reformation 1570-1640* (Princeton, 1961)

Gierke, Otto, *Natural Law and the Theory of Society 1500 to 1800*, translated and edited by Ernest Barker, 2 vols (1934; rpt. in one vol., Cambridge, 1958)

— *Political Theories of the Middle Age*, translated and edited by Frederic William Maitland (Cambridge, 1922)

Gilmore, Myron P., *The World of Humanism, 1453-1517* (1952; rpt. New York, 1962)

Gombrich, E.H., 'Botticelli's Mythologies: A Study in the Neoplatonic Symbolism of his Circle', *JWCI*, 8 (1945), 7-60

Graziani, René, 'Elizabeth at Isis Church', *PMLA*, 79 (1964), 376-89

Greenlaw, Edwin A., 'The Influence of Machiavelli on Spenser', *MP*, 7 (1909), 187-202

— 'Some Old Religious Cults in Spenser', *SP*, 20 (1923), 216-43

— 'Spenser and Lucretius', *SP*, 17 (1920), 439-64

— *Studies in Spenser's Historical Allegory*, Johns Hopkins Monographs in Literary History, II (Baltimore, 1932)

Haller, William, *Foxe's Book of Martyrs and the Elect Nation* (London, 1963)

Hamilton, A.C., '"Like Race to Runne": The Parallel Structure of *The Faerie Queene*, Books I and II', *PMLA*, 73 (1958), 327-34

— *The Structure of Allegory in 'The Faerie Queene'* (Oxford, 1961)

— (ed.), *The Faerie Queene*, annotated edn (London, 1977)

Hankins, John Erskine, *Source and Meaning in Spenser's Allegory: A Study of 'The Faerie Queene'* (Oxford, 1971)

— 'Spenser and the Revelation of St John', *PMLA*, 60 (1945), 364-81
Harbison, E.H., *The Christian Scholar in the Age of the Reformation* (New York, 1956)
Hardison, O.B., Jr., *The Enduring Monument: A Study of the Idea of Praise in Renaissance Literary Theory and Practice* (Westport, Conn., 1962)
Harris, Victor, *All Coherence Gone: A Study of the Seventeenth Century Controversy over Disorder and Decay in the Universe* (1949; rpt. London, 1966)
Haugaard, William P., 'Elizabeth Tudor's *Book of Devotions*: A Neglected Clue to the Queen's Life and Character', *SixCT*, 12 (1981), 79-106
Hawkins, Sherman, 'Mutabilitie and the Cycle of the Months' in *Form and Convention in the Poetry of Edmund Spenser*, edited by William Nelson, Selected Papers from the English Institute (New York, 1961)
Haydn, Hiram, *The Counter-Renaissance* (New York, 1950)
Heffner, Ray, 'Spenser's Allegory in Book I of the *Faerie Queene*', *SP*, 27 (1930), 142-61
Heninger, S.K., Jr., *The Cosmographical Glass: Renaissance Diagrams of the Universe* (San Marino, 1977)
— 'The Orgoglio Episode in *The Faerie Queene*', *ELH*, 26 (1959), 171-87
— *Touches of Sweet Harmony: Pythagorean Cosmology and Renaissance Poetics* (San Marino, 1974)
Herndl, George C., *The High Design: English Renaissance Tragedy and Natural Law* (Lexington, Ky., 1970)
Hieatt, A. Kent, *Short Time's Endless Monument: the symbolism of the numbers in Spenser's 'Epithalamion'* (New York, 1960)
Hofstätter, Hans H., *Art of the Late Middle Ages*, translated by Robert Erich Wolf (New York, 1968)
Holahan, Michael, '*Iamque opus exegi*: Ovid's Changes and Spenser's Brief Epic of Mutability', *ELR*, 6 (1976), 244-70
Holdsworth, Sir William, *A History of English Law*, 16 vols (1924, 3rd edn 1945; rpt. London, 1973)
Holland, Joanne Field, 'The Cantos of Mutabilitie and the Form of *The Faerie Queene*', *ELH*, 35 (1968), 21-31
Hollander, John, 'Spenser and the Mingled Measure', *ELR*, 1 (1971), 226-38
— *The Untuning of the Sky: Ideas of Music in English Poetry 1500-1700* (Princeton, 1961)
Hollander, Robert, 'Typology and Secular Literature: Some Medieval Problems and Examples' in Miner, pp. 3-19
Hopper, Vincent Foster, 'Spenser's "House of Temperance"', *PMLA*, 55 (1940), 958-67
Hoopes, Robert, *Right Reason in the English Renaissance* (Cambridge, Mass., 1962)
Hughes, Merritt, Y., *Vergil and Spenser* (New York, 1929)
James, E.O., *The Cult of the Mother-Goddess: An Archaeological Study* (London, 1959)
Javitch, Daniel, *Poetry and Courtliness in Renaissance England* (Princeton, 1978)
Jones, H.S.V., *A Spenser Handbook* (New York, 1930)
Judson, A.C., 'Spenser's Theory of Courtesy', *PMLA*, 47 (1932), 122-36
Jung, C.G., *The Archetypes and the Collective Unconscious*, translated by R.F.C. Hull (London, 1959)
Kantorowicz, Ernst H., *The King's Two Bodies: A Study in Medieval Political Theology* (Princeton, 1957)
Kelso, Ruth, *The Doctrine of the English Gentleman in the Sixteenth Century*, University of Illinois Studies in Language and Literature, XIV (Urbana, Ill., 1929)

Kendrick, T.D., *British Antiquity* (London, 1950)
Kermode, Frank, *Shakespeare, Spenser, Donne: Renaissance Essays* (London, 1971)
Knight, W. Nicholas, 'The Narrative Unity of Book V of *The Faerie Queene*: "That Part of Justice which is Equity"', *RES*, NS, 21 (1970), 265-94
Koebner, Richard, '"The Imperiall Crown of this Realm": Henry VIII, Constantine the Great, and Polydore Vergil', *BIHR*, 26 (1953), 29-52
Kolve, V.A., *The Play Called Corpus Christi* (London, 1966)
Leishman, J.B., *The Art of Marvell's Poetry* (London, 1966)
Levin, Harry, *The Myth of the Golden Age in the Renaissance* (London, 1969)
Levinson, Ronald B., 'Spenser and Bruno', *PMLA*, 43 (1928), 675-81
Levy, F.J., *Tudor Historical Thought* (San Marino, 1967)
Lewalski, Barbara Kiefer, *Donne's 'Anniversaries' and the Poetry of Praise: The Creation of a Symbolic Mode* (Princeton, 1973)
Lewis, C.S., *The Allegory of Love* (Oxford, 1936)
— *Studies in Words* (Cambridge, 1960)
Lotspeich, Henry Gibbons, *Classical Mythology in the Poetry of Edmund Spenser*, Princeton Studies in English, IX (Princeton, 1932)
Lovejoy, Arthur O., *The Great Chain of Being: A Study of the History of an Idea* (1936; rpt. New York, 1960)
Lovejoy, Arthur O. and George Boas, *Primitivism and Related Ideas in Antiquity* (1935; rpt. New York, 1973)
Lowance, Mason, I. Jr., *The Language of Canaan: Metaphor and Symbol in New England from the Puritans to the Transcendentalists* (Cambridge, Mass. and London, 1980)
McAlindon, T., *Shakespeare and Decorum* (London and New York, 1973)
MacIntyre, Jean, 'Spenser's Herculean Heroes', *HACB*, 17 (1966), 5-12
McLane, Paul E., *Spenser's Shepheardes Calender: A Study in Elizabethan Allegory* (Notre Dame, Ind., 1961)
MacLure, Millar, 'Nature and Art in *The Faerie Queene*', *ELH*, 28 (1961), 1-20
MacQueen, John, *Allegory*, The Critical Idiom, XIV (London, 1970)
Magill, A.J., 'Spenser's Guyon and the Mediocrity of the Elizabethan Settlement', *SP*, 67 (1970), 167-77
Major, John M., *Sir Thomas Elyot and Renaissance Humanism* (Lincoln, Nebr., 1964)
Mâle, Émile, *Religious Art in France: XIII Century*, translated by Dora Nussey (London, 1913)
Manley, Lawrence, *Convention, 1500-1750* (Cambridge, Mass. and London, 1980)
Manning, Stephen, 'Scriptural Exegesis and the Literary Critic' in Bercovitch, pp. 47-66
Marc, Olivier, *Psychology of the House*, translated by Jessie Wood (London, 1977)
Marshall, William, H., 'Calvin, Spenser, and the Major Sacraments', *MLN*, 74 (1959), 97-101
Mason, John E., *Gentlefolk in the Making: Studies in the History of English Courtesy Literature and Related Topics from 1531-1774* (Philadelphia, 1935)
Maxwell, J.C., 'The Truancy of Calidore', *ELH*, 19 (1952), 143-9
Miller, Lewis, H., 'A Secular Reading of the *Faerie Queene*, Book II', *ELH*, 33 (1966), 154-69
Millican, Charles Bowie, *Spenser and the Table Round: A Study in the Contemporaneous Background for Spenser's Use of the Arthurian Legend*, Harvard Studies in Comparative Literature, VIII (Cambridge, Mass., 1932)
— 'Spenser's and Drant's Poetic Names for Elizabeth: Tanaquil, Gloria, and Una', *HLQ*, 2 (1938-9), 251-63
Mills, Jerry Leath, 'Spenser's Castle of Alma and the Number 22: A Note on

Symbolic Stanza Placement', *NQ*, 212 (1967), 456-7

— 'Spenser and the Numbers of History: A Note on the British and Elfin Chronicles in *The Faerie Queene*', *PQ*, 55 (1976), 281-6

Mills, Laurens J., *One Soul in Bodies Twain: Friendship in Tudor Literature and Stuart Drama* (Bloomington, Ind., 1937)

Miner, Earl (ed.), *Literary Uses of Typology from the Late Middle Ages to the Present* (Princeton, 1977)

Musurillo, Herbert, *Symbolism and the Christian Imagination* (Dublin, 1962)

Nauert, Charles G., *Agrippa and the Crisis of Renaissance Thought*, Illinois Studies in the Social Sciences, IV (Urbana, 1965)

Neale, J.E., *Queen Elizabeth* (London, 1934)

Neill, Kerby, 'Spenser on the Regiment of Women: A Note on *The Faerie Queene*, V, v, 25', *SP*, 34 (1937), 134-7

Nelson, William, *The Poetry of Edmund Spenser* (New York and London, 1963)

Neuse, Richard, 'Book VI as Conclusion to *The Faerie Queene*', *ELH*, 35 (1968), 329-53

Nevo, Ruth, 'Spenser's "Bower of Bliss" and a Key Metaphor from Renaissance Poetic', *Studies in Western Literature*, edited by D.A. Fineman (Jerusalem, 1962), pp. 20-31

*New Catholic Encyclopaedia* (Washington, DC, 1967)

Nicolson, Marjorie Hope, *The Breaking of the Circle: Studies in the Effect of the 'New Science' upon Seventeenth-Century Poetry* (New York, 1960)

Northrop, Douglas A., 'Mercilla's Court as Parliament', *HLQ*, 36 (1973), 153-8

— 'Spenser's Defence of Elizabeth', *UTQ*, 38 (1969), 277-94

O'Connell, Michael, 'History and the Poet's Golden World: The Epic Catalogues in *The Faerie Queene*', *ELR*, 4 (1974), 241-67

— *Mirror and Veil: The Historical Dimension of Spenser's 'Faerie Queene'* (Chapel Hill, N.C., 1977)

O'Malley, John W., *Praise and Blame in Renaissance Rome: Rhetoric, Doctrine, and Reform in the Sacred Orators of the Papal Court, c. 1450-1521*, Duke Monographs in Medieval and Renaissance Studies, III (Durham, N.C., 1979)

Ornstein, Robert, *The Moral Vision of Jacobean Tragedy* (Madison, Wisc., 1960)

Oruch, Jack B., 'Spenser, Camden and the Poetic Marriage of Rivers', *SP*, 64 (1967), 606-24

Osgood, Charles Grosvenor, 'Spenser's English Rivers', *TCAS*, 23 (1920), 67-108

— (ed.), *Boccaccio on Poetry: Being the Preface and the Fourteenth and Fifteenth Books of Boccaccio's* 'Genealogia Deorum Gentilium' (1930; rpt. Indianapolis, 1956)

Owen, Lewis J., 'Mutable in eternity: Spenser's despair and the multiple forms of Mutabilitie', *JMRS*, 2 (1972), 49-68

Padelford, F.M., 'Spenser and the Puritan Propaganda', *MP*, 11 (1913-14), 85-106

— 'Spenser and the Theology of Calvin', *MP*, 12 (1914-15), 1-18

— 'Spenser and the Spirit of Puritanism', *MP*, 14 (1916-17), 31-44

— 'The Spiritual Allegory of *The Faerie Queene*, Book One', *JEGP*, 22 (1923), 1-17

Panofsky, Erwin, *Studies in Iconology: Humanistic Themes in the Art of the Renaissance* (1939; rpt. New York, 1962)

Parsons, A.E., 'The Trojan Legend in England', *MLR*, 24 (1929), 253-64, 394-408

Patch, Howard, Rollin, *The Other World* (New York, 1950)

Peterson, Richard S., *Imitation and Praise in the Poems of Ben Jonson* (New Haven, Conn. and London, 1981)

Phillips, James E., 'The Background of Spenser's Attitude toward Women Rulers', *HLQ*, 5 (1942), 5-32

— 'Renaissance Concepts of Justice and the Structure of *The Faerie Queene*,

Book V', *HLQ*, 33 (1970), 103-20
— 'The Woman Ruler in Spenser's *Faerie Queene*', *HLQ*, 5 (1942), 211-34
Porter, H.C., *Reformation and Reaction in Tudor Cambridge* (Cambridge, 1958)
Quinones, Ricardo, *The Renaissance Discovery of Time*, Harvard Studies in Comparative Literature, XXXI (Cambridge, Mass., 1972)
Raab, Felix, *The English Face of Machiavelli: A Changing Interpretation 1500-1700* (London, 1964)
Réau, Louis, *Iconographie De L'Art Chrétien*, 6 vols (Paris, 1955-9)
Ringler, Richard N., 'The Faunus Episode', *MP*, 63 (1965), 12-19
Rivers, Isabel, *Classical and Christian Ideas in English Renaissance Poetry* (London, 1979)
Robertson, D.W., Jr., *A Preface to Chaucer: Studies in Medieval Perspectives* (Princeton, 1963)
Roche, Thomas P., Jr., *The Kindly Flame: A Study of the Third and Fourth Books of Spenser's 'Faerie Queene'* (Princeton, 1964)
Rollinson, Philip, *Classical Theories of Allegory and Christian Culture* (Pittsburgh and Brighton, 1981)
Rose, Mark, *Heroic Love: Studies in Sidney and Spenser* (Cambridge, Mass., 1968)
Rosinger, Lawrence, 'Spenser's Una and Queen Elizabeth', *ELN*, 6 (1968-9), 12-17
Rowland, Beryl, *Blind Beasts: Chaucer's Animal World* (Kent, Ohio, 1971)
Shire, Helena, *A Preface to Spenser* (London, 1978)
Siegel, Paul N., 'Spenser and the Calvinist View of Life', *SP*, 41 (1944), 201-22
Smith, Bruce R, 'Landscape with Figures: The Three Realms of Queen Elizabeth's Country-house Revels', *RenD*, NS, 8 (1977), 57-115
Smith, Charles G., *Spenser's Theory of Friendship* (Baltimore, 1935)
Smith, Edward O., Jr., 'The Elizabethan Doctrine of the Prince as Reflected in the Sermons of the Episcopacy, 1559-1603', *HLQ*, 28 (1964), 1-17
Smith, Eric, *Some Versions of the Fall: The Myth of the Fall of Man in English Literature* (London, 1973)
Spencer, Theodore, *Shakespeare and the Nature of Man* (1942; 2nd edn, New York, 1961)
Spitzer, Leo, 'Classical and Christian Ideas of World Harmony: Prolegomena to an Interpretation of the Word "Stimmung"', *Traditio*, 2 (1944), 409-69; 3 (1945), 307-64
Stampfer, Judah K., 'The Cantos of Mutability: Spenser's Last Testament of Faith', *UTQ*, 21 (1952), 140-56
Stewart, Stanley, *The Enclosed Garden: The Tradition and the Image in Seventeenth-Century Poetry* (Madison, Wisc. and London, 1966)
Stirling, Brents, 'The Concluding Stanzas of *Mutability*', *SP*, 30 (1933), 193-204
Strong, Roy, 'The Popular Celebration of the Accession Day of Queen Elizabeth I', *JWCI*, 21 (1958), 86-103
— *The Cult of Elizabeth: Elizabethan Portraiture and Pageantry* (London, 1977)
Tayler, Edward William, *Nature and Art in Renaissance Literature* (New York, 1964)
Tillyard, E.M.W., *The Elizabethan World Picture* (London, 1943)
— *The English Epic and its Background* (London, 1954)
Tonkin, Humphrey, 'Discussing Spenser's Cave of Mammon', *SEL*, 13 (1973), 1-13
— *Spenser's Courteous Pastoral: Book Six of the 'Faerie Queene'* (Oxford, 1972)
Tuve, Rosemond, 'A Medieval Commonplace in Spenser's Cosmology', *SP*, 30 (1933), 133-47
— 'Spenser and the "Zodiake of Life"', *JEGP*, 34 (1935), 1-19
— 'Spenser's Reading: The "*De Claribus Mulieribus*"', *SP*, 33 (1936), 147-65

Waller, G.F., *The Strong Necessity of Time: The Philosophy of Time in Shakespeare and Elizabethan Literature* (The Hague, 1976)
Warner, Marina, *Alone of All Her Sex: The Myth and the Cult of the Virgin Mary* (London, 1976)
Watson, Arthur, *The Early Iconography of the Tree of Jesse* (Oxford, 1934)
Webb, Wm. Stanford, 'Vergil in Spenser's Epic Theory', *ELH*, 4 (1937), 62-84
Weiner, Andrew D., '"Fierce Warres and Faithful Loues": Pattern as Structure in Book I of *The Faerie Queene*', *HLQ*, 37 (1974), 33-57
Wells, Robin Headlam, 'Delight in Disorder: James Thomson and the Art of Landscape', *Comparison*, 8 (1978), 76-85
— 'Song from Spenser's *The Faerie Queene*', *CritS*, 6 (1973), 7-11
— 'Spenser and the Courtesy Tradition: Form and Meaning in the Sixth Book of *The Faerie Queene*', *ES*, 58 (1977), 221-9
Whitaker, V.K., *The Religious Basis of Spenser's Thought* (1950; rpt. New York, 1966)
White, Hayden, 'The Forms of Wildness: Archaeology of an Idea' in Dudley and Novak, pp. 3-38
Wickham, Glynne, *Shakespeare's Dramatic Heritage* (London, 1969)
Williams, Kathleen, 'Courtesy and Pastoral in *The Faerie Queene*, Book VI', *RES*, NS, 13 (1962), 337-46
— *Spenser's 'Faerie Queene': The World of Glass* (London, 1966)
— 'Venus and Diana: Some Uses of Myth in *The Faerie Queene*', *ELH*, 28 (1961), 101-20
Wilson, Elkin Calhoun, *England's Eliza*, Harvard Studies in English, XX (1939; rpt. London, 1966)
Wilson, Jean, *Entertainments for Elizabeth I* (Woodbridge, 1980)
Wilson, Rawdon, 'Images and "Allegoremes" of Time in the Poetry of Spenser', *ELR*, 4 (1974), 56-82
Wind, Edgar, *Pagan Mysteries in the Renaissance* (London, 1958)
Winters, Yvor, *The Function of Criticism* (Denver, 1957)
Woodhouse, A.S.P., 'Nature and Grace in The Faerie Queene', *ELH*, 16 (1949), 194-228
Woolf, Rosemary, *The English Religious Lyric in the Middle Ages* (Oxford, 1968)
Woollcombe, K.J., 'The Biblical Origins and Patristic Development of Typology' in *Essays in Typology*, edited by G.W.H. Lampe and K.J. Woollcombe (London, 1957), pp. 39-75
Yates, Frances, 'Queen Elizabeth as Astraea', *JWCI*, 10 (1947), 27-82
Zwicker, Steven N., 'Politics and Panegyric: The Figural Mode from Marvell to Pope' in Miner, pp. 115-46

# INDEX

Printed in the United States
by Baker & Taylor Publisher Services